GWENDOLYN BROOKS

GWENDOLYN BROOKS

POETRY & THE HEROIC VOICE

D. H. Melhem

THE UNIVERSITY PRESS OF KENTUCKY

Frontispiece: Gwendolyn Brooks,
courtesy of *The Contemporary Forum.*

The University Press of Kentucky
Scholarly publisher for the Commonwealth,
serving Bellarmine College, Berea College, Centre
College of Kentucky, Eastern Kentucky University,
The Filson Club, Georgetown College, Kentucky
Historical Society, Kentucky State University,
Morehead State University, Murray State University,
Northern Kentucky University, Transylvania University,
University of Kentucky, University of Louisville,
and Western Kentucky University

Editorial and Sales Offices: Lexington, Kentucky 40506-0024

Library of Congress Cataloging-in-Publication Data
Melhem, D. H.
Gwendolyn Brooks, poetry and the heroic voice.

   Bibliography: p.
   Includes index.
   1. Brooks, Gwendolyn, 1917-   . 2. Poets,
American—20th century—Biography. 3. Afro-Americans—
Intellectual life. 4. Afro-Americans in literature.
I. Title.
PS3503.R7244Z76   1987   811'.54 [B]   86-15737
ISBN 0-8131-1605-8

Contents

Abbreviations

The following abbreviations are used throughout the text and in the notes:

BSM   Dudley Randall. *Broadside Memories: Poets I Have Known.* Detroit: Broadside Press. 1975.

BWW   Claudia Tate, ed. *Black Women Writers at Work.* New York: Continuum, 1983.

EL   Elizabeth Lawrence

GB   Gwendolyn Brooks

GMR   Langston Hughes. *Good Morning Revolution.* Ed. Faith Berry. Westport, Conn.: Hill, 1973.

RPO   Gwendolyn Brooks. *Report from Part One.* Detroit: Broadside Press, 1972.

WGB   Gwendolyn Brooks. *The World of Gwendolyn Brooks.* New York: Harper and Row, 1971.

Acknowledgments

The idea for this study germinated in Gwendolyn Brooks's poetry workshop, which I audited at the City College of New York in 1971. Three years later, when there was still no book available on her, the work began its formal growth; its thesis persisted throughout many revisions. Happily, the field of Brooks scholarshp has blossomed in recent years. The debts I owe to fellow scholars, beginning with the late George E. Kent, are commemorated in the notes. I am obliged also to black fellow poets, who have always understood and sustained my approach.

My greatest debt is to Allen Mandelbaum, who initially approved and lent cogent criticism to the project begun at the City University of New York, and to John T. Shawcross, who unstintingly and formidably endowed the work with creative attention. Martin Tucker and Donald H. Reiman offered valuable criticism; James B. Gwynne lent his enthusiastic support at a critical time. And if my messages reach out with clarity, their precision has been rigorously enhanced by Kenneth Cherry, whose faith and editorial guidance never wavered.

I warmly thank Harper and Row, Publishers, Inc., for permitting me the perusal of their correspondence files regarding Gwendolyn Brooks, with her consent, in New York and at Princeton University Library; for their assistance in supplying information; and for allowing me to quote from the poet's published work with Harper's. I also thank the librarian of Princeton University Library for making available the earlier Brooks/Harper and Row

Authors' Files (1945-58) housed there. I have been fortunate in the cooperation extended me by Elizabeth Lawrence, the poet's former editor at Harper's. In Beryl Zitch, director of the Contemporary Forum, I have gained an indispensable source of information and continuing, friendly interest.

I am grateful to Dudley Randall, poet, pioneering publisher and editor of Broadside Press, for his patient kindness in answering research questions, and for permission to quote from Brooks's publications with Broadside. Appreciation is hereby accorded to Haki R. Madhubuti, poet, author, and publisher-editor of Third World Press and *Black Books Bulletin,* and to *Ebony* magazine, published by the Johnson Publishing Company, Inc., for permission to quote from their respective publications of Brooks.

My main research, conducted at the Schomburg Center for Research in Black Culture, the New York Public Library, received generous assistance from Ernest Kaiser, its librarian, and from his excellent staff. The central branch of the library, at Forty-second Street, particularly its General Research division; the Graduate School librarian, chief of Reader Services, and the library staff of the City University of New York have all provided significant help.

Friends have greatly enriched me. I think especially of conversations with Margaret W. Cook, the late Ree Dragonette, Vinie Burrows, Kay Leslie, Percy E. Johnston, Olga Cabral, Donald Phelps, Marc Crawford, Abby London, Isabel and Max Manes, and Claudia Menza. My family—my beloved late father, Nicholas; his wife, Theresa; Chester and our children, Dana and Gregory Vogel—each member, in a distinct way, has nourished this task.

My respect for Black culture began long ago with an awareness of the political realities of Black life, realities that engaged my own experience with a multicultural family background. I learned early that, as with people themselves, a literature of beauty and nobility could be ignored or depreciated because it diverged from prevailing norms.

And what, then, can I say to Gwendolyn Brooks, who read this study with impeccable care, offering suggestions and corrections, who inspired, and continues to inspire, its life?

For Gwendolyn Brooks:
*The Spirit and Struggle of Black People
Sounding in Her Work*

Introduction

Gwendolyn Brooks is a major figure in American literature. She has produced a body of work that extends over four decades. Yet, despite honors and esteem, it is mainly black scholars and critics who have accorded her poetry its due. This study will, in effect, examine Brooks's status and rank as one of the preeminent American writers of our time.

What shall the criteria be? Our academies generally accept T.S. Eliot, Ezra Pound, William Carlos Williams, and Wallace Stevens as major American poets. Why? Foremost on levels of craft and technique, modifications of form and language, scope or breadth or the work and its influence, the impress of personality. Although these criteria chart a final appraisal, the discussion here focuses on how poems are made. It is guided by the ideal principle: "Form is never more than an extension of content."[1] Historical considerations—personal, social, aesthetic—provide a context; pertinent correspondence, a background; cultural information, an aid to identifying, even valuing, what may inform a poem. But none of these suffice to evaluate the poetry; none measure the vital distance into the heart of composition. For this reason our basic task in furnishing a critical guide to Brooks's work is the analysis of poetic structures: by sight (on the page), sound, and sense; by prosody, diction, language, imagery, themes, motifs.[2] We ask not only how a poem is made or came to be, but also why it is made in a particular way.

Brooks remarks of the black writer: "He has the American

experience and he also has the black experience; so he's very rich."[3] Nevertheless, her work is grounded in a consciousness of race. Clenora F. Hudson observes, "Miss Brooks' poems accurately reflect what and how Blacks felt and feel about racial issues in this country."[4] Her view corroborates that of George E. Kent: "Gwendolyn Brooks shares with Langston Hughes the achievement of being responsive to turbulent changes in the black community's vision of itself and to the changing forms of its vibrations during decades of rapid change."[5]

Registering many forms of those "vibrations," the Harlem Renaissance of the twenties and thirties channeled and disseminated the influence of folk ballads, blues, jazz, and black speech. The black aesthetic resurgence notable since the sixties has been referred to as "Harlem Renaissance II" by writers like John A. Williams, who describes the first as primarily cultural, the second as essentially political.[6] It is within this mood of urgency that Brooks's poetry enters its dramatic phase of prophecy, invoking and ultimately fulfilling the need for leadership and "race heroes" in the black community.

From the beginning, humanism and heroism (or antiheroism) engaged Brooks's concerns.[7] Early works—*A Street in Bronzeville* (1945), *Annie Allen* (1949), and *Maud Martha* (1953)—are leavened by the pressures of daily life. *The Bean Eaters* (1960), charged with response to current events, reflects the polarizing of racial views that culminated in the "Black Rebellion" of the sixties.[8] *Selected Poems* (1963), largely culled from previous volumes, includes the remarkable "A Catch of Shy Fish" and the important political piece "Riders to the Blood-red Wrath."

In 1967, at the Second Fisk University Writers' Conference in Nashville, Brooks met with the artistic manifestation of the Black Rebellion. At the same time, the form of her verse—flexible—was opening more freely to content. The authority of prophetic voice became clearly audible. "My aim, in my next future, is to write poems that will successfully 'call' . . . all black people" (*RPO*, 183). *In the Mecca* (1968) marks a creative prime meridian for Brooks. There her oracular voice, prescriptive and prophetic, rings out. No facile demarcations exist, however, between "early," "middle," and "late" or "in-progress" Brooks. At times the past is "made new"; at others, it is discarded; there is always a willingness to take some degree of creative risk.

From *In the Mecca* on, we note the codifying of Brooks's heroic style. Two categories will be distinguished: the "grand heroic style," to borrow from Matthew Arnold's "grand style" (arising "when a noble nature, poetically gifted, treats with simplicity or with severity a serious subject"),[9] and the "plain." Homer's "simplicity" and Milton's "severity" impressed Arnold, and they are pertinent in Brooks: the bardic and narrative idiom of one and the politico-heroic-poetic immersion of the other channel two currents of her work. Though Wordsworth, the English pedagogical antecedent, reverts in Brooks to the Christian ideal of the good shepherd, she reflects further the heritage of didacticism in African and African American tales (see especially chapter 9, below, on *The Tiger Who Wore White Gloves*). In her, African griot joins Anglo-Saxon scop.

More frequently after *In the Mecca*, Brooks strategically employs black speech and music, features critical to black poetry.[10] W. E. B. Du Bois earlier identified "the Negro folk-song—the rhythmic cry of the slave" as "the singular spiritual heritage of the nation and the greatest gift of the Negro people."[11] The American slave system, its oral tradition nurtured by religion and the black church, encouraged the ties between speech and music, ties that came to involve the black tradition of fine oratory. The mediation, moreover, is fundamental to the African heritage of religiosity, imaged by the frequency and pervasiveness of the word "soul" in black life and culture. The word epitomizes Brooks's art.

Chapters of this book follow a chronological and textual sequence, except for topical groupings of *The Bean Eaters*. The first eight chapters are introduced by Brooks's correspondence with Harper and Row. Interaction with editorial opinion and guidance during the first twenty years of that association affords insight into Brooks's career, judgment, and work as published. It also records divergences of taste and viewpoint that accompanied some of the publications. Aiming to reflect the work at hand, style and management of the criticism will seem, by and large, to become more flexibly ordered.

Although there has been a tendency to replace the term

"Negro" with "Black," representing "the continuing decision of Essential Blacks," as Brooks points out, I use the former word where it reflects historical accuracy and/or represents usage by the speaker. "Black" is sometimes capitalized, in dealing with later works where "blackness" seems conceptually specified, and for emphasis or clarity.

Some interpolated remarks by the poet will be noted parenthetically in the text as "GB." Having most graciously read the entire manuscript, supplying both factual and interpretive information, Brooks kindly gave me permission to quote or paraphrase her comments.

1

Biographical

"Until 1967 my own blackness did not confront me with a shrill spelling of itself. . . . Yet, although almost secretly, I had always felt that to be black was good" (*RPO*, 83-84). Thus Gwendolyn Brooks expresses early self-acceptance and offers perhaps her greatest tribute to her parents. A psychological commonplace holds that firm ego-strength is built early and nurtured by a loving environment.

Brooks's parents gave her constant affection and respected her intellectual gifts. In the creative atmosphere, her father, a janitor with "rich Artistic Abilities" (*RPO*, 39), sang, told stories, and acknowledged charitably the poverty and misfortune of others. "His religion was kindness," she observes.[1] Her "Duty-Loving" mother played the piano and took her daughter to meet James Weldon Johnson and Langston Hughes in churches where they lectured. Many years later, in her eighties, Mrs. Brooks submitted a first collection of "storiettes" to Harper and Row, publishing them elsewhere the following year.[2] She figured actively in the poet's life until March 14, 1978, when she died at the age of ninety.

Brooks's reference to her father's chuckle epitomizes the family ambience: "It was gentle, it was warmly happy, it was heavyish but not hard. It was secure, and seemed to us an assistant to the Power that registered with his children" (*RPO*, 39). Warmth pervaded the family holidays, glimpsed in *Report from Part One*. The adult Brooks ruefully notes the absence of "black glory or greatness or grandeur" in the Euro-American celebrations. But growing up in a household where beggars were sometimes fed at the family table imparted communal awareness and nourished her generous sensibility.

David Anderson Brooks, her father, was the son of Lucas Brooks, a runaway slave. The poet's paternal grandfather took part in the Civil War, married, fathered twelve children, and had the highest regard for "family ties." His wife, Elizabeth, was affectionate and close to her children. David Brooks recalled an impoverished childhood of great hardship. In Oklahoma City, the family took in boarders and often gave free meals to the hungry, a tradition they continued in Chicago.

Mr. Brooks had a reverence for books and education. The sole member of his family who "stuck through school" (*RPO*, 52), he did chores, getting up at five in the morning to feed horses so that he might attend class. He loved to sing. At his high school graduation, the talented youth gave a speech, sang a song, and received on stage a bouquet of roses from the mayor, for whom he worked. Knowing little of her father's story that might account for his excellent qualities, Brooks concludes: "I think that his in-life, before he came to know Keziah and Gwendolyn and Raymond and cages nice and belts all tidy and snug, was of cinerama proportions, was suffused with wild organ music deep-center" (*RPO*, 53).

In a biographical "Document" written by the poet's mother at her daughter's request, Keziah Brooks allows a unique insight into herself as well as her family. Assuming the identity of Gwendolyn Brooks, she writes of herself in third person. The following information is drawn from her summary (*RPO*, 46-50).

In 1914, Keziah Corine Wims, a fifth grade teacher in Topeka, Kansas, met David Anderson Brooks, who had spent a year at Fisk University, Nashville, Tennessee, hoping to become a doctor. Both native Kansans (the latter born in Atchison, the former in Topeka), they were married after a two-year courtship and moved to Chicago. Two and half months before the birth of her daughter, Mrs. Brooks returned to her parents' home in Topeka, where she awaited the event of June 7, 1917. Five weeks later, she returned to Chicago with her firstborn, Gwendolyn Elizabeth Brooks.

Keziah Brooks remarks that her daughter was not allowed to crawl. Instead, Gwendolyn was eased (or hastened) into the next stage by members of the family, who helped her to walk around chairs and led her about the apartment. The poet's earliest childhood was solitary until her brother, Raymond, was born sixteen months later. When Gwendolyn was four, the family moved to their permanent home at 4332 Champlain Avenue, where there were playmates, a front and a back yard, a porch, a hammock, and a sandbox. The poet had planned to make this house into a small arts center in tribute to her parents before the building was tragically destroyed by fire in September 1984.

Gwendolyn and Raymond regularly attended Sunday school at the Carter Temple Methodist Episcopal Church, where their mother taught classes. Of the religious framework, Kent observes, "On the basis of Miss Brooks's well known devotion for her fellow man and the values informing her poetry, I would say that one source of her sensibility is a religious consciousness, from which dogma has been ground away."[3] She herself has stated, "My religion is . . . PEOPLE. LIVING."[4]

As a child, the poet reports, she "dreamed freely, often on the top step of the back porch" (*RPO*, 55). Her romantic imaginings about gods, angels, heroes, and future lovers were envisioned in the changing sky. She wrote constantly in notebooks, rhyming from the age of seven, casting her thoughts into didactic verse about nature, love, death, the sky.[5] Her mother assured her that one day she would achieve the excellence and renown of a *"lady Paul Laurence Dunbar"* (*RPO*, 56). Mrs. Brooks describes her own excitement at discovering her daughter's ability, whereupon she assumed most of the household chores, assisted by her husband and her son.

Admiring dramatic recitations, Mrs. Brooks rehearsed her daughter at age four and five in their public delivery. Her musical interest, like her husband's, illustrates the pervasive black heritage, religious and secular, reflected in her daughter's poetry. Mrs. Brooks trained a group of ten- to thirteen-year-olds in special musical programs at Carter Temple Church. She encouraged Gwendolyn to write plays for the children with acting ability. Brooks remarks in an interview with Ida Lewis that her mother had "all kinds of 'nerve' " (*RPO*, 173-74). After the young girl decided to send poems to James Weldon Johnson, who wrote back suggesting she read modern poetry, Mrs. Brooks took her to meet the austere poet during his visit to a neighboring church. Later, when Langston Hughes visited the Metropolitan Community Church, which Brooks still attends, the mother again escorted her child with a sheaf of poems. Hughes read them on the spot. Noting Brooks's talent, he advised her to go on writing, and became an inspiration to the sixteen-year-old.

Socially, her disposition to write, her "decent dresses" made by her Aunt Beulah, and her lack of skill at sports set Brooks apart among her peers at the elementary school and the several high schools she attended (graduating from Englewood High School in 1934). She experienced discrimination by white *and* black people because of her deep coloring. Hoping for "achievement of reverence among the Lesser Blacks" (*RPO*, 38), she early pursued and attained publishing success. At thirteen her first poem, "Eventide," was published in *American Childhood*; by sixteen she was a weekly contributor to the *Chicago Defender* column "Lights and Shadows," and had seventy-five of her poems printed there within two years. In 1937, at the age of twenty, her work appeared in two anthologies.

Having been graduated from Wilson Junior College (now Kennedy-King) in 1936, she worked as a maid in a North Shore home for a month, when the *Defender* failed to offer her a job. She then spent four "horrible" months as secretary to a spiritual adviser who specialized in patent medicines.[6] He was housed in the Mecca, an apartment building complex she had not visited until the Illinois State Employment Service sent her there to "a typing job." Many years later, the Mecca became the setting of her poem.

Gwendolyn Brooks met Henry Lowington Blakely II in 1938, observing immediately, "That is the man I am going to marry" (*RPO*, 58, where "That" appears as "There," corrected by Brooks). A Wilson student, he was a "fella who wrote" and still does,[7] and was eager to meet the "girl who wrote" of whom he had been told. The couple were married the following year. On October 10, 1940, Henry L. Blakely III was born; daughter Nora was born eleven years later, September 8, 1951. There was a hiatus in the marriage from 1969 to 1973, when the Blakelys lived apart. During that time, Brooks wrote her autobiography. In it she describes Henry as "a man of intellect, imagination, and dynamic 'constitution' " (*RPO*, 58). A lifelong integrationist, he maintained his political conviction throughout his wife's approach toward a Black Naitonalist/separatist position.

Teachers in school had admired and encouraged the poet's creative writing. Early, along with the regular program of English and American literature, she read *Caroling Dusk* (1927), Countee Cullen's anthology in which she was introduced to many Harlem Renaissance writers.[8] Brooks was greatly impressed by Hughes's *The Weary Blues* (1926) and Ralph Waldo Emerson's "Self-Reliance" and "Compensation." Later, her reading of Chekhov, Whitman, Eliot, Pound, Joyce, Hemingway, Frost, Dickinson, John Crowe Ransom, Merrill Moore, and occasionally Millay registered.

The mature honing of her talent took place in 1941, when Inez Cunningham Stark, elegant upper-class rebel from Chicago's "Gold Coast," brought her capabilities to the South Side Community Art Center. A reader for *Poetry* magazine who served on its board after 1938, Stark conducted a class in modern poetry that combined stringent poetry workshop standards, readings from the work of prominent poets, and prosodic instruction, using Robert Hillyer's *First Principles of Verse* as a text.[9] Both Henry and Gwendolyn were regular members, as were Edward Bland, to whom *Annie Allen* is posthumously dedicated; William Couch; John Carlis, a California painter; Margaret Taylor Goss (Burroughs), now director of the Museum of Afro-American History; and Margaret Danner Cunningham, the poet who became, for a short period, an associate editor of *Poetry*. The obituary of Inez Stark Boulton which appears in the *Chicago Daily News* of August 19, 1957, is quoted in its entirety in the Brooks autobiography (*RPO*, 68). The account cites Mrs. Boulton for bringing Le Corbusier, Léger, and Prokofiev to this country when she was president of the Renaissance Society of the University of Chicago (1936-40), but overlooks her work with the South Side Community Art Center.

Brooks also pays the highest tribute to Langston Hughes, "the noble poet, the efficient essayist, the adventurous dramatist," who strongly influenced her life and her art (*RPO*, 70-71). Striking parallels may be drawn between their commitment to expressing Black experience; their Garvey heritage of African nostalgia; and the absorption of blues, jazz, and common speech into their poetry. Brooks characterizes Hughes as a man of great understanding who (like herself) befriended and aided many black writers, an "easy man." This was a matter of personality, not principle, whose firmness clearly shows in recently published material and evaluations.[10] Along with Sterling A. Brown, she observes, Hughes celebrates the richness of Black personality, subscribes to Black hope, and features them in his work. As noted by Alain Locke and others, he is a poet of the urban masses. "Poet of the city," Jean Wagner calls him, naming Brown his "antithesis . . . poet *par excellence* of the soil."[11]

Like Hughes, Brooks adapts older forms while she develops the new. Both experiment with visual emblems, and both adopt the venerable practice of initial capitalization for types of emphasis. *Aloneness* appears in script; *The Tiger Who Wore White Gloves* in full capitals. Hughes capitalizes throughout *Ask Your Mama—Twelve Moods for Jazz* (1961). Antipodal to e. e. cummings's lowercasing, it reflects, nevertheless, the latter's explorations in typography.

Hughes devoted several of his newspaper columns to the young poet and later dedicated to her a book of short stories, *Something in Common* (1963). Brooks also acknowledges assistance from a number of writers, critics, and editors, such as Paul Engle, whose review of *A Street in Bronzeville* in the *Chicago Tribune* "initiated My Reputation" (*RPO*, 72), and Elizabeth Lawrence, whose warm and critical presence will be accounted.

The poet's recognition grew: she received an award in 1943 ("my first public prize") at the Midwestern Writers' Conference, directed by Alice Manning Dickey. She began in 1948 to review books for Van Allen Bradley, literary editor of the *Chicago Daily News*, Hoke Norris and Herman Kogan of the *Chicago Sun-Times*, and Robert Cromie of the *Chicago Tribune*. She also reviewed for Hoyt W. Fuller's *Negro Digest* (later titled *Black World*), the *New York Times*, and the *New York Herald Tribune*. Eventually concluding that a reviewer as well as a critic "should have read Everything," she declined to review any further. From the selected excerpts of her reviews, the reference to Randall Jarrell's *The Lost World* (1965) bears special mention. Her straightforward approach to criticism, like her "straight" approach to writing, admired by Richard Wright in a 1945 letter to her, is epitomized in the following:

> "The Lost World" poems are interesting. Again we must be grateful, in this day when poets offer verse that is exquisite but not interesting, scintillating but not interesting, shrewd and controlled and carved with terribly serious care—but not interesting. (*RPO*, 75)

Given the positive reinforcements provided by family and by early publishing experience, book publication increased the poet's confidence and sense of achievement. When interviewed in 1950, she was described as "a shy brown young woman of thirty-two" who explained thus her reluctance to speak on race relations: "There's nothing like knowing your limitations. The reason I'm a writer is because I'm no good at expressing myself orally. When you make a mistake on paper you can correct it, but you have to live with a mistake when you express it while speaking."[12]

Although she still seemed reserved by temperament in 1960, there were a number of other factors in her growing self-assurance. Before 1967, for example, in addition to the publication of five more volumes, generally well received, there was a succession of prizes: the *Mademoiselle* Merit Award (1945); an American Academy of Arts and Letters grant in literature (1946); Guggenheim fellowships (1946, 1947); the Eunice Tietjens Memorial Prize of *Poetry* magazine (1949); the Pulitzer Prize in poetry for *Annie Allen* (1950); the Friends of Literature Poetry Award (1963); the Thormod Monsen Literature Award (1964); and Litt. D. from Lake Forest College (1965). She was invited to teach, first at the University of Chicago (1962), then at Columbia College in Chicago (1963-69), which conferred an honorary L.H.D. in 1964.

By 1951 the poet had borne two children of whom she was proud. Her body had performed as "it was *supposed* to do. . . . I wanted my body, as well as my mind and spirit, to succeed, to reach an appropriate glory" (*RPO*, 204). She was deeply moved by the death of her father in 1959, to whom she dedicated *The Bean Eaters*. Significant repercussions of a parent's death are partly explained by the Freudian concept of "introjection," psychologically "taking in" the important figure to preserve its life. The salient qualities of David Brooks suggest the buttressing of strength and aspiration already raised in his daughter. This firming permitted reverberations of the Civil Rights Movement to sound directly in her work. Just as World War II had animated "Gay Chaps at the Bar" and "Negro Hero" in Brooks's first volume, specific political events charged with urgency the humanism of *The Bean Eaters* and *Selected Poems*.

The visionary moment occurred in 1967 at the Second Fisk University Writers' Conference. Describing the awe and excitement of finding herself, together with Margaret Danner Cunningham, "in some inscrutable and uncomfortable wonderland" anticipating the arrival of Amiri Baraka (then LeRoi Jones), she comments, "Until 1967 I had sturdy ideas about writing and about writers which I enunciated sturdily. . . . Until 1967 my own blackness did not confront me with a shrill spelling of itself" (*RPO*, 73, 84).

Returning to Chicago in May, Brooks met Walter Bradford through Oscar Brown, Jr., via a telephone conversation. Brown had culled a musical talent show, *Opportunity, Please Knock*, from the Blackstone Rangers, a large, teen-aged gang with which Bradford worked as a social organizer. Brooks began a poetry workshop for interested Ranger members at the First Presbyterian Church, where rehearsals for the production took place. As the members gradually returned to their rehearsals, others, intent on poetry, came to her and began meeting at her house— youth organizers and students from Wilson Junior College, including don l. lee (now Haki R. Madhubuti) and Carolyn M. Rodgers, the former having already published *Think Black*, the latter to be nominated for a National Book Award (1976) in poetry for *How I Got Ovah*. The group increased slightly; the workshop became an integral part of their lives and of Brooks's life. From this workshop, Brooks later produced the anthology *Jump Bad*.

Some of the students also registered in the Organization for Black American Culture (OBAC, pronounced Oh-bah'-see) workshop program. Brooks, too, involved herself, assisting in the dedication of OBAC's "Wall of Respect" in Chicago (see Brooks's poem "The Wall"). This slum ruin, proudly decorated with a mural featuring black heroes, has since been torn down by the city. Brooks's importance to the community at large was recognized the following year by her 1968 appointment to succeed Carl Sandburg as Poet Laureate of Illinois.

As a principal figure of the Contemporary Forum, a lecture bureau under the energetic direction of Beryl Zitch, Brooks toured widely. She gave readings and conducted poetry workshops at many universities. Her own reading favored African writers, such as the Ugandan poet Okot p'Bitek, whose *The Song of Lawino* particularly impressed her. And she turned to Dudley Randall's pioneering Broadside Press for the publication of *Riot*. Brooks's gesture of commitment to Black solidarity meant leaving a secure position without any financial guarantees. Typically, however, she had always shared her "wealth," as Madhubuti comments in his introduction to *Report from Part One*. His own work, in which Brooks firmly believes, has received her financial as well as spiritual assistance.

After the Gwendolyn Brooks Cultural Center was opened at Western Illinois University in Macomb, Illinois, March 1970, 1971 saw further developments in Brooks's career. She started an annual magazine, *The Black Position*. Its auspicious first issue featured articles by Dudley Randall, Hoyt W. Fuller, Lerone Bennett, Jr., don l. lee, Curtis Ellis, Larry Neal, Francis and Val Gray Ward, and Carolyn M. Rodgers. A volume, *To Gwen With Love*, was dedicated to her by members of the Black artistic community. *The World of Gwendolyn Brooks* completed her publications with Harper's. At Broadside, in addition to *Jump Bad*, she edited *A Broadside Treasury*, an excellent anthology that includes "Martin Luther King, Jr.," a Memorial Broadside published April 5, 1968, the day after the assassination. The poet visited East Africa for the first time, an epiphanic experience described in her autobiography. That fall, she served as Distinguished Professor of the Arts at the City College of New York.

Brooks's reading and lecturing schedule had grown intensive during the sixties. In 1966 she suffered a mild coronary attack complicated by influenza. In 1971 she suffered another heart seizure around Christmas. The City College term was nearly over; the strenuous weekly commuter flights ended. Convalescing the following year, the poet prepared her autobiography for publication by Broadside Press. Afterwards, she journeyed to England with her husband in 1973, marking their reconciliation.

The couple traveled to Ghana and parts of England and France in the summer of 1974.

Along with other distinctions, including the 1973 appointment as honorary Consultant in American Letters to the Library of Congress, Brooks has received more that fifty honorary doctorates from American colleges and universities. She became, in 1976, the first black woman elected to the National Institute of Arts and Letters. In the same year, she was given the Shelley Memorial Award by the Poetry Society of America; a theater piece based on her poetry, "Among All This You Stand Like a Fine Brownstone," was produced in Washington, D.C.[13] Her honors continue to increase. In 1984 she received the Johnson Publishing Company's Black Achievement Award in Fine Arts.

By 1977, health problems, her own and those of her mother, increased. Mrs. Brooks was hospitalized, then moved to her daughter's house, where the poet undertook full nursing care. Two months after Brooks helped celebrate Carl Sandburg's one hundredth birthday memorial in 1978, her beloved mother died. The poet grieved deeply and sought to work out her own recovery. After receiving an honorary doctor of letters degree from the City College of the City University of New York, she visited England and France. Brooks resumed her extensive travels in the United States, giving readings and workshops, participating in various aspects of black life and culture.

On January 3, 1980, she read at the White House in the company of twenty other distinguished poets, including Robert Hayden and Stanley Kunitz, at "A Salute to Poetry and American Poets." One might interpret as a feminist gesture her selection of "the mother," a controversial poem on abortion, which had appeared in her first volume thirty-five years before. She was subsequently appointed to the Presidential Commission on the National Agenda for the Eighties.

The Gwendolyn Brooks Junior High School, at Harvey, Illinois, was dedicated on November 24, 1981. In 1982 Brooks visited the Soviet Union as guest of a conference of prominent Soviet and American writers. In 1983 she returned to England to judge the Sotheby's International Poetry Contest. More recently, she was named Consultant in Poetry to the Library of Congress (1985-86).

Brooks's values animate her advice to young writers: that they be educated, read widely, write, and "live richly with eyes open, and heart, too."[14] An unflinching responsibility reflects the "Duty-Loving mother" she admired. Her talent retains its youthful capacity for growth and change:

> I—who have "gone the gamut" from an almost angry rejection of my dark skin by some of my brainwashed brothers and sisters to a surprised queenhood in the new black sun—am qualified to enter at least the kindergarten of new consciousness now. New consciousness and trudge-toward-progress.
>
> I have hopes for myself. [*RPO*, 86]

2

A Street in Bronzeville

On July 18, 1944, Gwendolyn Brooks submitted her first collection, *A Street in Bronzeville*,[1] to Harper and Brothers.[2] His interest immediately stirred, senior editor Edward C. Aswell sent the manuscript to Richard Wright for an evaluation. Wright responded enthusiastically to the work and its accurate portrayal of Negro life, although he judged the manuscript too slight for a volume. He took exception to only one poem, "the mother," because of its subject matter, abortion. Wright felt that the poet's strength lay in ballads and blues and the glimpses of lost people in an urban black society. The title seemed esoteric; nor did he favor drawings, as Brooks had suggested.

Aswell agreed with all of Wright's comments. On September 22, 1944, Elizabeth Lawrence, who was to become the poet's editor of twenty years, wrote the letter of acceptance.[3] A copy of the Wright letter was enclosed. Lawrence inquired about the poet's life as it might affect her productivity, and whether Brooks had any prose projects like a novel or short stories in mind.

Brooks wrote back on September 28, a happy letter that first mentions *American Family Brown*. This proposed series of related poems underwent numerous metamorphoses of conception and execution over the years, emerging as *Maud Martha* in 1953. Brooks enclosed a sonnet sequence, "Gay Chaps at the Bar," with which she hoped to end the book (as it does), and expressed dissatisfaction with her prose. She told Lawrence that, as a wife and mother of a four-year-old son she worked between chores. But writing was the only "work" that interested her. She aimed to continue to present Negroes as people, not exotics, whether in prose or verse. She would avoid, however, merely propagandistic poetry. Although she appreciated Richard Wright's letter, she felt that the stressed element in "the mother" was not abortion but the poverty that made for ambivalence in the mother, thwarting her maternal desire. Brooks hoped, moreover, to retain the title "A Street in Bronzeville." It had occurred to her first, and most of the poems had been written especially for it.

In October, Lawrence journeyed to Chicago, and the two met. Apologizing for her shyness, Brooks confessed in a subsequent letter that she had drunk her first martini on the occasion. She defined her concept of poetry as truth and beauty. Yet the former was no substitute for the latter, which could exist without it. (Note the later shift in theoretical emphasis.)[4] She also included part of the first draft of "The Sundays of Satin-Legs Smith," which reveals the typically hard work of revision that went into her poems. On October 30, Lawrence replied with a warm and reassuring letter, enclosing a contract. Brooks promptly accepted (Nov. 2) with a courteous tribute to the editor's judgment on publication date, manuscript length, and arrangement of pieces, but she retained the final decision on sequence. She disclosed that she was planning to write fiction next. Predictably, the news pleased the editor. Most publishers whose writers leave narrow sales precincts for potentially broad ones rejoice.

By February 1945 (when two pages of her poems appeared in *Harper's Magazine*) the poet was working on *American Family Brown*, then projected as her first novel. Having conceived the order of the poems, she requested that the heading "A Street in Bronzeville" be retained for the first section. Brooks agreed to begin with "the old-marrieds," but objected to "Negro Hero" as following the sonnet sequence "Gay Chaps at the Bar." (Note that the proximity would have appended the poem to the sonnets, blurring their differences.) She was pleased that her editor still favored the title *A Street in Bronzeville*.

In March, Lawrence endorsed the poet's arrangement. Despite one editor's objections to "Ballad of Pearl May Lee," Lawrence liked it, she maintained, as did the majority of editors in the office. Brooks wrote back that she was not certain enough of her own feelings to withstand serious objections. Interestingly, William Rose Benét (to EL) singled out the piece for special praise. In response to Lawrence's query, Brooks's March 24 letter included her favorable, perceptive views on Wright's *Black Boy*.

The next month, Lawrence acknowledged receipt of a new poem, "People Protest in Sprawling Lightless Ways," which appears in *Annie Allen*. She observed that, like the poem, a new volume of Brooks verse should possibly command a more universal appeal than *Bronzeville*. She reported general delight with Benét's warm approval, which would accompany Wright's comments on the jacket. The publication date was set for August 15.

In July, Brooks wrote her editor that chapter 19 of *American Family Brown* would appear in the magazine *Portfolio*, and that Paul Engle would review *Bronzeville* for the *Chicago Tribune*. Engle had conferred poetry workshop awards upon the poet in 1944 and 1945 at the Annual Writers' Conference of Northwestern University. On August 3, Gwendolyn Brooks received her first copies of *A Street in Bronzeville*.

On August 14, V-J Day (formally celebrated September 2), Lawrence remarked the propitious timing of the publication, which corresponded with the historic event. Advance sales figures (including books to reviewers and consignment bookshop purchases) had already exceeded 2,500 copies; a second printing appeared the following month. Reviews, generally quite favorable, were published in *The New Yorker, Poetry,* and the *Saturday Review of Literature*, among other magazines, and in newspapers like the *Chicago Tribune* and the *New York Times*.

Brooks's career was fully and splendidly launched. News that she was one of ten young women to receive the *Mademoiselle* Merit Award for Distinguished Achievement in 1945 would bring her to New York for a first visit in December, a visit she anticipated in a letter to Lawrence (Dec. 3). The editor replied immediately that December 28 should be set aside for a reception at which Brooks would meet Richard Wright. Brooks's excitement and delight mark the tone of the correspondence during these months, continuing through the spring of 1946 when she was notified of the Guggenheim Fellowship and the American Academy of Arts and Letters Award ($1,000). Work on *American Family Brown* seemed promising in January 1946 when a synopsis and ten chapters were sent to Lawrence; they served to renew the Guggenheim in 1947.

"Bronzeville," Brooks remarks, was a name invented by the *Chicago Defender* (*RPO*, 160). She described it to Lawrence as a South Side area of about forty blocks, running north and south from 29th to 69th Streets, and east and west about thirteen blocks from Cottage Grove to State Street (Sept. 28, 1944). An anatomy of Bronzeville appears in the important sociological study *Black Metropolis*, by St. Clair Drake and Horace R. Cayton.[5] These authors analyze the nature and consequences of segregated black life and call for integration to combat its evils. In "Bronzeville 1961," a new chapter for the 1962 edition, Drake and Cayton find that their foci of investigation or "axes of life" remain what they had been in 1945 when the study was first made. The categories are " 'staying alive,' 'getting ahead,' 'having fun,' 'praising god,' and 'advancing the Race' " (Drake, xv). In some respects these topics gloss *A Street in Bronzeville*, although skepticism tinges "praising god" and irony touches the "Race Hero" who is "advancing the Race."

A corollary aspect of "advancing the Race" by individual achievement or through social action is "the demand for solidarity" (Drake, ch. 23). This longstanding desire roots Brooks's later concern, most marked in *Beckonings* and "In Montgomery." It partly explains the early sources of her interest and the depth of her later chagrin at the erosion of unity.

Brooks initially planned *A Street in Bronzeville* to portray a personality, event, or idea representing each of thirty houses on a street in the vicinity (GB/EL, March 12, 1945). The sequence of twenty poems in the first section, "A Street in Bronzeville," is close in tone[6] and milieu to the following five, grouped here as "Five Portraits." All the poems give humanistic and compassionate glimpses of black life. The first section focuses on common existence; the middle one, except for "Hattie Scott," offers longer poems that probe distinct and dramatic characters. The third and last section, "Gay Chaps at the Bar," comprises the sonnet sequence. Thematically, the volume is largely structured around two units: local/black and national/multiracial. Brooks exposes their interrelationships—personal, social, and national. The theme of entrapment, by community norms, socioeconomic forces, and personal psychology, underlies the whole.[7]

"Negro Hero" and "The Sundays of Satin-Legs Smith" form a central contrast near the middle of the book. In the latter poem, a politically apathetic dandy reflects material values of the dominant white culture around him, while the black blues "weep" for him out of juke boxes. Smith filters both a white cultural and sociopolitical exhaustion, and a pre-Black Rebellion seeming quiescence. Beside the Negro Hero who is "advancing the Race," he functions as reality and contrast, epitomizing "staying alive," "having fun," and perversely "getting ahead." "Negro Hero," following "Satin-Legs," looks past "Hattie Scott" and "Queen of the Blues" to the forthright announcement of "Ballad of Pearl May Lee." Its subject connects with national segregation in "Gay Chaps at the Bar" and carries forward the social criticism, overt and implied, of previous poems.

Through the poet's humane purview, local boundaries include more than limit: we enter a microcosm.[8] A *Street in Bronzeville*, furthermore, represents a prevailing social and literary temper. The wartime and postwar impetus toward racial integration, present in a poem like the seventh sonnet in "Gay Chaps," "the white troops had their orders but the Negroes looked like men," rarely appears without irony. One recalls Richard Wright's observation (true, perhaps, of women's writing, also) that black people's early, repressive experiences made their inner lives necessarily rich and complex. He sometimes envied, nevertheless, white children's simple and unconvoluted encounters with society.[9]

Developments in modern poetry, the Harlem Renaissance, and her reading preferences imprint Brooks's first volume. In one source, she lists as favorites Chekhov, Dickinson, John Crowe Ransom, Langston Hughes, the Joyce of *Dubliners*, the Eliot of "Portrait of a Lady," "The Love Song of J. Alfred Prufrock," "The Hollow Men," and "The Waste Land," and Merrill Moore's conversational sonnets.[10] In her poem to Robert Frost she observes, "He is splendid. With a place to stand." All the admired writers listed share qualities of tight structure, apt detail, and delight in language.

The shadows of Pound, Eliot, and Hemingway, which Houston A. Baker, Jr., sees in the antiwar theme of "Gay Chaps at the Bar," accompany "the metaphysical complexities of John Donne and the word magic of Apollinaire, Eliot, and Pound. The high style of both authors [Brooks and W.E.B. Du Bois], however, is often used to explicate the condition of the black American trapped behind a veil that separates him from the white world. What one seems to have is 'white' style and 'black' content—'two warring ideals in one dark body.' "[11] ("Two warring ideals" is a quotation from Du Bois in *The Souls of Black Folk*.) Kent, on the other hand, emphasizes "the powerful negatives and positives" in her poetry: "We find them yoked and coordinated. . . . Her sensibility produces a unified confrontation with life and art."[12]

Since this study aims to discern the dynamic confluence of black and white poetic energy in Brooks's work, the latter view applies here. For example, the ballad (an English and/or "white" form), the sonnet (an Italian-originated and/or white form), the blues (a black form), syncopation (a black-adapted and developed form)—all meet in *A Street in Bronzeville*. "Black content," however, like "white content," holds properties common to all human experience and is no more exclusive or homogeneous, necessarily, than black or white form. What bears the most fruitful observation in Brooks and, indeed, any good poet, is the close relation of form to content.

Thus, within *Bronzeville*'s multivoiced abundance and through its mixture of black and white elements, Brooks employs and modifies the ballad form, adapts the blues into a pattern with the ballad in "Queen of the Blues," and melds Petrarchan and Shakespearean sonnet forms into contemporary modes and themes. Finally, it is music we hear in these poems, whether in the ballad, a poem meant to be sung, in the blues, or in the lyrical sonnets (as are most of the "Gay Chaps" sequence). Brooks gathers the several strains—religious, chiefly the spirituals Du Bois refers to as "sorrow songs,"[13] and secular—into her oral poetry. Her sure ear demands that her poems, like those of nearly all the best poets (including Milton, a poet-hero who also was "musical" and had a musically oriented father), be read aloud.

Irony[14] and technique unify her vision without reducing its range. This range confronts us in *Bronzeville* and resonates throughout even the simpler pieces. Brooks dramatizes everyday existence while her prosodic variations support its diversity. Regarding "white influences" mentioned above, such as the discernible Eliot in "kitchenette building," "obituary for a living lady," and "when you have forgotten Sunday," the pertinence is not Eliot's whiteness but the character, usage, and meaning of his work for Brooks. It represents a Western bourgeois, post-World War I weariness, anomie, and acedia; a quest for faith; an expatriate mentality that led him, Pound, Stein, Hemingway, and others to flee their American roots. Brooks, however, exchanges enervation for social criticism.

I. "A Street in Bronzeville"

This sequence of vignettes gives a cross section of the residents. Young, old, middle-aged, mostly poor, they reveal their hopes, needs, commonality, and differences. The seemingly heterogeneous order of the poems keys their mosaic pattern.

"[T]he old-marrieds" introduces the section with an ironic view of constrained, respectable life. The hyphenation to which Brooks will turn increasingly for her compounding appears in title and verse; the lyricism introduces the music of the poems. The three couplets, varying from six to eight feet, suggest the septenaries favored in Medieval and Renaissance English poetry; their stanzaic length wryly acknowledges pairing. The old-marrieds are not swayed by the May season, the call of "pretty-coated birds," or the sight of lovers in "little side-streets." Alienated as much from the romantic scene as from each other, they are doomed to voyeurism. He hears the birds and sees the lovers; she hears "the morning stories," soap opera accounts of love "clogged with sweets." The word "clogged," the presence of the silent couple amid happy sounds, and the repetition of the first line at the close, "But in the crowding darkness not a word did they say," indicate an eroded relationship rather than tacit intimacy. Repetition encircles the couple in muted announcement of the volume's major theme: entrapment.

"[K]itchenette building" steps past façade into an apartment. Taking an Eliotic wryness from "The Hollow Men" Brooks begins, "We are things of dry hours and the involuntary plan." The

Latinate verbal tendency, favored by Eliot, is suggested by "involuntary," but gives way immediately to terse phrasing that evokes the local scene. Irregular rhyme, slant rhyme, and meter move toward pentameter. The thirteen lines present a kitchenette milieu where things incline askew. Nothing works well: yesterday's garbage remains "ripening in the hall"; patience is rewarded by tepid water in the communal bathroom on each floor ("We think of lukewarm water, hope to get in it").

The poem poses the question of dreams deferred, the "raisin in the sun" that Langston Hughes feared they would become. The poet-narrator wonders whether aspiration can survive its fight with "onion fumes" and "fried potatoes" and the entire constellation of poverty. Colors of the dream are "white" and "violet." Brooks has commented that the colors were chosen for their "delicacy," and that, although dreams can be nightmares, she preferred to deal with them in the poem as "lovely lightsome things." White is partly ironic. Violet, color of the flower that figures in the tenth sonnet of "Gay Chaps at the Bar," is a solitary flower, honeyed, self-pollinating. The speaker doubts that art, "an aria" sung by the dream, can survive its physical habitation.

From the interior view of the staid "old-marrieds" and "kitchenette," Brooks probes deeper. "[T]he mother" is a dramatic monologue on abortion, a controversial topic then, as now. She comments: "Hardly your crowned and praised and 'customary' Mother; but a Mother not unfamiliar, who decides that *she*, rather than her World, will kill her children. The decision is not nice, not simple, and the emotional consequences are neither nice nor simple" (*RPO*, 184).

The poet employs full rhyme with a touch of slant in this thirty-two-line poem, very irregularly metered. The first stanza rhymes five couplets; the second alternates rhyme in the first six lines, then continues the couplet pattern. The meter, rolling insistent, often anapestic, conveys the profound agitation of the speaker. Tonal control, epecially in the first stanza, heightens tension. The mother begins rhetorically, "Abortions will not let you forget," addressing the reader/listener in impersonal second person. She reviews the loss judiciously: the children will not be neglected; she will not be burdened. But during the second stanza, her defenses fall away: "I have heard in the voices of the wind the voices of my dim killed children." The woman then justifies herself to the aborted children, confessing that her "crime" was not "deliberate." She wanted to shield them from a painful existence. She loved them all, she insists, the last line univerbal, emphatic: "All."

We leave the strong emotions of "the mother" for the light "southeast corner," a poem of three unbroken ballad stanzas. Here "The School of Beauty," whose "Madam" has died, has been replaced by a tavern. This opening information comments iron- ically on the concept of beauty ("Madam" suggests the manager of a bordello, which Brooks did not intend, as well as the director of a school) and the state of society. Vulgarized art cedes to the tavern's illusory companionship, release, and escape. Alcohol connotes the flight from entrapment.

The Madam lies in her grave "Out at Lincoln," beneath the grandest monument in the cemetery, buried in a fine, "right red" ("bright" is a printer's mistaken correction in the omnibus vol- ume), velvet-lined steel casket and a lovely gown that have con- sumed her entire fortune, testaments to her isolated existence which left no heirs, "While over her tan impassivity / Shot silk is shining." A mischievous elegiac connects "Lincoln" (the most notable black cemetery in Chicago and the name of the assassi- nated president) in the third line with "shot silk" in the last line. The lack of separation between the three ballad stanzas (a joining that will serve other purposes in "In the Mecca") suggests a monumental effect for this small gem.

From the death of the Madam, we revert to life and procrea- tion. "[W]hen Mrs. Martin's Booker T.," a dramatic ballad, adds the desire for "respectability" to the sociological picture of Bronzeville. Thus Mrs. Martin's feelings of acute disgrace when her son "ruins" Rosa Brown lead her to move from her neigh- borhood to "the low west side of town." She says she will have nothing to do with Booker T. until he marries the girl he has impregnated. The son's name is highly ironic, since Booker T. Washington, founder of Tuskegee Institute and recipient of many honors, is the paragon of the respectable, industrious Negro. Booker T. dashes any hopes he or his mother might have enter- tained for his "getting ahead" or "advancing the Race," let alone maintaining respectability. He has, of course, avoided personal entrapment by rejecting marriage with someone he apparently does not love, but the social consequences are high, including rejection by his mother. (GB: "For the record, or just your private information, the *real* Booker T.—not, unfortunately, his name— DID succumb to his mother's blandishments and DID marry the girl, living many years of misery and thwart, until he finally left her and married, later, an older woman who made him very happy. [The 'ruined' girl's name was poetic—Pearl.]")

The lean verse features one telling simile. Mrs. Martin assures us that her son has "wrung my heart like a chicken neck." The chicken, which will become a recurrent symbol of the innocent victim throughout Brooks's work (see especially *Annie Allen* and *Maud Martha*), here suggests violation of the mother's innocent hopes and the humble circumstances that "chicken neck" evokes.

From the wayward Booker T., Brooks turns to "the soft man," who seeks to escape the crudities and spiritual poverty of his days by weekly church attendance. His solitude and despair recall the old man who sits outside the cafe in Ernest Hemingway's "A Clean, Well-Lighted Place," a title echoing in the "clean, unanxious place" to which the soft man will "creep on Sundays." Partly in pentameter, irregularly rhymed, the poem marks the first appearance of Brooks's emphatic capitalization in the volume. "Being seen Everywhere (keeping Alive)" also partly approximates "staying alive." Brooks turns here to black vernacular speech, dance/music ("Rhumboogie"), and local place-names (see n. 21).

After the pious "soft man," "the funeral" skeptically views mourning conventions and hypocrisies. The ambling, irregular meter and random rhyme suggest disorientations of thought and image. In "sweet clichés," the "dishonesty of deft tact" that avoids confronting death, the mourners take comfort. Images, like odors of the flowers, wind about them as they turn to each other to pray "vaguely." "The flowers provide a kind of heat" sets a richly connotative image between the cold and decay of the corpse and the fear of the mourners. Extolling Heaven and its spiritual rewards ("'Heaven is Good denied, / Rich are the men who have died.'") typifies solaces welcomed in Bronzeville, as elsewhere. Religious pieties portrayed as "a dear blindfold," cherished, but costly, subdue the clamor of real social and economic problems. "I hope you hear," Brooks told an interviewer, "how this poem cries out for our doing something about our plight right now, and not depending on acquiring God or whatever."[15]

Following the general critique in "the funeral," Brooks examines a specific quest for grace. "[H]unchback girl: she thinks of heaven" is a fine lyric of ten lines (a classical number of perfection), mainly iambic pentameter, random rhyme, and pronounced alliteration. It presents a view of normalcy toward which the "crooked" girl's dreams are projected. She addresses God as her Father in heaven, which is surely "a blue place, / And straight. Right. Regular." Alliteration emphasizes the desired vertical correctness and uniformity. "Out of coils, / Unscrewed, released, no more to be marvelous," she will not need to sublimate emotions into scholarship. Rather than a place where her lovely spirit will shine through, however, heaven becomes conformity, "proper halls" where she, too, will be "proper." Held in a disdainful society, yet accepting its values, the girl's twisted body turns social emblem.

A "normal" young girl, also dissatisfied, appears in "a song in the front yard." In this ballad variation, the girl describes her quarrel with respectable life. Confined "in the front yard," she wants "a peek at the back," at the weeds and roughness of "untended," spontaneous existence, because "A girl gets sick of a rose." Not without humor, her refractory vision takes in the exciting backyard world. The child's eyes romanticize poverty; they do not see its restrictions. The insight appears obliquely in her mother's sneering pronouncements that "the charity children," forbidden companions, will grow up to be "bad" or go to "Jail" (capitalized) like the boy who stole and sold her family's back gate. Significantly, the back rather than the front gate was removed, for through this opening the child's dreams escape her environment. Freudian interpretation works here—suggesting the superego front yard and the ego/id/libido backyard.

The young girl would be intrigued with the subject of "patent leather." Like "the soft man," the poem utilizes Black English. A ballad variation with marked alliteration, it tells of "That cool chick down on Calumet" who "got herself a brand new cat, / With pretty patent-leather hair." The speaker, a macho neighbor, envies the man who has intrigued the good-looking woman. The syncopated first line also begins the third stanza. "Hair," slant rhymed with "her" in the following line, "And he is man enough for her," pokes sly fun at the style popular among black (and, to an extent, white) men in the forties—the pomaded Italian and Latin movie star look that white men had seriously emulated in the twenties and thirties. The second stanza continues critique of the subject's "shrill" voice and "pitiful" muscle. The stanza's rhythmic irregularity emphasizes roughness and the speaker's disapproval, setting off both against smoothness and the stylistic conventionality of the "new cat."

In the next poem, a third young black girl faces still another type of social problem. "[T]he ballad of chocolate Mabbie," like the "Ballad of Pearl May Lee," epitomizes what Arthur P. Davis calls the "black-and-tan motif" in Brooks's poetry, i.e., the white culture-inspired valuing of lightness among blacks themselves.[16] "Chocolate" recalls both the color and the food made from cocoa beans; the young Annie Allen in "The Anniad" will be compared with "sweet and chocolate." Associated with childhood and youth, desired by black and white alike, the irony of its taste figures here. Mabbie at seven breaks her heart over Willie Boone who "wore like a jewel a lemon-hued lynx / With sand-waves loving her brow." With compassion, the poet views the child who stands alone at the gate, watching her beloved Willie. Joined by the "chocolate companions" of her future self (according to Brooks, "*other* dark girls, now & in the future"), Mabbie, trapped in the hue of her skin, will surely experience disappointments in love. Transitions are skillfully handled in the six quatrains. Variations on the initial line move subtly from an image of "Mabbie without the grammar school gates," thinking that they were "the pearly gates" of heaven, until her rude encounter with Willie.

The spiritual question in the previous poem and the spiritual presence of the Black church in Bronzeville introduce "the preacher: ruminates behind the sermon." A notably contemporary piece, it was cited in 1974 as a source of controversy in Charleston, West Virginia, public school education.[17] Brooks opens, "I think it must be lonely to be God. / Nobody loves a master." God may feel the lack of a "hand to hold." He is both remotely omnipotent and humanly deprived. God as "master" invokes the concept of "slave" and slavery, adding political irony to the religious subject and skepticism to the humanist tact. Images of the Deity suggest a fearsome employer; creatures "running out / From servant-corners" recall Milton's "Sonnet 19," in which God's "state is Kingly. / Thousands at his bidding speed." In Milton, God's yoke is "milde," not heavy as in Brooks, where no one dares befriend the Deity. To "slap Him on the shoulder" or buy him a drink would be unthinkable. But he may tire of perpetually looking down upon the world, says Brooks, and might prefer a more equitable relationship with his worshippers. Questioning the idea "of being great / In solitude," the poet indirectly invokes her own concept of greatness and the heroic ideal. A leader must be close to his followers, she implies. Her view on leadership is democratic, not authoritarian.

The four quatrains, based on iambic pentameter, rhyme in the second and third lines of each stanza and irregularly slant rhyme in the others. The effect recesses the rhyme as a harmony withdrawn into the stanza and shielded or disguised by the outer lines. It is as if God were withdrawn into the stanzas, himself entrapped by ritual and remoteness.

"Sadie and Maud" poses a humanistic answer. Another ballad, verbally spare, it advances the theme of "a song in the front yard." It matches Sadie's involved spontaneity (like that envied by the young girl in the other poem) against Maud's conventional respectability (what the young girl might actually have become). "Sadie" recalls Sadie Thompson, the prostitute in Somerset Maugham's classic *Rain*. Maud's name derives from "Magdalene," the reformed adulteress in the New Testament, and recalls Tennyson's romantic heroine in the poem "Maud," so that for the reader— exceeding the poet's intention—there is further irony. Like Mrs. Martin, Booker T.'s mother, Sadie's parents react strongly to her out-of-wedlock childbearing: they nearly "died of shame." Sadie leaves her two daughters the expansive heritage of the "fine-tooth comb" with which she has scraped life. Maud goes to college, as the hunchback girl and chocolate Mabbie may do (GB: "Mabbie, maybe; the hunchback girl, no."), and remains unmarried, "a thin brown mouse" living alone in her house.

"Having fun," Sadie escapes from society's mores. Yet "staying alive," she accepts responsibility. Her daughters emulate her;

identification betokens affection. Sadie's life, financially and socially restricted, holds a spiritual vigor not accessible to Maud or even, perhaps, to "the mother." The speaker's colloquial tone and the lean toughness of the verse refine an implicit message: "Live!"

"[T]he independent man" avoids either woman's example: he deliberately escapes marriage. Sensing himself a fine vintage wine, he avoids the "cork" or trap of a dreary future like that of "the old-marrieds." The irony of conventional form (basically iambic pentameter, rhymed) represents a tensional grid for the man's struggle against society's expectations. In a closing heroic couplet, the poet lightly assures us that such a man, self-indulgent, inconstant, makes a better weekly visitor than a husband. He would give his wife "a good glee" as he showed "his leaping ruby," with its possible sexual connotation, to a friend. The word "glee" perversely suggests the happiness he will not provide. It also ironically invokes Emily Dickinson's "lonesome Glee."[18] Since a glee, moreover, is a song for three or more solo voices, it may connote the music, speech, and gossip in which the man's infidelities will be notoriously celebrated. (Ambiguity of the word foreshadows the interesting usage, on a larger scale, of "catch" in "A Catch of Shy Fish," *Selected Poems*.) The "independent man" presumably is "having fun."

More sophisticated than Maud, the heroine of "obituary for a living lady" recalls, in ironic tone and landscape of restraints, Eliot's "Portrait of a Lady." Eliot's rhyme varies; Brooks's eleven rhymed couplets are far more irregular in length. The terminal pull of her rhyme becomes an amused postscript, drawing attention to the subject's conventionality and timid, probably doomed gestures toward romance. The poet/speaker describes her friend paradoxically as a "decently wild" young woman, respectably shy of physical intimacy with the man she loves. He stops calling; by the time she relents, he has found "a woman who dressed in red." Discovering "the country of God" further entraps her libido, which can escape only through her "neutral kind bland eyes that moisten / the first pew center on Sunday—I beg your pardon /— Sabbath nights." (Contrast the earthy fervor of St. Julia Jones in "In the Mecca.") The poem's inconclusive ending (will the preacher's overtures succeed? will the young woman rebuff him?) hints that the "obituary" has already been written.

"[W]hen you have forgotten Sunday: the love story" affirms the durable coexistence of passion and respectability. The poem begins abruptly, like Eliot's "Prufrock." (Compare "Let us go then, you and I" with "—And when you have forgotten the bright bedclothes on a Wednesday and a Saturday.") But Brooks is not Prufrock, the "patient etherized." She enjoys her robust recollection of the past more than she mourns its losses.

Technically, the compound phrasing ("nothing-I-have-to-do and I'm-happy-why?") looks ahead to later style. Brooks organizes the verse (free, except for the three end rhymes, *bell, tell, well,* at lines 11, 27, and 29, respectively) in parallel syntax, introduced by adverbs and conjunctions. She ends with three lines whose rhyme (*a b a*) reinforces their summarizing. The poem maintains a long verbal breath. The twenty-nine lines essentially comprise one sentence that lists in sensuous detail the homely images of affection. Feelings, physical satisfactions, and tactile images which begin and end with the "bright bedclothes" revive the past. The poet closes, self-confident that if these items were forgotten, she would be, also. One may compare with "Ballad of Pearl May Lee": abrupt beginning, persistent feeling, intense focus; and contrast as to speaker, style, theme.

Noting that the poem " 'takes place' *in its present*," Brooks informs me that it refers to herself and Henry Blakely in the early days of their marriage, when they lived "at 623 East 63rd Street, our most exciting kitchenette," a corner apartment with a view of constant street activity (*RPO*, 69; also cited in "Langston Hughes," chapter 6).

From strong love to violence, the sequence shifts to "the murder," based on a neighborhood incident from Brooks's childhood. Returning to the ballad form, its five quatrains tell of the year-old baby, "poor Percy," whose brother Brucie "Burned him up for fun." Spareness and the paradox of complex simplicity remind us of William Blake's cognates of innocence and experience. Violent subject matter and the Anglo-Saxon names "Percy" and "Brucie" bespeak ancestry in the old English and Scottish popular ballad. Images stun grotesquely: Brucie delightedly watching his burning brother; Percy watching the fire "Chew on his baby dress" and "enjoying too / His brother's happiness."

Brucie, uncomprehending, expects his brother to return and play. Percy, who "wondered at the heat," dies still loving his brother "Who could, with clean and open eye, / Thoughtfully kill." By disregarding consequences, the poem suggests, people may "innocently" commit deadly acts, as in war. "Thoughtfully kill," ironic and ambiguous, stresses the inadequacy of intention divorced from feeling. Without what Wordsworth called the "feeling intellect," "thoughtful" may transpose into thoughtless, innocence into guilt.

Another death, undramatic, yet one implicating society, moves "of De Witt Williams on his way to Lincoln Cemetery." The poem was banned in 1962 by two radio stations (see chapter 6). Their officials decided that the musical version, "Elegy for a Plain Black Boy," composed by Oscar Brown, Jr., might offend by using the word "black." During the forties, however, WNEW, the New York station involved, had broadcast Brooks's reading of poems from *A Street in Bronzeville*, including the disputed work. An exquisite, ballad-type elegy, the poem celebrates the individual in his commonness. The main repetend, "He was nothing but a / Plain black boy," affirms ordinary humanity. The repeated verse from the spiritual, "Swing low swing low sweet chariot," posits death as release. Like Brooks's other protagonists, the young man has been trapped. "Having fun"—women and "liquid joy"—he escapes finally into the casket, his "chariot."

Brooks combines refrain and metrical elements of the ballad and Negro spiritual. She strategically deploys the lines of its five quatrains and two couplets: 4, 2, 4, 4, 4, 4, 2. The first and last two stanzas, nearly identical, frame the funeral procession as it passes the dead man's favorite retreats.

De Witt Williams has lived only minimally. "Matthew Cole" ("Here are the facts. / He's sixty-six.") has barely lived at all. Detail and imagery render the man's bleak life in a furnished room (actually that of Henry Blakely's aunt), where disorder retreats behind a defensive, public smile. Cole's dismal present, portrayed in the first stanza, is hardly brightened by "the whiteless grin" of the housekeeper, who collects four dollars on Saturday night and blares her radio at him on Sunday. The irregular, dominant trimeter of the stanza (mainly assonant and slant rhymed) expands to the regular tetrameter, rhymed and slant rhymed, of the second. The latter's form helps to project its images: a remote, orderly past of modest cheer.

The series ends with "the vacant lot"—still vacant on the street where Brooks was raised. Lines of the slight ballad vignette run together like the three stanzas of "southeast corner." The speaker observes matter-of-factly: "Mrs. Coley's three-flat brick / Isn't here any more." No one misses the family: Mrs. Coley, her arrogant, African son-in-law ("Rightful heir to the throne"), her adulterous daughter. Like a Greek chorus expressing the "respectable" voice of the community, the speaker takes malicious satisfaction in the son-in-law's cuckoldry. The block of verse, epitaphial, sounds an epilogue to the "Street in Bronzeville" group. A vague malaise abides. What will occupy the vacant lot? Change and empty space suggest possible counters to the entrapment theme as the portraits begin.

II. Five Portraits

"The Sundays of Satin-Legs Smith," a major work of one hundred fifty-nine lines, is the longest poem in the book.[19] Careful and extensive revising is apparent in two handwritten worksheets enclosed with the poet's letter to Lawrence after their first meeting (Oct. 25, 1944). Brooks's own note of criticism to herself that interpretation was needed appears after line 56, "Like narrow banners for some gathering war," a line in which she strove for an onomatopoeic rendering (GB: "like a gathering war, coming on, coming on—faint to loud"). In the published poem, however, the rhetorical information inserted amid the description of Satin-Legs's closet "innards" (ll. 57-61) seems dispensable. Generally, the poet hones the verse. Pentameter, often iambic, rhymes irregularly in couplets or randomly. Latinate -*tion* suffixes favored by Eliot and the balanced alliterations lend ironic elegance.

The poem opens with a couplet (below) and three tercets followed by three longer stanzas, then breaks into irregular stanzaic lengths. Structural tension between freedom and order mirrors the man's life, his desire for "having fun," and, through petty wardrobe luxuries, "getting ahead."

Inamoratas, with an approbation,
Bestowed his title. Blessed his inclination.)

As a dandy, a ladies' man, his closet, toiletries, and mirror ticket escape. The closet, a marvel of literature, is crammed like Gatsby's patent cabinets with suits, dressing gowns, ties, and shirts. Those "beautiful shirts" in "sheer linen and thick silk and fine flannel,"[20] tearfully admired by Daisy Buchanan, are parodied by the "wonder-suits in yellow and in wine, / Sarcastic green and zebra-striped cobalt" of Satin-Legs, best admired by himself. His closet, moreover, stands in a cheap hotel, not a mansion. "Let us proceed. Let us inspect, together," says the poet, showing us—with amusement and pity—the holdings of a scrubby lifetime. Although sedulously stylish, with the extreme padded shoulders of a forties "zoot suiter," even the colors of Satin-Legs's wardrobe mock him. Proud, pleased with his image ("Here is all his sculpture and his art"), his self-engrossed creativity footnotes Thorstein Veblen's "conspicuous consumption." Satin-Legs's body provides both art and industry: he is "reimbursed" for what skill and inclination lead him to perform.

The man arises from his Saturday night indulgences in "a clear delirium"—Brooks's oxymoron for an ecstatic residue. Fragrances of his luxuriant Sunday bath contrast with the smells of his impoverished childhood. "Lotion, lavender and oil" substitute for the elegant garden he will never cultivate. He breakfasts, walks among sounds of the everyday, respectable life closed to him. The restaurant juke boxes play "The Lonesome Blues, the Long-lost Blues, I Want A Big Fat Mama"—black music, it has been noted.[21] Names of the songs express Satin-Legs's own yearning. Again, as sculpture, art, and architecture of the outside world congeal into concern with body and dress, the blues replace classical music: Saint-Saëns, Grieg, Tschaikovsky, Brahms. "But could he love them?" the poet asks, then explains that "a man must bring / To music what his mother spanked him for." Brooks limns Satin-Legs's background: his father's small dream, his sister's prostitution, the poverty of "all his skipped desserts." Next she depicts his retreat from reality. He attends the movies where both hero and heroine are booed as they kiss. Only Mickey

Mouse, the tough, clever little rodent (trickster), receives general approval.

At "Joe's Eats," accompanied by his flamboyant date replaced each week, they eat and "go out full. / (The end is—isn't it?—all that really matters.)." The end for Satin-Legs is sex and death, though he would translate the sex into love. The lyric epilogue, a tetrameter sestet, its delicacy emphasized by *"Her body is like new brown bread,"* closes on a startlingly romantic note. The subject's tawdry existence can offer him meager authenticity. Like his father's "little dream," like the size of the lyric itself (six lines out of the hundred fifty-nine), the fantasy is a small one. Elusive as Gatsby's failed image of Daisy, Satin-Legs's submerged dreams of love, appended to his life, importantly end the poem.

"The Sundays of Satin-Legs Smith" is an achievement. Longer than "Prufrock," it similarly deals with an antiheroic vision, but it places the protagonist solidly in his environment, with a past and intimations of a future. Prufrock, of course, lives chiefly in his mind. His account differs from "Satin-Legs" more critically in social attitude than the obvious narrative contrasts. Eliot would improve us morally and spiritually. Brooks, no less concerned, probes social ills at their roots in poverty and discrimination.

In "Sundays," the sympathetic narrator rhetorically addresses the reader ("Would you have flowers in his life?"). In "Negro Hero / to suggest Dorie Miller," Brooks moves inward, presenting a dramatic monologue with the power of Robert Browning. Lengthy verses, forty-four lines in seven stanzas, extend its fullness. The World War II hero embodied the fate of Negro servicemen who were often rewarded with second-class treatment for risking their lives. Miller is the paradigm of one who "advances the Race." Born in 1919 near Waco, Texas, he was a messman on the U.S.S. Arizona. At Pearl Harbor, on December 7, 1941, he manned a machine gun and brought down four of the attacking Japanese planes as the battleship was sunk. Decorated with the Navy Cross, he served on the aircraft carrier Liscome Bay as a mess attendant, third class. On November 24, 1943, Miller was killed in action in the South Pacific when his ship was torpedoed and sunk by a Japanese submarine in the Makin battle. He was twenty-four years old.

Brooks conceives Miller as speaking in life; at the same time, the soliloquy is retrospective. A complex, wrenching mixture of anger, affirmation, and self-solace, like the sonnet sequence ahead it debates the paradox of patriotism and prejudice. Intricately combining free and metrical verse, moderate-to-strongly alliterated, using slant, full, and internal rhyme, with variations on an original stanzaic pattern, the work takes a hard-eyed view of the situation. For Miller knows, from his opening lines, that "I had to kick their law into their teeth in order to save them," just as a rescuer may have to fight a drowning man—a reference to the sinking Arizona. As messman, in keeping with pre-World War II practice, he was confined to the galley on the rigidly segregated ship. When it was attacked, he rushed topside and took command of a machine gun in the chaos. In shooting down the Japanese planes, Miller was technically violating the regulations which confined blacks to menial and noncombative duties. This is why he maintains that his fight was even more against discrimination at home than it was against the Japanese.

The sailor's intoxication with satisfying his "boy itch to get at the gun" sobers to reflections on democracy, his "fair lady" with a knife hidden in her sleeve (st. 4). In stanza 5, he bitterly reviews his treatment by the Navy.

> Still—am I good enough to die for them, is my blood bright
>   enough to be spilled,
> Was my constant back-question—are they clear
> On this? Or do I intrude even now?
> Am I clean enough to kill for them, do they wish me to kill
> For them or is my place while death licks his lips and strides
>   to them
> In the galley still?

Note that line length, irregular, mostly long, contracts at the end of each stanza, the way psychic ambivalence and rhetorical flow (including compulsive near-triple rhymes) imply turbulent rhythms of the sea.

Foregrounding Miller's outcry, a rhyming cinquain (unique among the six- and seven-line stanzas) follows, in which a Southern white man insists he would rather be dead "Than saved by the drop of a black man's blood." (Cf. "Riot," chapter 8). At the close, while the seaman poignantly affirms that it was "a good job," he becomes archetypal of the exploited, unappreciated Negro. Overt violence of war complements covert violence at home, inflicted by hypocritical democracy, the fair lady with the concealed knife. Proximity of sex and death suggests the options of Satin-Legs Smith. But democracy's embrace is provisional: Miller's love goes unrequited. Even after throwing back her sleeve, he represses the painful memory, refusing to "remember / Entirely the knife." He chooses, instead, to affirm his own actions and his hopes. The poet's ease of projection continues in this poem's important intimation of the heroic voice. Inclusion of the rhymed cinquain portends the formal flexibility of "In the Mecca."

"Hattie Scott," a sequence of vignettes, sets five brief monologues carefully between the public, meditative soliloquy of "Negro Hero" and the portrait/blues soliloquy, "Queen of the Blues." Shifts in mood, pace, and length add energy to the poem and its neighbors. The rhythm combines intervals of speech and music; rhyme follows the usual *a b c b* of the ballad. Hattie Scott is a diligent houseworker whose menial occupation parallels Dorie Miller's in the U.S. Navy. Unlike the standard English of "Negro Hero," however, diction in the five poems moderately uses black English vernacular.

"[T]he end of the day," the first poem, views the mature Hattie at sunset, the rhythm of her life patterned after the natural course of the day. Overworked, she identifies with the weary sun, "Pullin' off his clothes and callin' it a day." Yet by kinship with the source of natural energy, Hattie conversely takes on his power and thus becomes a dual emblem. "[T]he date," an octet, humorously portrays Hattie's impatience to finish her chores, while her employer attempts to keep her working overtime. Hattie rebels. Soliloquy reveals her anger; refusal establishes her dignity. In "at the hairdresser's," four syncopated quatrains, Hattie wants to "show them girls" her glamour. She orders hopefully, "Gimme an upsweep, Minnie, / With humpteen baby curls." Her tastes emulate the dominant white culture, with whom upswept hair was popular in the forties. The "girls" whom she seeks to impress "Think they so fly a-struttin'." "Fly" is an expression of the

1900-1940s, meaning "fast and ecstatic; brash" (Major, 54). Brooks is amused by the woman's fashionable yearnings.

"[W]hen I die," a lyrical ballad of three tightly made quatrains, meditates upon death. While Hattie can anticipate "NO LODGE with banners flappin' " after her casket, her "one lone little short man / Dressed all shabbily" will be there with flowers, "his buck-a-dozen." He will mourn her briefly, then find a replacement. Hattie accepts this pattern, just as she has accepted her laboring relationship to the sun. "[T]he battle" closes the group with a ballad narrative of three quatrains. Hattie recounts the domestic battle between a sadomasochistic couple, Moe Belle Jackson and her husband. The houseworker expresses her own repressed anger by describing how she would retaliate lethally with a knife. She ends sarcastically with an image of Moe Belle timidly offering her husband more grits the following morning. The poems contrast Hattie's healthy mind to the couple's pathology.

Ending with "the battle" instead of "when I die" points to continuities beyond the scene: strength and the potential for change. Though Hattie tolerates her life, determined to enjoy it, she progresses from fatigue to submerged hostility to a violent act of imagination. The sequence foregrounds the Dorie Miller image of confrontation and heroism, as well as exploitation, three aspects that shift to another level in the next poem.

While "Queen of the Blues" shows the influence of Langston Hughes in style and subject, it remains technically unique.[22] Brooks employs both a recast ballad form and the blues proper, the former in third person, the latter in the woman's confessional song. Speech and music commingle. The ballad/blues confluence displays Brooks at her best "Tuned Ear," at ease with Southern black musical and linguistic elements. The blues itself is the musical genre developed out of Negro work songs, hollers, and spirituals, popularized through the vocal style of W. C. Handy around 1912 (Major, 29). Its lyrics involve repetition at the beginning of each passage, with a rhyming conclusion. Poets, in modifying the traditional three-line, twelve-bar pattern, have expanded the variations which appear to some extent in music.[23] Brooks's twelve stanzas suggest the twelve bars of the form.

Mame was singing
At the Midnight Club.
And the place was red
With blues.
She could shake her body
Across the floor.
For what did she have
to lose?

The closing couplet (repetend) establishes the narrator's presence.

The first five stanzas of the ninety-two lines describe the Queen's background, her unknown father, her love for her mother, whom she mourned "with roses and tears," her lack of a family life, her essential solitude. These facts lend context and continuity to the blues soliloquy that follows. The Queen sings the loneliness of her life, how she loved a man who left her for another woman after she worked as a domestic for whites, "Scrubbed hard" in their kitchens, and gave him her earnings. As "daddy" he connotes her disappointing father.

After the M.C.'s introduction, Mame reflects on her wounded majesty. Why don't men tip their hats to her? Stanza 11 functions as chorus, a ragtime-sounding, huckstering quatrain, repeating the M.C.'s public appraisal, "Strictly, strictly, / The queen of the blues!" In stanza 12, however, the M.C.'s voice merges with the woman's private, closing lament and develops an ambiguous yet dramatic identity into choral comment, as in classical Greek plays.

Mame/narrator/chorus concludes that "Men are low down / Dirty and mean." John T. Shawcross reminds that "low down and dirty" is a frequent epitome in jazz lyrics and card playing. He suspects that in the background is a blues called "Jelly, Jelly," written by Earl "Fatha" Hines and Billy Eckstine, and well known as performed by Hines and Josh White. In the song, "jellyroll," which has sexual connotations, has killed the narrator's mother and blinded his father, and the human condition is referred to as "low down and dirty."

The Queen feels empty and abandoned. Respectability

eludes her eminence as "Queen of the Blues." If her father had been available, we are told, she would not be at the "Midnight Club," itself the emblem of her low social status. The name of the club suggests a critical point for the singer, the end of her day (cf. "Hattie Scott"). The title "Queen" provides the supreme irony: trapped in dissatisfactions, the Queen is powerless to command respect on her own terrain. Ambivalence toward men, beginning with her father and reinforced in her relationship with "daddy," catches her between longing for love and esteem, and anger with those who withhold it.

Images are distinct and simple; color, extreme: black, brown, white, primary. The Club, in "red / With blues," suggests basic feelings; the "brown-skin chicken" other woman will be made "Black and blue" by the Queen. The singer's imaginary child is a "Baby girl / With velvet / Pop-open eyes," textured after her own flamboyant style.

Linguistic ironies abound. The word "holler," for example, which appears differently in the first sonnet of "Gay Chaps at the Bar," refers to the M.C. who shouts the identity of the singer as "Queen." The "holler" is an animated religious song associated with revival meetings. "Hollering" about the singer, the M.C. peddles her status like a surrogate slave auctioneer and doubly barbs the conception. Exploited by business and society, which is represented by the M.C., at the mercy of arm-pinching patrons, her position matches that of the woman who scrubs kitchen floors and is manipulated by her boyfriend, the abused woman whose life she sings, and lives.

The "Ballad of Pearl May Lee" (Hughes's favorite, recalls Brooks, who usually includes it in her readings) ends the group preceding the sonnet sequence. Its 107 lines (exceeded in the volume only by the 159 of "The Sundays of Satin-Legs Smith") are grouped in seven- and six-line stanzas. It should be compared with *The Bean Eaters'* "A Bronzeville Mother" and "The Last Quatrain of the Ballad of Emmett Till," which also approach black presumption of white womanhood. But treatment of the subject matter differs. The "black-and-tan" motif underlying the earlier poem fades in later work as unity and Black Nationalism gain prominence. White perfidy, however, figures importantly throughout. In the "Ballad of Pearl May Lee," intimacy has taken place in the white woman's Buick, token of the white middle class. Her seductiveness implicates a hypocritical society.

"Then off they took you, off to the jail," begins this lament or coronach ballad. With the abrupt, adverbial clause introduction of "when you have forgotten Sunday," it similarly addresses an unseen listener. But one speaker remembers happiness; the other, anguish. "You paid with your hide and my heart, Sammy boy, / For your taste of pink and white honey," Pearl's repetend grieves. Her lover, falsely accused, wrongly jailed, is lynched. Pearl, her name a symbol of purity as well as ironic reference to her dark color, notes bitterly that her Sammy felt "Black" was "for the famished to eat" even while they were together. She often wished him dead, but despite her ambivalence, betrayed love impels her rage and grief. Deeper still runs guilt over her terrible vindication.

Pearl's emotion invades the entire narration, destroying temporality, merging past and present. Intense feeling charges the first stanza. Pearl recounts, "I cut my lungs with laughter," when Sammy was taken to jail. The hideous visual and aural imagery abates in the second stanza where Pearl confesses misery over her lover's fate. These extremes highlight the color imagery: the vicious sheriff is "red" (st. 3), suggesting a "redneck" or segregationist; Pearl wants a red gown to "dig" her out of despair (sts. 5 and 16, the last), an activity comparable to her lover's being "dragged" to jail. The verb "dig," of course, also suggests the digging of Sammy's grave where Pearl's sympathies lie. The other primary color, yellow, is admired by Sammy, along with white. Physical imagery pertains to the senses of taste and touch: the heat (fire) of Sammy's passion and the cold of his disdain for Pearl.

The basically standard English suits both style and subject matter, the latter's violence typical of the old English ballad. Stanzaic length augments by linear repetitions and by suggestion of parallel repetitions like those found in the folk ballad "Edward," where the repetitions "Mither, Mither" and "Edward, Edward" alternate to the end. Alliteration predominates. The simple, terse language favors monosyllabic, Anglo-Saxon verbs. Note the effective use of "cut," for example, in the first stanza, where Pearl cuts her lungs with laughter over Sammy's fate, and, in stanza 7, where she addresses the murdered lover as having often "cut" her cold. Her laughter, finally self-punitive, sends a grotesque wailing to Sammy's grave.

The five portraits bridge the transition from local emphasis in the "Street in Bronzeville" sequence to national emphasis in the sonnet sequence. The portraits spotlight characters relating to both the smaller and the larger contexts. In so doing, they signal heroic concerns that will eventually define Brooks's art. We learn more fully what it means to live and die in Bronzeville, trapped in poverty, trying to maintain dignity, struggling to survive. "Having fun" is often tinged with melancholy and frustration. Personal and social entrapment abide. But the blues are not the whole story, nor is grief their total meaning. Strength imbues the surface angers and their vehicles of endurance: labor and mere "staying alive."

III. "Gay Chaps at the Bar"

The sonnet form was not an eccentric choice for Brooks. It had already been favored by many Harlem Renaissance (or "Harlem Awakening," in Arna Bontemps's preference) poets such as Claude McKay, Countee Cullen, and Langston Hughes.[24] The sequence of twelve sonnets is based on letters to the poet written by black soldiers. Each fourteen-line poem is composed in pentameter, mainly iambic, with modifications of Shakespearean/Petrarchan rhyme schemes. The alternate scansions possible in several poems, and elsewhere in Brooks's metrical work, attest to the theoretical difficulties of accentual-syllabic meter,[25] as well as to the poet's intuited sense of rhythms that derive from content. She herself depreciates her own concern for meter or stress, preferring their spontaneous apprehension.

Dedicated to "Staff Sergeant Raymond Brooks and every other soldier," the poems represent contemplations of and by American servicemen in World War II. The sequence merits close attention for several reasons. First, formal confines are meaningfully relaxed by slant rhymes and assonance in terminal and internal positions, with the important line initial carefully attended. Second, dramatic rendering of contemporary life deep-

ens. Bronzeville and even the individual portraits are largely
sociological in conception; "Negro Hero" is archetypal. The sonnets, however, probe subtleties of situation and psychology and
test the meaning of black life and American ideals under fire.

Of the twelve poems (numbering added), the rhyme scheme
of one (no. 7) is Petrarchan, identified as "P"; another (no. 1) varies
the Petrarchan, identified as "Pv"; six (nos. 2, 6, 8, 10, 11, 12)
combine the Shakespearean, "S," with the Petrarchan—the latter
appearing in the sestet—and such combinations are identified as
"S/P"; three (nos. 3, 4, 5) are Shakespearean ("S"); and one (no. 9)
varies the Shakespearean, identified as "Sv." The Petrarchan is
rhymed as octet and sestet; the Shakespearean/Petrarchan as two
quatrains and sestet; the Shakespearean as three quatrains and
couplet. Prosody of the first sonnet, examined in detail, typifies
the careful crafting of the rest.

1. "gay chaps at the bar" (Pv). The slant rhyme, subtly de-
ployed, offers no trite or predictable couplings. Surprise
abounds, along with the intellectual quality of half-rhyme. The
poem takes its title from a letter written to Brooks by William
Couch, an American officer in the South Pacific during World War
II (see chapter 4, *Maud Martha*, and *RPO*, 191). He saw men
return from the front crying and trembling, men who had been
"Gay chaps at the bar in Los Angeles, Chicago, New York." The
poet speaks through the collective voice of such an officer: black,
schooled in the social codes of segregation ("bar" especially evokes
the color bar, justice, and the "bar" between life and death, as in
Tennyson's "Crossing the Bar"). Limits and dimensions of such
conduct determined "Whether the raillery should be slightly
iced / And given green, or served up hot and lush" (ll. 3-4). But
the soldiers were not taught "to be islands" or "how to chat with
death." The color green is central. Transposed into the tropics it
becomes an island, untamed, menacing the soldiers who have not
been prepared "To holler down the lions in this air." Linguistic
levels, from "raillery" (l. 3) to "holler" (l. 14), which also summons
the Negro "holler" in music, move the language from standard to
vernacular as the soldiers move into the untamed environment.
References to learning and knowledge emphasize the youth of the
servicemen who are mostly fresh out of school, with its mock-

battle sports, and cast into deadly encounters for which they lack "smart, athletic language" (l. 10).

"We knew how to order. Just the dash / Necessary. The length of gaiety in good taste" (ll. 1-2). The break after "dash" punctuates as a dash itself might do, further emphasizing "Necessary." The sentence fragments connote restrictions of decorum and indirectly comment on the brevity of life itself. Yet the second line struggles successfully to escape the confining pentameter. "Necessary," ordinarily a four-syllable word, can be compressed in quick, affected or Anglicized speech, the latter plausible following "Just the dash." Still, the meter breaks into six stresses. The long *a*'s of *gaiety* and *taste* reinforce each other so that, again, a limit (*taste*) is imposed upon feeling (*gaiety*) through the connection.

> And we knew beautifully how to give to women
> The summer spread, the tropics, of our love.
> When to persist, or hold a hunger off.
> Knew white speech. How to make a look an omen.
> But nothing ever taught us to be islands. [ll. 5-9]

Images of heat, food, and instruction continue as they will to the end of the poem. But the "tropics" of love hardly prepare anyone for the heat of the island, of war, solitude, death. And what is taught? To whom? Roles become tentative, arbitrary, confused. The lexical mode of this theme appears in *white*, which connects through consonantal *taught* with assonant *islands*, associating the ironic *white / taught / islands*. (*Taught* will also be recalled in *brought*, l. 12.) *Islands* refers by consonance to *omen*. (Note that *women*, deprived of its first letter, yields its half-rhyme *omen*, the *look* which now replaces the feminine presence.) Along with *white / taught*, it bridges the octet to the sestet:

> But nothing ever taught us to be islands.
> And smart, athletic language for this hour
> Was not in the curriculum. No stout
> Lesson showed how to chat with death. We brought
> No brass fortissimo, among our talents,
> To holler down the lions in this air. [ll. 9-14]

But, pivotal, turns from positives in the octet—the known and comfortable, the lexicon of decorum—toward negatives in the sestet—the unknown and threatening, the ferocity of death. *But* echoes the *b* of *beautifully* and alliterates with *brought* and *brass*, which accompany *no*.

The linking of positive with negative underscores the thematic irony and ambivalence. *Brass*, an almost comic touch, connotes army "brass," or officers. The eccentric "fortissimo" clips exactly the right pretension. And "brass fortissimo," very loud brass, invokes "sounding brass" (1 Cor. 13:1). Devoid of charity and, therefore, of spiritual power (note allusiveness of *talents*), brass can provide no sound/force to defeat the *lions* (a power image, also biblical) "in this air"—literally the attacking bombers. The last line's colloquial and unrestrained "To holler," an inappropriate if not useless defense, offers antithesis to the restrained beginning, "We knew how to order." And how ineffectual the knowledge, the order, and, finally, how false! The poem moves from social restraints to natural ones—death and the jungle; from the officers' known place in the ordered, white-dominated world of the past toward the spontaneous, unknown islands of their present and future and, by analogy, of their selves.

2. "still do I keep my look, my identity . . ." (S/P). Leaving the collective "we" for third person, the poet meditates upon death that fixes the body in the meaning of its days, so that the look "Shows what / It showed at baseball. What it showed in school." General observations open each quatrain of the octet ("Each body has its art . . . / Each body has its pose"), then shift to concrete images (*castle, shack, rags, robes*). Harsh alliteration counters the liquid *l*'s. Placed on a "crawling cot" or "hasty pall," released from grimace and pain into the benign past, the anonymous casualty claims identity.

3. "my dreams, my works, must wait till after hell" (S). A soldier tells of the honey and bread of his past life that must, during war, be stored "In little jars and cabinets of my will." He seeks patience to endure hell, "keep eyes pointed in," that his spirit not be coarsened by this experience; and hopes not to become "insensitive / To honey and bread old purity could love." (Cf. the "labeled cabinet" where "the Keeper" stores the chains of enslavement in "The Third Sermon on the Warpland.") Tight structure probes anxiety lest the soldier be unable to resume his past life and sensibility, to "remember to go home."

4. "looking" (S). The poet urges a mother to look at her soldier son in farewell, since words are inadequate. Although the poem enriches the sequence thematically, several problems make the piece less successful than the others. In the first line, "You have no word for soldiers to enjoy," the plural is used, rather than the singular, but an individual soldier, the son, "him," is referred to from the fourth line on. " 'come back!' the raw / Insistence of an idle desperation / Since could he favor he would favor now" addresses the mother with a terseness verging on the cryptic. Nor does "beat back the storm" contribute more than a stock image.

5. "piano after war" (S). This is the most Shakespearean sonnet of the group, in structure and style. "But suddenly, across my climbing fever / Of proud delight" recalls the Bardic turn. Brooks makes all features of the poem her own, however. A soldier imagines what peace will be like, a room in which a woman will play the piano, retrieving the "old hungers" which "will break their coffins." But the Lazarus allusion collapses into "A cry of bitter dead men." Their intrusion on the speaker's reverie connotes not only human sacrifice, but also the inevitable postwar reappraisal. Premature, useless death serves an embittering retrospect to survivors and casualties (their shades) alike. And so the future will always be fingered by that cold. The "thawed eye will go again to ice. / And stone will shove the softness from my face." "Shove," crudely suggesting "shovel," provides the poem's inexorable moment.

6. "mentors" (S/P). The soldier continues to meditate upon his dead comrades, knowing that "my best allegiances are to the dead," and "all my days / I'll have as mentors those reproving ghosts." In the sestet, terminal full rhymes of the second tercet (*wears, theirs*) rhyme with each other and half-rhyme with *whisper* and *her* in the first. The quatrain rhyming is also complex. Terminal words in each group slant rhyme consecutively as well as alternately.

Brooks will not permit "mentors" and "piano after war" to be quoted separately. As a unit, they consider the tainting of postwar life. All is "changed utterly," Yeats observed—more positively—in "Easter 1916."

7. "the white troops had their orders but / the Negroes looked like men" (P). This excellent sonnet, the only regular Petrarchan, is the most impassioned. Severely controlled, it gains strength from the tension. White soldiers reluctantly prepare to accept the strange Negroes with "A type of cold, a type of hooded gaze," and are perplexed by their ordinariness. The apartheid of coffins ("A box for dark men and a box for 'Other' ") had, nevertheless, become a nuisance; often "the contents had been scrambled." The four feminine endings in the sestet contribute to the sarcasm about such mishaps that seemed to offend neither the universe nor the weather. At this dramatic turning point of the sequence, the critical edge sharpens. The incident jolts faith—in American democracy and its God. Brooks takes the path of *style indirect libre* (third person narration in a subjective mode; see chapter 4, *Maud Martha*).

8. "firstly inclined to take what it is told" (S/P). "Thee sacro-sanct, Thee sweet, Thee crystalline, / With the full jewel wile of mighty light—". These words introduce the soldier's profound reassessment of his patriotism, addressed within the context of received beliefs.[26] Alluding to "America" (the lyrics proclaim, "My country, 'tis of thee, / Sweet land of liberty," whose fathers' God is the "author of liberty"; a country that enjoys "freedom's holy light" and will "Protect us by thy might, / Our [or 'Great'] God our King."), the sonnet dissects the unrealized pretensions of the anthem. There is an interesting aural association, with vital semantic difference, between Christ (from the Greek *chriein*, to anoint) and crystalline (from Greek *krystallos*, ice, crystal; *kryos*, *krymos*, icy cold, frost), reinforcing the God/country duality. The Trinitarian emblem appears clearly in the three *Thees* of the first line and three *Thys* of the fifth. In the poem, unlike the song, duality becomes duplicity, betrayal of the youthful inclination toward belief and the soldier's need to be committed "To a total God. / With billowing heartiness no whit withheld" (ll. 13-14). "Freedom's holy light" has hardened into "jewel wile of mighty light," precious yet stony (unfeeling), deceitful power. After the harsh reality and irony of no. 7, succession by no. 8 stresses the idea that conventional beliefs are also becoming war casualties. The remarkable phonic density, with its complex internal assonance and consonance and terminal ambiguities of half-rhyme render the ambivalences here as Brooks pushes allusion and metaphor toward symbolism.[27]

9. " 'God works in a mysterious way' " (Sv). The quotation ironically adapts a title from William Cowper's devotional *Olney Hymns* (1779), where the verb is "moves."[28] Brooks continues to probe and prod the God/country duality. She uses double and internal rhyme to lighten the first quatrain, in which "the youthful eye cuts down its / Own dainty veiling, Or submits to winds." In effect she approaches the theme obliquely, even mysteriously. The objective tone of third person gives way to imperative address in the sestet, whose agitated rhythmic shifts subside in the closing tercet. At last the soldier directly petitions God, asking, "Step forth in splendor, mortify our wolves. / Or we assume a sovereignty ourselves" (ll. 13-14). If we were comparing the religion here with Eliot's in *Four Quartets*, three-quarters a wartime effort, we would conclude that the last line is one he could not possibly have written. Relentlessly devotional, he pursues an ecstatic personal redemption that Brooks's humanism—pained, skeptical, critical, hopeful—must forgo.

10. "love note / I: surely" (S/P). In the next two poems, the soldier turns his skepticism to earthly attachments. "Surely you stay my certain own, you stay / My you. All honest, lofty as a cloud" (ll. 1-2). Brooks augments the flag symbol into an astute conflation of personal/political allegiance, of flag and absent beloved. Together with the next poem, it deepens the resonance of doubt. The soldier knows he can still find his love's "gaze, surely ungauzed" (l. 7). But the flag, like democracy in "Negro Hero," is a woman the soldier has learned to mistrust. "Surely" ironically punctuates six times. No longer will the man believe her "Why, of course I love you, dear" (l. 6). (Compare also the personification in "Riders to the Blood-red Wrath.") Withdrawn from certainty, "From the decent arrow / That was my clean naïveté and my faith" (ll. 10-11), he has learned to "doubt all. You. Or a violet" (l. 14). He questions every aspect of his life, his received politico-religious beliefs and, by implication, his personal relationships. The violet, a spring flower, connotes modesty, among other associations, and symbolizes a love returned.

11. "love note / II: flags" (S/P). "Still, it is dear defiance now to carry / Fair flags of you above my indignation," (ll. 1-2). The soldier's love of country is costly because it postpones addressing his racial indignation. (Cf. "fair fables," l. 3, "In the Mecca.") He will pull "a pretty glory" (Old Glory) into a foxhole, remembering "dandelion days, unmocking sun" of his freedom and innocence, before the present "scattered pound of my cold passion." "Glory," especially in context of flower imagery here and throughout the sequence, also invokes morning glory, spring, youth. "Pound" reverberates with its various other meanings: domesticated animal confinement, weight, a monetary unit, to crush, to pulverize, and it echoes Shakespeare's "pound of flesh." "Cold" evokes "crystalline" of no. 8 and hints of death. "The blowing of clear wind in your gay hair" conveys the beautiful image of a personified flag. The word "gay" summons both the "gay chaps" in their innocence and a woman with hair streaming in the wind—her fickle love, "Love changeful in you." (The related "coquettish death" image of "the sonnet-ballad" develops in "The Anniad" and its "Appendix.")

12. "the progress" (S/P). "And still we wear our uniforms, follow / The cracked cry of the bugles" (ll. 1-2). Now speaking for all troops, the soldier returns to the collective "we" of the first poem. "Still" in the first line and beginning lines 5 and 6 emphasizes the "Initial ardor" that has been lost, persisting as a "cracked cry" recalling the cracked Liberty Bell in Philadelphia and the broken coffins of no. 5. We shall salute the flag, applaud the President, and celebrate, "rejoice / For death of men who too saluted, sang." The "soberness" and "awe" of the soldier turns to fear and "a deepening hollow through the cold." "Cold" here connotes death. Victory will be ephemeral.

The word "hollow" and the line beginning, "How shall we smile, congratulate" (l. 12) somewhat evoke, respectively, Eliot's *The Hollow Men* and *Prufrock* ("And how should I presume?"). Both works also address will and belief. But while apathy, timidity, and *Angst* flatten into social alienation or cosmological egoism in Eliot's works, Brooks's soldier faces concrete fears. These culminate in the poem's last, terrifying image, prescient in 1945 with the end of the war in sight:

> How shall we smile, congratulate: and how
> Settle in chairs? Listen, listen. The step
> Of iron feet again. And again   wild.

Even so, this is a call to resistance. Brooks has projected strength, not elegy, throughout the sequence. The space between "again" and "wild"—missing in *Selected Poems*—suggests a leap across an abyss, a giant step conjuring for this reader a soldier's marching stride.

"Gay Chaps at the Bar" meditates on war, the Black American experience, and postwar expectations. The sonnet sequence casts a periplum (in Ezra Pound's sense) of discovery. Each review plumbs interpretation as we mine the semantic ore. Slant rhymes throughout (together with assonance and consonance) help convey instability and tension and further the intellectual content. Brooks's tone is usually conversational as well as contemplative. Her strengths lie in powerful images, often paradoxical, striking concepts, such as the God/country duality and the woman/flag personification, both pairs involving the presence of death. She employs allusion, metaphor, symbolism, but little simile. Homogeneity of language, text, and context afford greater modulation, subtlety, irony, and complexity of psychological and thematic detail than in the preceding sections. Like the other poems, however, the sonnets demonstrate Brooks's dramatic projection, while they philosophically augment the volume's central theme of entrapment.

Note that the first word of the sequence is "We"; the last is "wild." Brooks has described both personal and social communities and their feral environment. The sonnets decry war, racism, hypocrisy, and unreflecting acceptance of beliefs, including patriotism, social codes, and God. They broaden the meditation of "Negro Hero." "At the bar" of life, the gay chaps judge the world that judges them. The future will be haunted by "a cry of bitter dead men" who are uncertain that they have not died in vain. The soldiers' "best allegiances," to the dead, will continue the war against social injustice.

Important Postscript

A technically significant poem, "Death of the Dinosaur," appears in *Cross-Section 1945*.[29] Although it is one Brooks no longer cares for, it links early and later work, as "The Anniad" does, with respect to an important heroic feature. While *A Street in Bronzeville* employs heavy alliteration incidentally, the dinosaur poem of the same period does so systematically. Weight of consonants and the lumbering line represent the dinosaur's physical and symbolic reality. The first and last lines of this irregularly metered, rhymed and slant-rhymed piece wonderfully express the animal clumsily approaching extinction: "They are done, the days of easy and dank food . . . / Dust to themselves but themselves dismally to dust." Phrases such as "walks without wisdom," "Big and booming," and "A terribly dry death" typify the style.

Of related interest, "One wants a Teller in a time like this" also appears in the volume. The plea for guidance suggests a call for leadership. Together with prosodic elements of the dinosaur poem, it indicates the poet's basic concerns and future development.

3

Annie Allen

During the postwar period, after *Bronzeville*, Brooks worked concurrently on two projects: the *Annie Allen*[1] manuscript and a novel, *American Family Brown*, which became *Maud Martha*. One should note the dynamic interaction between the two forms, poetry and prose, through which the poet was broadening her range. In fact, the bulk of correspondence between poet and editor from the publication of *Bronzeville* to the publication of *Annie Allen* deals with the novel until, in October 1947, it was rejected.

Annie Allen correspondence began on March 24, 1948, when Brooks submitted the work to Lawrence under the title "Hester Allen." Its major piece, "The Anniad," was then called "The Hesteriad." Editorial opinion was so mixed that, considering her own reservations, Lawrence felt the manuscript should be seen by another reader. She sent it to the poet Genevieve Taggard, who submitted a detailed criticism of the work. Taggard's comments, eight pages in longhand on legal-sized ruled paper, focused negatively on "The Hesteriad," taking up three and one-half pages. She felt the lack of a real human story and found the writing monotonous, an exercise more than a poem. (Cf. Brooks's later comments, "The Anniad" introduction, below.) Of the other poems, "the birth in a narrow room" seemed unfinished. Regarding the manuscript as a whole, Taggard wondered whether it should be published.

Lawrence sent Brooks (who later guessed the author's identity) a copy of this criticism, along with her own reactions on July 14. While assuring the poet that Harper's wished to publish the volume, the editor felt the new work to be transitional, its author developing stylistically toward something new. The emphasis on form and the occasional obscurity troubled her. She sensed an interest in words and sounds for their own sake rather than as communication.

Three days later, after briefly expressing satisfaction at acceptance, Brooks vigorously defended her work, especially from the criticism of the unidentified reporting poet. She withdrew for revision "The Egg Boiler" (it appears in *The Bean Eaters*), a closing sonnet group, and a poem, "from flabby shadows my out-leading strings." She admitted disinterest in writing more poems like "the date" in the "Hattie Scott" *Bronzeville* sequence, though she still respected "obituary for a living lady." Brooks also acknowledged her quest for a new style. In "The Hesteriad" and "the children of the poor" she was seeking greater linguistic precision. Disagreeing with the reporting poet on an absent story line in "The Hesteriad," Brooks insisted she had selected each word with meticulous care. "[T]he birth in a narrow room" seemed clear. She firmly defended "the children of the poor," a sequence which Thornton Wilder's brother Amos had especially liked. Brooks revealed that "she has sprinkled nail-polish on dead dandelions" (in "the ballad of the light-eyed little girl") referred to an incident in which her son, Henry Jr., had tried to revive the appearance of the dandelions for his pigeon's grave. "A light and diplomatic bird" was not derivative; it approached a "universality" she thought the editor would appreciate. The phrase "got square with us" (in "intermission") seemed patently to connote "getting even." Nor did Brooks feel that the line "that wish of kind to kennel kind" (one of five concluding lines dropped from the original version of "People protest in sprawling lightless ways") should present any difficulty. In guessing correctly the identity of the poet-critic, Brooks remarked that Babette Deutsch was a possibility but would have been more daring in judgment. The poet closed with the hope that her defense was not too strenuous; she wanted her offspring to be properly understood.

On August 11, Lawrence wrote that a contract was being sent with an offer of a $100 advance, one-half of that offered for *A Street in Bronzeville.* The book would be published in 1949. Brooks answered straightway that she planned twenty more poems to follow "the birth in a narrow room." Shortly afterward, she decided to change the title to *Annie Allen* and sent Lawrence a telegram, soliciting her opinion. Lawrence replied immediately that she liked the title, particularly its alliteration. The poet continued working on the manuscript until its submission on January 14, 1949. In this final form, ten of the eleven pieces in "Notes from the Childhood and the Girlhood" were new, as was the third sonnet in "the children of the poor." Brooks had omitted many poems previously included in the last section ("The Womanhood"), and had revised and pared down others. She mentioned acknowledgments that were to be made, and added that she now proposed to rewrite *American Family Brown.*

Lawrence met Brooks on January 26 in Chicago, while the editor was en route to California. On March 3, Lawrence wrote that *Annie Allen* was scheduled for August publication. She made several suggestions, but admitted they might be wrong. In "Maxie Allen" the third and last stanzas (later omitted) seemed forced. She did not care for "Downtown Vaudeville," and was troubled by the personal pronoun in the line, "I bear to such brusque burial" (pronoun subsequently omitted) in "Throwing Out the Flowers." "The Contemplation of Suicide" (omitted, but included in *The Bean Eaters*) had a troublesome phrase, "surf's epileptic" (retained). "That" in "that is dolesome and is dying" ("The Anniad," st. 37) seemed unnecessary. The poems entitled "Food Car in Front of a Mortuary" and "Child's Nightmare" (both omitted) seemed problematic. "I Like [*sic*] Those Little Booths at Benvenuti's" seemed too reportorial. Lawrence's last query regarded *American Family Brown*: had the poet thought further about doing it in verse?

Brooks's quick reaction to the tactful, tentative criticisms was positive rather than defensive, as with the Taggard letter. She promised some immediate manuscript revisions. She confirmed her wish to do *American Family Brown* as a verse novel and was examining ways to present it effectively. A few days later she proposed the following changes: two new poems, "the rites for Cousin Vit" and "the parents: people like our marriage" were to replace "child's nightmare" and "food car in front of a mortuary."

All the poems were to remain in their sequence. Brooks was willing to remove "I love those little booths at Benvenuti's," but her brief justification of the poem on poetic and sociological grounds sufficed. Her defense of "downtown vaudeville," which describes the reactions of white audiences to Negro performers, was impassioned and unequivocal. She defended the last stanza of "Maxie Allen." Although the editor still queried the section, it was published.

Of the advance galleys sent by Lawrence, Langston Hughes wrote the editor that he was pleased to receive them and suggested sending them to Richard Wright in Paris for review in Hughes's new magazine *Voices* (June 16, 1949). William Rose Benét was not enthusiastic, preferring *Bronzeville*; Selden Rodman was destructively critical. J. Saunders Redding, highly enthusiastic, gave *Annie Allen* a very favorable notice in the *Saturday Review of Literature*.[2] He did caution the poet, nevertheless, against a tendency toward obscurity. Paul Engle wrote John Fischer at Harper's that he thought quite highly of Brooks, who had been in a summer workshop of his at Northwestern University years before and whose book he had helped launch (via his 1945 review of *Bronzeville* in the *Chicago Tribune*). Alfred Kreymborg was out of town when the galleys arrived, but found the new work fully as rewarding as *Bronzeville* and admired its technical range.

On July 11, Brooks received her first copies of *Annie Allen*. Her plans for an autographing party in Chicago were cancelled, but she was pleased by a letter from Inez Boulton, part of which she quoted (GB/EL, July 25). The poet's former mentor noted considerable poetic growth. Although Boulton approved of Harper's advice, she was concerned that some Negro poets had been exploited. Brooks did not wish to be spared adverse criticism, however, and wanted to see the Rodman comments as well as all the others (GB/EL, Sept. 5). She mentioned her pleasure with Eve Merriam's review, which she found helpful.

Financial difficulties were again pressing. Her employment ending, Brooks applied unsuccessfully for a John Hay Whitney Fellowship with a recommendation from her editor. There were few bright spots until May 1, 1950, when the poet's life was suddenly rekindled by a new recognition: the Pulitzer Prize.

Critical reaction to *Annie Allen* reflected the Harper editors'
reception. Favorable response was tempered by reservations
about its "obscurity" and linguistic dazzle, especially in "The
Anniad." Phyllis McGinley found this poem the most praisewor-
thy.[3] But a careful review by Stanley Kunitz puzzlingly omitted
reference to "The Anniad" by name, apparently ignoring or missing its satire, and Kunitz made several cautionary criticisms.[4]
While admiring the honesty and technical skill of the poetry, he
observed that the occasional excess of "Oh mad bacchanalian lass"
("The Anniad," st. 22) and archaisms like "such rubies as ye list"
("The Anniad," st. 28) were "not faults of incapacity or pretension:
what they demonstrate at this stage is an uncertainty of taste and
direction" (Kunitz, 54). Rolfe Humphries, while locating the
poet's strength in daring and invention, was concerned "when she
seems to be carried away by the big word or the spectacular
rhyme; when her ear, of a sudden, goes all to pieces."[5] It is useful
to place this extravagant language, however, not only in its ironic
and satiric context, but also against the discussion of speech traits
in black poetry, especially the "elegant black linguistic gesture" of
unusual words (Henderson, 33, 37).

Some of the problems in *Annie Allen* are real. The intense
compression of language and symbols at times may strain comprehension. But such obscurity usually yields to scrutiny of the
text. Difficulties result mainly from syntactical inversions, covert
ironies, and whittling away of deictics, which all culminate in "The
Anniad."[6] Even more recently, the obstacles have led don l. lee to
criticize *Annie Allen* as an "important" book, but one written for
whites and unread by blacks (*RPO*, preface, 17). "'The Anniad'
requires unusual concentrated study," he writes, and "the sonnet-
ballad in part 3 of the poem 'Appendix to The Anniad' . . . leaves
me completely dry." But the "flaws" mostly reflect the experimental nature of the work with its oblique ironies, and represent a
stride forward, even outward, toward utilizing more poetic mate-
rials, notably those which will culminate in the concision and
muscularity of the heroic style.

In *Annie Allen*, words are enjoyed for their own sake. The
flavor of the folk ballad (whose incremental repetition connects
with the blues "worrying the line") appears in some poems. Slant
rhyme may be related to musical "blue" notes. Brooks's poly-

phonic mode—her orderly varieties of rhyme and rhythm—look ahead to the flexible polyrhythmic diversity of *In the Mecca*. The bravura use of language and rhyme, moreover, helps to identify an Annie Allen poetically "black" as well as "white," a heroine the teen-aged Nikki Giovanni could recognize as "my mother."[7]

Annie Allen is dedicated to the memory of Edward Bland, "killed in Germany March 20, 1945; / volunteered for special dangerous mission / . . . wanted to see action." Bland was a fellow-member of the poetry workshop conducted by Inez Stark (later Boulton). The introductory "Memorial to Ed Bland," first published in Edwin Seaver's anthology *Cross-Section 1945*, sets the tone of tightly controlled yet accessible feeling. Irregular scansion, rhythm, line length, and varied rhyme help to portray the truncated life of one who "grew up being curious / And thinking things are various."

The book divides into three parts: "Notes from the Childhood and the Girlhood" (11 poems), "The Anniad" (43 stanzas and 3 "Appendix" poems), and "The Womanhood" (15 poems). Less organically shaped than *Maud Martha* (also a Bildungsroman), it is a poem sequence, pyramidal in form, with its apex at "The Anniad." As for the book's alliterative title, note also the semantic difference between "The Hesteriad" and *Annie Allen*. "Hester" derives from the name "Hestia," the Greek goddess of the hearth; "Ann" originates in the Hebrew name meaning "grace." "Annie," a diminutive, connotes a small (or youthful) grace. Annie seeks her romantic image of a graceful (if not gracious) lover and a graceful life. For her, the two are nearly identical. Hearth-oriented she is not. Even the sound of "Hester" has a serious, substantial ring. (Recall Hester Prynne in Nathaniel Hawthorne's *The Scarlet Letter.*)

I. "Notes from the Childhood and the Girlhood"

In these poems (numbered by the poet) we glimpse Annie's birth; her practical and didactic mother; her "settled" parents; her responses to racism, to killing, and to death. We see the roots of Annie's mythologizing, the shape of her dreams, her character and sensibility. "1 / the birth in a narrow room" remarkably relates the impressions of a newborn infant. Framing the adjective "pinchy" ("How pinchy is my room!"), it coins a word that Stanley Kunitz called "a little masterpiece all by itself" (54). The poem begins: "Weeps out of western country something new. / Blurred and stupendous. Wanted and unplanned." Opening portentously with the word "weeps," sentence order reverses the usual sequence of subject and predicate, forcing the subject out of its expected place (like a baby's headlong entrance and first cry), ahead to "something new." This "something new" connotes the new elements in Brooks's work. The original published version, for example, refers to "Kansas country" in the line, naming the state where Brooks was born.[8] The change to "western" moves from local to general. The third line in the poem, "Winks. Twines, and weakly winks" is indented, a device the poet previously reserved for ballad refrains. Indentation here subordinates (even contracts, like a birth contraction) the line to the previous one.

Alliteration promptly subsides into a Keatsian richness of detail. Imagery draws the small, momentous fact of birth into the splendid warmth. The china child, trapped on the milk-glass fruit bowl like a figure on Keats's Grecian Urn, represents an illusory ideal of beauty. This early, romantic presence hovers over Annie's life. Like the immortal china child (the east, as opposed to the mortal child from "western country"), the baby has nothing to do,

> But prances nevertheless with gods and fairies
> Blithely about the pump and then beneath
> The elms and grapevines, then in darling endeavor
> By privy foyer, where the screenings stand
> And where the bugs buzz by in private cars
> Across old peach cans and old jelly jars.

Annie is born into a world of old peach cans and old jelly jars,[9] utilities unknown to "the bashful china child," who also enters Annie's consciousness with the societal image of pretty things. "Darling endeavor," somewhat Shakespearean, buffs the ironic sheen.

Although the poem suggests a sonnet variant, like the sixteen-liners of George Meredith in *Modern Love*, it is actually a series of dispersed couplets. The only paired rhymes end the poem in transition to rhyme patterns that follow. Like *Maud Martha*, child

Annie seeks love, symbolized by the rhyme. Through the basically iambic pentameter that—with opening sestet (*a b c d e f*) and a ten-line second stanza (*c g d a f g e b h h*)—hints of a sonnet, birth in the narrow room of formal strictness can still make new the form ("something new"). Novelty also implies Annie's coming struggle with reality.

"2 / Maxie Allen" identifies the conflict between the stern mother who teaches her daughter to count her blessings, mostly material and physical, and "Sweet Annie," who tries to inform Maxie Allen "of something other," mystery and human warmth. Tetrameter portends "The Anniad" meter, emblem of Annie's romanticism. The rhyme scheme is based on the couplet which, together with the meter and full rhyme, propels the poem's didacticism and carries through the important coupling motif of the volume. In the shift from third person to first, half-way into the last stanza, we see that Mrs. Allen's own dissatisfactions ironically parallel her daughter's. The transition accompanies a linked rhyme between the second and third stanzas. Insistent rhyming marks the operative compulsions, conflicts, and identities.

"[T]he parents: people like our marriage / Maxie and Andrew" (poem 3) portrays Annie's parents. Having forfeited their illusions to moderation and dullness, they "settled for chicken and shut the door" on the "swans and swallows" of their dreams. In a metaphor of tame dessert, "Pleasant custards sit behind / The white Venetian blind," the parents secure the quotidian by the protective blind, itself foreign—and white. While the poem's meter is irregular, the rhymes win out.

"Sunday chicken," "old relative," and "downtown vaudeville" (poems 4, 5, and 6) develop Annie's rebellious consciousness. Technically interesting, each piece comprises three rhyming tercets and a concluding couplet, all in iambic pentameter; tercets within each poem slant rhyme. "Sunday chicken" shows Annie's dislike of killing anything, even the once-lovely chicken. She compares this execution with the practices of cannibals and tigers. Subject and theme reappear in "brotherly love" (*Maud Martha*). For Brooks, chickens and other forms of life are people, defined as "things of identity and response" (*RPO*, 193).

A special view of death expresses a child's egoism in "old

relative." Annie respects life, but she understands it only in immediate terms. The dead chicken is a personal confrontation; death of the anonymous old relative means not being permitted to play her favorite popular records. The "Anniad" Annie who rebukes death invokes the child Annie who sticks out her tongue at the corpse in the casket.

"[D]owntown vaudeville" introduces the young girl to white racism. The gifted Negro clown amuses whites by virtue of his color. They are "so joined to personal bleach" that they also feel superior to the blacks in the audience. The clown performs "downtown," a location defining his subservient position. He entertains like a jester at court. The clown image will recur as "fool" in "The Anniad" (st. 39). The performer doffs "his broken hat," which represents his broken spirit. This tragic intimation, following the sacrificial theme of "Sunday chicken" and the rejected death image of "old relative," suggests Annie's fate.

"[T]he ballad of late Annie" and "throwing out the flowers" poems 7 and 8) employ the ballad stanza to continue the mythic augmenting. Annie, lying late abed in her "bower," expects a marvelous man of "gist and lacquer. / With melted opals for my milk, / Pearl-leaf for my cracker." Her hero, a suave man of substance, will feed her the ambrosia of romance. Opal, a complex image referring to heaven, as in "Opal Towrs" of the Empyrean in Milton's *Paradise Lost* (Book II, l. 1049), is regarded by some superstitions as unlucky. The latter connotation implies that Annie's dreams bring her misfortune. Pearl-leaf suggests her innocence. Sequential pairing of the two poems evokes the love and death themes encountered in *A Street in Bronzeville* and developed in "The Anniad."

"[T]hrowing out the flowers" gives another dimension to the sacrificial victim theme (poem 4) and the rejected intrusion theme (poem 5). The piece wryly mythologizes Thanksgiving dinner into symbols of recurrence, death, and renewal. "The duck fats rot in the roasting pan," the dead flowers are borne "to such brusque burial" in the garbage can, relieving the vase of its malodorous charge. Incremental repetition ("Before it was over and all," "Are dead with the hail in the hall," "Since it's over and over and all," "Just over, just over and all") gives the ballad its sense of enduring ritual, touched with whimsy.

" '[D]o not be afraid of no' " (poem 9) is Annie's motto. Refusing to emulate her mother's submission, she wants to face life's negatives. After the opening rhymed tetrameter couplet, the motto (followed by "Who has so very far to go") is unsettled by the next lines:

> New caution to occur
> To one whose inner scream set her to cede, for softer
>   lapping and smooth fur!

The continued linear irregularity of rhymed couplets suggests a puzzling over and thinking through. Verbal play, which will be one of the delights of "The Anniad," appears in the phrase "set her to cede." The punning on "cede" ("seed") involves both a yielding and a setting of the seed (ideas) for materialism, and going to seed or losing vitality. "Lapping" invokes sitting on the lap, as well as wrapping (with "soft fur").

Conflicted, about to make a crucial choice, Annie would be "like a candle fixed" against disappointments and the "countershine" of an untamed moon and sun, symbols of romantic love. (The combining form "counter-" will reappear in stanza 34 of "The Anniad" where the desert of reality "countercharms.") The ambivalent language indicates that Annie Allen's dreams, like Maud Martha's, tilt at reality. The candle image, critical in Brooks, will recur negatively in "A Catch of Shy Fish," where "Big Bessie throws her son into the street," and in the "Don Lee" section of "In the Mecca" (st. 41). Annie, rejecting facile solutions, "not fearful to be unresolved," shows the "negative capability" Keats admired. She also knows "it is brave to be involved," the idea confirmed personally in "The Anniad," then socially in "The Womanhood."

"'[P]ygmies are pygmies still, though percht on Alps' / Edward Young" (poem 10), like the previous poem, indicates Annie's potential for intellectual independence. The epigraphic title, from Young's "The Complaint; or, Night-Thoughts on Life, Death, and Immortality" (1742-43), quotes a prophetic work that influenced William Blake's apocalyptic *The Four Zoas*.[10] A popular example of the "Graveyard School" in English poetry, "Night-Thoughts" offers a vision of the Judgment Day and eternity thereafter. The reference signals Brooks's early interest in the prophetic. The two pentameter quatrains, rhymed and slant rhymed, bear heroic touches of alliteration, heavy stressing, and compounding ("giantshine" and "breast-bone," the latter a readymade form). Pygmies, Annie says, disagreeing with the negative implications of the title, have their own excellence. They can see better on Alps, heights of experience, and "can expand in cold impossible air" of the imagination. They can pity the giants who, "wallowing on the plain," are confined to the space of physical experience. The pygmies become spiritual giants, reversing roles. The inversion also provides an oblique political and religious metaphor: the meek (though not so meek here) inheriting the earth.

Although Annie would go her own way bravely, "my own sweet good" (poem 11) depicts her succumbing to romantic expectation, itself as conventional as her mother's materialism. In the three-stanza ballad, a quotation, Annie imagines her lover kissing "all the great-lipped girls" he can while riding to meet her. Simplicity and directness of thought and form mask a linguistic sophistication, as in the play on "good," "god," and "gold" in the first stanza, a sentence fragment beginning "Not needing, really, my own sweet good" (compare the abrupt beginnings of "Ballad of Pearl May Lee" and "when you have forgotten Sunday"). Gold as a pejorative image is introduced in the next section; in stanza 7 of "The Anniad," the heroine will submit to her lover with "gilt humility."

The kind of man Annie imagines—or has already encountered—is bound to give her grief. Half-god, good from her point of view, he contents her with "promise so golden and gay." His dimple, considered a sign of handsomeness, is noted in the fourth stanza of "The Anniad" where the hero or "paladin," awaited by Annie, retains a dimple in his chin. This closing poem bridges "The Childhood and the Girlhood" to "The Anniad," and anticipates the difficulties that Annie's romanticism will incur.

II. "The Anniad"

It should be observed that the suffix *-ad* is a Greek form, denoting descent from a period of time (in Annie's case, an updated Medieval); a group (the poems); an epic in celebration. Here Brooks continues to celebrate the common life with its potential grandeur, in a way both critical and compassionate.[11] "What a pleasure it was to write that poem!" Brooks exclaims in the Stavros craft interview (*RPO*, 159). And yet, eight years later she observes, somewhat self-deprecatingly, "I enjoyed being technically passionate. I think 'The Anniad' is just an exercise, just an exercise" (Hull, 32. Cf. Genevieve Taggard's comments, above). The form, nevertheless, emerged initially from the content. "I imagine I finished one stanza," she remarks, "then decided that the rest of them would be just like that" (*RPO*, 158). The singular form of this forty-three-stanza poem, whose septets have been classified as a version of rhyme royal, bears a resemblance to the tetrameter of the long-meter hymn stanza. But the Brooks stanza, to be further examined, is unique. Her poem contains an elaborate scheme of rhyme and half-rhyme, a tetrameter line (foot to be discussed) using three or four rhymes per stanza, varying greatly the initial *a b (a) c (a) b (a) d d c* with closing couplets and other modifications. Trotting rhythm suggests the "paladin" in Annie's fecund imaginings (see st. 4). The word "paladin" itself, reminiscent of Carolingian romances, refers to a member of the twelve douzepers or noble companions.

"The Anniad" is a mock heroic, more compassionate than critical or satirical. Mention of "higher" and "lower" gods in the first stanza hints of a missing invocation, usually found in the mock epic. The genre reverts to the Homeric "Batrachomyomachia" ("Battle of the Frogs and Mice"), which served as a model for many eighteenth-century pieces. (See John Dryden's "MacFlecknoe" and Alexander Pope's "Rape of the Lock," both in heroic or iambic pentameter rhyming couplets.) Long before the eighteenth century, however, the legends of Charlemagne, popular in Italy during the Middle Ages, were adapted to Renaissance tastes. The bourgeoisie of the Italian city-states enjoyed the broad comedy which reduced chivalry to a realistic and farcical view of life.[12]

The stanzaic form used in the genre by Pulci, Boiardo, Ariosto, Tasso, and others is ottava rima, attributed to Boccaccio, and comprising eight hendecasyllabic lines rhyming *a b a b a b c c*. Transformed into the English iambic pentameter, the stanza was used by Milton, Keats, and Byron. The close rhyming and quick rhythms of "The Anniad" relate it to ottava rima. Its rhyme also suggests rhyme royal, whose iambic pentameter rhymes *a b a b b c c*. Brooks diverges from both, however, not only in her tetrameter, but also in varying the pattern of her rhyme. There is a heptasyllabic bias to her lines, which mostly begin with headless iambs. The tendency shortens the verse, giving an impression of a rocking trochaic meter (the way Milton does in "L'Allegro": "Meadows trim with Daisies pide, / Shallow Brooks, and Rivers wide").

The interesting question here is why Brooks chose mock heroic, unusual for a modern poem. One explanation may be a continuity with the antiheroic tendency in literature after World War I and the angry skepticism notable after World War II. The mock epic, like other forms of satire, has always afforded a means of social criticism, protected from political or literary reprisals by not seeming to take itself too seriously. Though satire and wit may be deeply felt (witness Jonathan Swift's *Gulliver's Travels*), the full impact of feeling is not communicated by intellectual appeals. So while "The Anniad" repeatedly enjoins us to "Think," "Appendix to The Anniad" directly appeals to our emotions.

Annie is a "thaumaturgic lass" (st. 5), pitied for her magical aspirations. These become villainous as "the culprit magics fade" (st. 30). Her lover, unnamed, personifies a mythology of golden, romantic dreams, like the "gold half-god" of "my own sweet good." He offers only "a fictive gold that mocks" (st. 36), like the mock heroic itself.

Throughout "The Anniad," appearance and reality, dream and destiny, struggle variously in the half-rhyme against full rhyme, two-stress against two-stress, trochaic sound against iambic meter, and strict compression against expansive ideal. A sense of doubleness, a consciousness of one's own role in the poem, gives a strange depth to the narrative. Poet and reader join in the work of observation and analysis. Stanley Fish uses the term "reader harassment," the ancient sermonic device whereby the reader's own values are illuminated by those of the subject.[13]

Engagement of the reader, a venerable, bardic function, further connects Brooks's mock heroic style with her movement toward heroic genre. The later, Anglo-Saxon elements, already glimpsed in individual poems, can be noted even in the rarified precincts of "The Anniad." It should be remembered, also, that the Anglo-Saxon scop, "mindful of saga and lay" (*Beowulf*, l. 783),[14] interpreted his narrative as part of his delivery. As distant as the four-stress with caesura of "Hwaet! we Gar-Dena   in geardagum, / þeodcyninga þrym gefrunon" (the opening lines of *Beowulf*) may be from "The Anniad" in meter and texture—not to mention language—there is a positive affinity in the alliteration, which will become an increasingly important source of vigor in the heroic works, and perhaps even in the ironic relation of four feet in "The Anniad" to four stresses in the earlier poem. Negative relationships also obtain: epic to mock epic, sonority to a clopping pace. Here is the first stanza:

> Think of sweet and chocolate,
> Left to folly or to fate,
> Whom the higher gods forgot,
> Whom the lower gods berate;
> Physical and underfed
> Fancying on the featherbed
> What was never and is not.

The trochaic/iambic tugging within the above lines, which seem to begin trochaic and end iambic, lends several ambivalences to the poem. The sound is an emblem of heroic pretension, evoking the trot—not gallop—of a horse, while at the same time pulling toward a conventional, iambic rhythm. Annie is not anchored like Maud Martha; she is buffeted by her foolish fancies and by the political world she did not make. Rhyme reinforces the complexity. The first four and the last lines above rhyme and half-rhyme, like some profound counterpointing between personal impulse and social determinism, reason and emotion.

Alliteration increases in the stanzas. "Buxom berries beyond rot" (st. 2); "Think of ripe and rompabout" (st. 3); "Think of thaumaturgic lass" (st. 5); "Garrulous and guttural" (st. 12); "Hies him home the bumps and brindles" (st. 15); "Rot and rout you by degrees" (st. 35) are typical lines. The firmness of masculine endings at line terminus matches the near elimination of articles and pronouns, usually at line initial. Without deictics, verbs and objects bear a dual responsibility, for themselves and for their subjects. Such compression may tax comprehension.

The first line of "The Anniad" links with the "black-and-tan motif" running through Brooks's work. The "sweet and chocolate" young Annie who dreams of a gallant lover is enchanted by the "man of tan." She tries to "improve" her appearance, "Printing bastard roses" upon her image in the looking-glass, "the unembroidered brown," and dresses her "black and boisterous hair, / Taming all that anger down" (st. 5). (Cf. the "untamableness" of Maud Martha's hair as symbol of rebellion, *WGB*, 163.)

But Annie does not rebel. Her lover, a "Narrow master," paladin of her dreams, displays a virulent male chauvinism. The word "master" (like the observation "Nobody loves a master" in "the preacher: ruminates behind the sermon") summons the word "slave." The lover esteems neither Annie's color nor her sex. That Annie tolerates, even welcomes the subjugation, implicates her self-denigration in terms of color, her romanticism, her upbringing, and beyond these, the dominant culture contempt for women in Western society. Even the chivalric code, despite its adoration of the Virgin Mary, usually assigned women an object status as trophy or emblem. Ideological entrapment signals Annie's bondage to her illusions. The "lowly room" to which she is taken in "gilt humility" becomes "a chapel." The lover, reminiscent of Satin-Legs Smith in his attractions for women and somewhat mysterious means, respects Annie merely as a trophy of innocence. He reduces and perverts the chivalric mystique in her consciousness.

"Doomer, though, crescendo-comes" (st. 12). War and the draft, personified as menacing and cynical, supposedly provide channels for chivalric and romantic expression. Language here bears affinities with heroic literature. "Doomer," characteristic of "The Anniad," is close in spirit to the Anglo-Saxon kenning, to compounds like "ring-giver" (king), "whale-road" (sea), etc. Elimination of articles accompanies semantic compression, so that the noun carries a heavier load than in a normal sentence. To do this, the noun often expands into epithet, frequently compound or kenning, or distills into a metonym. Other linguistic associations with the heroic genre appear in "man of tan," later "tan man," and "ocean-eyed lover" (st. 3), which bears direct comparison with Homer's "all-seeing Jove."

"Tamed" by military training into conformity, the way Annie tames her angry, rebellious hair (also a sexual symbol), her lover goes off to "The hunched hells across the sea" (st. 13). He returns, a grotesque of himself, chasing his lost wartime image, which Annie's adoration cannot revive. Victimized like her by illusions of male supremacy, he has obeyed a romantic code, replete with the false glamour of war. A black man, he endures a painful descent from his status abroad. War has debilitated him physically and morally and has lowered his regard for human life. At home, "This white and greater chess / Baffles tan man" (st. 18). He wants his power restored, together with the easy amatory encounters of war, its "candy crowns-that-were" (st. 19). The crowns evoke the wartime favors and status purchased with GI candy bars and revert to the "sweet and chocolate" of the first line.

Reference to "a green / Moist breath" (st. 17) alludes to the man's war-contracted illness, tuberculosis. The color green, like that of gold, connects his disease (sometimes associated with green-sickness and itself a symbol of the destruction and destructiveness of his illusions) with Annie, her youth and her parallel self-deceptions. She "Seeks for solaces in green" (st. 25), comforting emblem of her youth and of the spring. Throughout the seasons, she continues to romanticize her unhappy relationship. (Her quest for "solace" anticipates Maud Martha's finding "self-solace" at the hairdresser's.) "Sweet," collocated with images of the disease, also invokes Annie—referred to several times as "sweet and chocolate"—and couples the lovers in the imagery. This bonding has already attached to "gold" (associated with the lover), the "fictive gold" of their mutual illusions and Annie's absorption of the images of both man and dreams into a "gilt humility." The poem is dappled by images of subtle color (fuchsia, apple-green, maple, half-blue, silver, and crimson, in addition to gold, green, and skin tones), of taste (berries, candy, confection, and vinaigrette), of jewels, ornaments, perfume, flowers, and other tactile and sense imagery, and of mythological beings. All of these express, by their rarified quality, together with the somewhat artificial diction in both language and syntax, Annie's grand extravagance of imagination.

While the young woman is content to have her lover back, he cannot deal with civilian realities. Venting his displaced anger and frustration, he rejects her and seeks to recapture his wartime status in the arms of "a gorgeous and gold shriek / With her tongue tucked in her cheek, / Hissing gauzes in her gaze, / Coiling oil upon her ways" (st. 21). The snake imagery recalls Keats's "Lamia" and Geraldine in Coleridge's "Christabel." The "tan man" does not limit his philandering to the "gold shriek" (gold again used negatively). He finds a "maple banshee" and "A sleek slit-eyed gypsy moan" (st. 22). His tastes, though different from Annie's, are no less exotic. Mystery and irony assume archaic and poetic language: "passing-lofty light," "Hyacinthine devils," "scenic bacchanal," "droll prodigal," a language that, even when turning opaque, as in "violent vinaigrettes," conveys the sense. Amusing yet bizarre, the last refers (like "bad honey") to the man's unsatisfying affairs with the banshee and the gypsy. "Vinaigrette" is an ornamental container, usually for smelling-salts, as well as a sauce for cold meats or vegetables.

The strange women, like the other densely packed images and symbols, reward scrutiny. They hold an Eros/Thanatos key (that major presence in post-Freudian Western literature) as death images: a banshee presages death; the gypsy is a "moan" like the banshee's wail. The gypsy wanders, mirroring the man's restlessness; the maple of the banshee is color, physical gratification (including sex), and the questionable taste of death—a "Moist sweet breath," a "bad honey." The "Hyacinthine devils" that Annie hears singing in the upper air present another death image, alluding to the mythological youth loved by Apollo who changed him into a flower upon his death. The sonnet-ballad ending the section clearly states that the man has learned to court "Coquettish death." Thus the women, together with other images, foreshadow the tragedy in a carefully mounted series.

Having fathered Annie's children, the lover (marital status ambiguous in the text, but clarified as "husband" in Brooks's letter to Lawrence, March 12, 1949) leaves her for pleasure without responsibilities. Annie looks to consolation in nature and in books, Greek and Roman classical wisdom. A magic, surreal aura prevails. The terrifying "desert" of reality "countercharms." The poet, functioning as a kind of Greek chorus, advises the ex-soldier to return home and tells Annie to tend her children. "Kill that fanged flamingo foam" (st. 36), the man is warned. The flamingo, a tropical and subtropical bird (from "overseas" like the "overseas disease"), is pink and red, strangely long-necked, and emphasizes the throat, coughing, and other symptoms of tuberculosis, particularly the spitting of blood. Fangs suggest a snake so that the throat, the bird's neck, flamingo-colored foam (phlegm), and the snake—resembling the bird's neck and serving as symbol of temptation and evil—are collocated images. Fangs, often containing a poisonous venom, are long, sharp teeth for seizing and tearing prey. The disease tears increasingly at the lover who, lacerated by his own debauchery, goes home to Annie, and to death.

The word "That" in "That is dolesome and is dying" (st. 37), which troubled the editor, is also explained in the Brooks letter of March 12. The relative pronoun signals the dying lover (husband) as reduced to object, unworthy of personal pronouns at this point because of his moral and physical decay, the latter due to tuberculosis. "Now she folds his rust and cough / In the pity old and staunch." Annie forgives the man as she always does, having borne his children and learned to see him with "his feathers off" (st. 37). She is still incorrigibly romantic. "Posies" and "quaff" (st. 39) typify the vocabulary. In the same stanza the bereft Annie, drinking at a bar, waits to pick up "her fool"; the noun exemplifies the exact diction. "Fool" suggests Annie's harshened vision of the world, while it connotes a jester at court. Thus Annie, as if introjecting her dead lover, continues his quest for what has become a mocking vestige of her dreams. Concluding stanzas reveal her at a sorrowful twenty-four, drinking at taverns with strangers. Finally, like a disenchanted and hopeless Penelope "In the indignant dark," she is left in her kitchen with a violet, a symbol of her solitude. (Cf. violet in "Gay Chaps," no. 10.) As she kisses "The minuets of memory" in the last line of the poem, we find her still embracing the illusive past, the elegant and antiquated dance of life that it "was never and is not."

From this nostalgic moment, "Appendix to The Anniad / leaves from a loose-leaf war diary" again shudders into gear. "1 /

('thousands killed in action')" revives the horror of battle, the repression necessary to bear what cannot be shared, and carries the romance of the previous poem into reality. Relaxing the Anniad line into an irregular, basically iambic pentameter with varied rhymes, the four stanzas comprise 6, 3, 2, and 2 lines, the last a near-heroic couplet. Their form struggles toward—or away from—the sonnet, a presence in "2."

The second poem, an exquisite lyric, is both elegy and hymn to life. Its eight iambic pentameter lines, with a ninth in hexameter, suggest a slant-rhymed Spenserian stanza, beginning:

> The Certainty we two shall meet by God
> In a wide Parlor, underneath a Light
> Of lights, come Sometime, is no ointment now.
> [st. 1, ll. 1-3]

The capitals, reflecting the bigger-than-life manner in which Annie previously experienced life, set her fallen ideals and illusions into an ironically devotional context. Physical life and love yield to truth of the senses, a vitality of "Bees in the stomach, sweat across the brow. Now." The poem's capitalization, imagery, and compressed passion recall Dickinson (cf. her poem no. 511, for example).[15] Brooks's poetry will focus more specifically on postwar questioning of beliefs and institutions as the Civil Rights Movement develops. But the roots are here: "We never did learn how / To find white in the Bible." Hudson, writing of the *Selected Poems*, views "Now" as emblematic of the new "young Black" who refuses the deferred dreams and gradualism of the "older Blacks," and cites "First fight. Then fiddle" as another example from the *Annie Allen* poems in the volume.[16] Note also that "Now" occurs twice, at the beginning (l. 3) and as the final, emphatic word of the poem.

Of "3 / the sonnet-ballad," the poet writes, "Its one claim to fame is that I invented it" (*RPO*, 186). The moving coronach, in iambic pentameter (*a b a b / b c b c / d e d e / f f*), begins and ends with "Oh mother, mother, where is happiness?" so that the question-lament encircles the poem as it does Annie's life. Diction contrasts with the first two sections, expressing the battered romanticism that still clings to her psyche. "They took my lover's tallness off to war," she cries. He learned to court "Coquettish death" (see the banshee and the gypsy, above). Thus his faithlessness to Annie intersects with his loss of faith in life. Spiritually and physically diminished, his "tallness" becomes a casualty of war. The adjective "tall" will recur importantly in Brooks's compound for the new black as "a tall-walker" (*RPO*, 82, 85).

"The Anniad," together with its "Appendix," is a unique achievement, deserving the closest study. Experimental, it reverts to an ancient genre while pressing form and language to extremes. As Mallarmé effaces the connectives between images, Brooks realizes the purpose of the narrative by strictest paring, offering a spare meter and style that lend themselves to symbolism, packing each word with meaning, choosing a language, syntax, meter, stanza, and varied rhyme to convey "What was never and is not . . . / What is ever and is not," and then taking fantasy and myth into the dimension of reality where all may be newly perceived.

This bridging is accomplished by the tripartite "Appendix." First, its realism draws the romance of mock heroic into the present and "countercharms," in Brooks's word, breaking the self-deluding spell. Afterwards, "the sonnet-ballad" uses prosodic icons of romantic myth against themselves. As epilogue, the trio completes the tale and foregrounds its genre. Decrying war as illusive waste, the "Appendix" reappraises human love and sacrifice in terms of an antiromantic humanism.

III. "The Womanhood"

"The Womanhood" poems, fifteen in number (including "the children of the poor" sequence), return to the humanistic ground of the first section. Brooks carries forward "The Anniad" 's delight in language. Alliteration, punning, and word-play abound, but they merge, for the most part, with the emotional current, its depth and swiftness measured by "I / the children of the poor." These five superb sonnets are at once meditative and heroic. They nurture the strength and freedom of Brooks's later style of grand heroic. The quintet of Petrarchan/Shakespearean variations balance alliteration with lyricism. Except for the Latinate closing line of the first sonnet, the verbal pairings and compounds, rhymes, punning, and alliteration show a somewhat greater tendency toward the Anglo-Saxon than "Gay Chaps at the Bar." Alliteration continues the style of "The Anniad"; the language faintly echoes its romantic imagery. But while the "Appendix" seems to reach toward sonnet form, the "children" sequence fully engages its rhetorical/personal mode. And while "Gay Chaps" protests war and racism, "children" skeptically considers postwar society, church, and state from a mother's point of view. The children of the poor are the offspring—and orphans—of war. Complementary, the two sequences give male and female perspectives on history, morality, and individual destiny.

> People who have no children can be hard:
> Attain a mail of ice and insolence:
> . . . .
> And when wide world is bitten and bewarred
> They perish purely, waving their spirits hence [ll. 1, 2, 5, 6]

The first poem distinguishes between the simple "purity" of death in battle (world war) and the complex imperfections of ordinary existence, the poor left to struggle with childrearing. The dead, like Annie's lover, are frozen in war's rage. (Cf. "untranslatable ice" in the "Appendix.") But pain is the legacy of the living who attend its residue: children, their "queer / Whimperwhine" through "a throttling dark" of racial and economic oppression. The children's "unridiculous / Lost softness," their "trap" and "curse" of sweetness, finally "makes a sugar of / The malocclusions, the inconditions of love." "Malocclusion," an imperfect or incomplete bite, contrasts with the complete "bitten" of "bitten and bewarred." ("Unridiculous" recalls the clown in "downtown vaudeville" and the unclowning colored people in "I love those little booths at Benvenuti's".)

> What shall I give my children? who are poor,
> Who are adjudged the leastwise of the land,
> Who are my sweetest lepers, who demand
> No velvet and no velvety velour; [ll. 1-4]

"2" asks bitterly. The caustic oxymoron "sweetest lepers" accompanies insistent alliteration. The fatherless children are "quasi, contraband / Because unfinished." "Quasi" and "contraband" suggest, among several apt meanings, legal status (quasi) rather than intent of the party in interest (the lover), and forbidden status (contraband), which includes allusion to Negro slaves who escaped behind Union lines in the Civil War. Annie cannot realize her plans and dreams for her children. In a metaphor of sculpture, she observes, "I lack access to my proper stone." Wondering in "3" "And shall I prime my children, pray, to pray?" she decides they should be "metaphysical mules," stubborn in belief. She will stand by them, supporting their faith, should it falter.

"First fight. Then fiddle. Ply the slipping string," begins "4," the famous sonnet which had especial currency during the Civil Rights Movement. Brooks/Annie maintains that politics must precede art, and she enjoins, "But first to arms, to armor":

> Win war. Rise bloody, maybe not too late
> For having first to civilize a space
> Wherein to play your violin with grace. [ll. 12-14]

War has moved from foreign battlefields to home, to the self that must shape the dignity of its destiny before creating other beauty. The children's anger ("Carry hate / In front of you and harmony behind") will be their armor, their arms.

In the last poem, Annie reflects upon "When my dears die," whether at the end they will perceive any semblance of justice, "something to recognize and read as rightness." Because faith and life have prepared them, and experience has made them "adroit" or resourceful, Annie, not without irony, thinks they may "Accept the university of death," that universal knowledge and indiscriminate condition. The sequence thus comes to terms with faith, mortality, and personal responsibility. Bitterness against war and its social detritus transmutes into construction. Though religious faith will help Annie's children to endure, they must actively challenge social injustice.

"II / Life for my child is simple and is good" sounds a coda to the sonnets. Its free verse, buoyant tone, and plain diction express the fearless child who, like his mother, enjoys life in a direct and unaffected way. Though he has known physical injury ("his lesions are legion") as opposed to Annie's psychic ones, "reaching is his rule." A fine parallel between mother and son projects a dauntless vitality, as if the sonnets have worked through Annie's despair.

"III / the ballad of the light-eyed little girl" joins the themes of innocent victim and casual murder (cf. "the murder," as discussed in chapter 2). Sally does not mean to kill "her passive pigeon poor"; linguistic inversion adds to the ballad's archaic flavor. "The bird's name, "Confederate," denotes both an ally and a rebellious white Southerner, ipso facto an upholder of slavery. Sally, identified as "brown," "could not find the time" to feed her bird. The domesticated pigeon suggests the innocent or sacrificial victim image of the chicken in Brooks's work. "Light-eyed" connotes a lightness in feeling and associates light color with superficiality. The brown girl's light eyes also indicate both inner conflict and ambivalence toward "Confederate" and her responsibility for feeding him his "crumb." Complexity of the poem, structural and semantic, explains why Brooks passionately defended its inclusion in *Selected Poems* (see the correspondence, discussed above and in chapter 6). In the last lines, "whose epitaph / Is 'PIGEON—Under the ground,' " full capitals add to the epitaphial image.

"IV / A light and diplomatic bird / Is lenient in my window tree"(ll. 1-2) sets its regard for small forms of life in the company of Emily Dickinson and Robert Burns. "Light," "bird," "window" suggest the soul or spirit. "Bird" and "tree" may be transcendental. "Diplomatic" and "lenient" imply the mercy Annie seeks to "make miniature Valhalla of my heart." Brooks notes: "Valhalla: where my strifes, like heroes, may lie at last to rest" (*RPO*, 187). The ultimate destruction of mythic Valhalla lends further irony. The word and concept, nevertheless, balance the Christian symbolism of the poem.

Vocabulary in "He can abash his barmecides; / The fantoccini of his range / Pass over" (st. 3) poses the kind of "elegant black linguistic gesture" that might also be at home in Dickinson, as is the hymn stanza. (The earlier poet usually prefers short measure, 4-3-4-3, to the iambic tetrameter, long measure, of the six stanzas here.) "Barmecides" is the name of a family in the *Arabian Nights;*

one member invited a hungry beggar to a feast and pretended to
serve and eat an imaginary repast. The Italian word "fantoccini"
refers to puppets moved by machinery. Thus the bird can put to
shame those who pretend to feed (or serve) him, those who, like
the speaker seated behind a closed window, appear like puppets
and may actually be moved by powers beyond them. Their secu-
larity, moreover, emphasizes the bird's spirituality. Intense compression conveys Annie's cri-de-coeur to the "lenient" creature,
who becomes a religious emissary and symbol ("Oh open, apostolic height!") of heavenly peace. The foreign words support the
universal theme.

   In "V / old laughter," Annie's vestigial romanticism yearns for
the joyful, unspoiled culture of a vanished Africa, "Old laughter
chilled, old music done." Following this slight, ballad variation,
written at nineteen, is the strong "VI / the rites for Cousin Vit."
An elegiac sonnet (Pv), it robustly portrays the deceased, who is
being carried out the door in her casket. Her name derives from
the Latin *vita*, meaning life; even in death, the woman is true to
her name. En route, she rises to return to her bar haunts, where
she dances "the snake-hips with a hiss," drinks and gossips, and,
in the last word set monumentally apart as a sentence, "Is."[17]

   "VII / I love those little booths at Benvenuti's" returns to the
Bronzeville of "obituary for a living lady," "when you have forgotten Sunday," and "The Sundays of Satin-Legs Smith." It shares a
similar ironic stance; the use of couplet, varied rhyme patterns
and line length; and the suggestion of Eliotic distance and selective listing of objects, situations, and events ("objective cor-
relatives"). Unlike the clown in "downtown vaudeville," "The
colored people will not 'clown,' " implying Annie's growing sense
of racial pride and self worth. They refuse to "take the part of
jester" (Annie's terminology) for the visiting whites. The name of
the restaurant means "welcome" in Italian.

   "VIII / Beverly Hills, Chicago" belongs to the Eliot genre of
the previous poem ("The dry brown coughing beneath their feet";
"we drive on, we drive on"). Again, however, Brooks makes the
style her own as, intensified by ironic restraint, the poem sardonically depicts economic injustice. The epigraph, "('and the
people live till they have white hair')," quotes the late E. (Ernest)

M. Price, friend of Henry Blakely. There is envy of the "golden gardens," the lives whose trouble appears with "a gold-flecked beautiful banner"—"gold," the image of economic illusion here. "Beautiful," also illusive, will appear importantly in the "beautiful disease" of "Big Bessie" (*Selected Poems*). While it sounds no early Eliot weariness of tone, the piece tends toward discursiveness.

The lyric "IX / truth," strangely beautiful in its rhythmical shifts within a predominantly two-foot line, becomes a working through of ideas. The poet begins by imagining the belated appearance of unfamiliar truth: "And if sun comes / How shall we greet him? / Shall we not dread him, / Shall we not fear him / After so lengthy a / Session with shade?" Although "shade" denotes deprivation of sunlight, it connotes the "shade" or spirit in classical mythology, and reinforces a Homeric presence. Perhaps, says the poet, we have waited too long through the "night-years," a kenning-type compound, joined by the epithets "shimmering morning" in the same stanza and "propitious haze" in the next. The sun (son) becomes an awesome image of personified truth, awaited like a Messiah whose hard-knuckled knocking may inspire flight to the familiar haze. Homeric intimations also suggest a conflation of the Messiah with Ulysses' tumultuous return to Ithaca. The five stanzas, of irregular length, number 6, 7, 5, 3, and 2 lines, as if tapering down to the expectant yet fearful retention of ignorance, where "the dark hangs heavily / Over the eyes."

"Exhaust the little moment. Soon it dies" urges "X," an aphoristic tercet, confirming the "Now" of the "Appendix." It rhymes with the last line of "truth" and slant rhymes with "XI," which begins:

> One wants a Teller in a time like this.
>
> One's not a man, one's not a woman grown,
> To bear enormous business all alone. [ll. 1-3]

Initially published in *Cross-Section 1945*, the work holds primary significance here. "Teller," capitalized, a metonym for prophet, represents the first such poetic recognition in Brooks. References to solitary bearing of burdens occur in the Bible, notably where Moses tells the Lord, "I am not able to bear all this people alone, because *it is* too heavy for me" (Num. 11:14). The poet meditates, as if "calling" her own spirit to the task. On the narrative level, the speaker is Annie—wishing for guidance, continuing her reflections from "IX"—whose personified "truth," the sun, is analogous to the Teller. The latter will give practical, homely advice and encouragement, while fortifying belief in love and God. The play on telling time recalls Sojourner Truth's words in 1853 to a women's rights convention: "I wanted to tell you about Woman's Rights . . . and every once and a while I will come out and tell you what time of night it is."[18] Parent and prophet, the Teller expresses spirit-nurturing values.

Although the lines following are rhymed couplets, their irregular meter indicates uncertainties with which they grapple. The last stanza, a meditative dialogue (the Teller's anticipated words italicized), comprises a sestet, rhymed and slant rhymed, and continues the pattern of pentameter with variations. The change from impersonal indicative to imperative culminates in "*Behold*" and concludes strongly with alliteration and spondaic stressing. "*Behold,*" a univerbal line, connects four lines back with its end-rhyme, "cold," and with the half-rhymes in the poem. Its brevity weights the conclusion, "*Love's true, and triumphs; and God's actual,*" truths that Annie still struggles to maintain.

"XII / beauty shoppe," in three parts, "facial," "manicure," and "shampoo-press-hot-oil-&-croquignole," relates to the "Hattie Scott" vignettes and other realistic portrayals in *Bronzeville*. Madame Celeste (heavenly) works assiduously on the patrons; male and female purchase dreams of physical charm. Annie views the clients with amused good humor. The macho client's obvious sexual maneuvering in "manicure" contrasts with the ironic mode of the following trio, a love sequence where she is protagonist.

"XIII / intermission," also tripartite, begins with "1 / deep summer)." Linguistic excess ("By all things planetary, sweet, I swear"), the "early Millay inflection" noted by Kunitz, actually serves, here and elsewhere in the volume, especially in "The Anniad," to project both Annie's ebullient romanticism and the poet's gently mocking tone. The "gloves of ice" she requests, half-jesting, are not only a shield against the lover; they will surely melt, like ice cubes in the "whiskey" of his speech or the "gin" of his grin, beverages from whose natural source she is intoxicated ("well drunken"). The alliterative and semantic play on water, whiskey, weather, wildness, and seasons jostles against the remote and decorous "planetary" and the unleashed feelings of the speaker. There are no Shakespearean hymns at heaven's gate in this sonnet, no Millay postponement to retain joy, as in "I know I am but summer to your heart."[19] The cry, like that of "Appendix to The Anniad," is "Now."

Brooks's humor, slyly satirical, demands close reading. In this poem, as in later works such as "An Aspect of Love, Alive in the Ice and Fire," extravagant language signals the ironic mode. "2," a pleasant love lyric, tells of a seaside interlude in which the lovers' speech contends with the waves' movement. "3" begins archly, "Stand off, daughter of the dusk." A "black-and-tan motif" poem, it advises the dark young woman (Annie) not to "wince when the bronzy lads / Hurry to cream-yellow shining." Regular meter of "2" turns irregular. Thus the "intermission," an experience with a new lover, ends badly, reinforcing Annie's sense of rejection.

A poem of acerbic perceptions, "XIV" begins, "People protest in sprawling lightless ways / Against their deceivers." The lyric is shorter by five lines than the version submitted to *Cross-Section 1945* (which published, instead, the three poems mentioned). "Deceivers" was originally "deprivers," less forceful yet internally rhymed with "reviver" (st. 2). Lines 6 and 7, "To win. / To," abruptly break the metrical symmetry (basically pentameter), in suggesting that humanity, complex and ineffectual, turns to anyone, including the devil ("many a cloven foot"), who promises power or material gain. Note the deprecatory "golds goldly."

"XV" presents Annie at her apex of maturity. The poem's "freedom within form," mainly iambic pentameter though metered and rhymed irregularly, comprises five stanzas of varying lengths. Lines 27 through 46 are indented. (The stanzaic numbering follows that of the *Selected Poems* edition; in *The World of Gwendolyn Brooks*, stanzas 4 and 5 are combined.) The poem begins:

> Men of careful turns, haters of forks in the road,
> The strain at the eye, that puzzlement, that awe—

Grant me that I am human, that I hurt.
That I can cry.

Although Brooks came to disavow this kind of "appealing to whites to help us" (*RPO*, 175), the poem is rich in thought and complex in execution. The plea for integration, for Negroes to be judged as "human," perceives a newly disguised prejudice. Personified by the educated, "graceful glider," it requests patience since "prejudice is native" and our only "hope is that intelligence / Can sugar up our prejudice with politeness" (st. 4). Visually foregrounded and segregated by indentation, the Glider whispers, Satan-like, his fallacious argument that "prejudice is native" into Annie's ear. In the passage, Brooks alludes to her technical maneuver: "For the line is there. / And has a meaning": the color line. After the Glider quotation, the closing six verses return to left alignment and the poet's (Annie's) voice. "There are no magics or elves" aims a final thrust at Annie's own romanticism ("culprit magics" of "The Annaid"). Having requested "Admit me to our mutual estate" and understood the social realities, the poem concludes in 1949 with a conciliatory, "Let us combine. . . . We are lost, must / Wizard a track through our own screaming weed."

There will be no such invitation in the Brooks of *Mecca* and after. The imperatives of "Rise" and "combine," however, directed at the reader/audience (the rhetoric of the poem invites a public platform), intimate a prophetic voice in which Brooks seems to make Annie clearly her persona. Also significant is that the poem addresses men—power symbols for Annie throughout the sequence, particularly in "The Annaid"—and the rulers of government and society that they largely continue to be.

"The Womanhood" poems diverge from "The Anniad" in several directions. They leave tetrameter for the ample pentameter, importantly in sonnet form; abandon third person for monologue—at times dramatic—in first person singular and plural (the latter engaging a new consciousness); and drop uniform stanzas and intricate full and slant rhyme in favor of more varied and irregular rhymes, stanzas, and line lengths that at times break to free verse. Whether lyric or ironic; angry, elegiac, or hopeful—in their structural diversity they reflect maturely upon life. Annie, impelled by motherhood, looks bravely at a world she would like to reform. Her growth from egoistic romanticism into a realistic idealism draws the volume into unity. At times Brooks seems to anticipate criticism with conscious attempts to universalize her poetry. By keeping sight of Annie as a specific human being, however, she averts the dangers from which her own talent and good judgment protect her.

4

Maud Martha,
Bronzeville
Boys and Girls

American Family Brown, the source of Maud Martha,[1] was conceived as a series of twenty-five poems about an American Negro family (GB/EL, Sept. 28, 1944). In her letter of acceptance for *Bronzeville*, Lawrence had inquired about a prose project and encouraged one as artistically feasible. The poetic conception, never completely abandoned, infuses both the lyric passages and the narrative. The first published section appeared in *Portfolio* (Summer 1945). With minor changes, it is chapter 18 of *Maud Martha*, "we're the only colored people here." Lawrence mildly faulted the use of italics, but admired the universal quality of the work.

Brooks initially submitted *American Family Brown* on January 25, 1945, as a synopsis and ten chapters. These earned her Guggenheim Awards in 1946 and 1947. The poet's covering letter assured that she had eliminated all the italics she could. Having immediately acknowledged the manuscript, the editor wrote back in February, expressing her reactions and those of several readers. Lawrence felt the original plan was hampered by a self-consciousness more suited to poetry than prose. She thought Brooks potentially a first-rate novelist. She commended the author's knowledge of character and her economy and distinctive rhythm in style. But plot, suspense, and dramatic conflict were to be pursued. The editor wondered whether the story was actually a series of vignettes. One reader liked the lyrical writing but was disappointed by the sociological tone and patent concern with problems of Negro life. The poet would be more successful, the reader felt, if the themes were implicitly expressed through individuals rather than types, plot instead of perspective. Lawrence reminded that Brooks herself wished to present her people as individuals.

Brooks's warm response (Feb. 25) relieved the editor, who replied the next day. The poet did not see her work as near-static vignettes, but something close to that. Although Helen had been the protagonist, her sister, the more emotional Evelina (later Maud Martha), seemed to upstage her in the plot. In the new, proposed synopsis, Brooks would return to her initial focus on Helen, a reversion justified by Evelina's weakness as a character. She accepted elimination of chapter subheads at the editor's suggestion. On March 15, Lawrence wrote back, again with criticisms culled from several readers. Helen, an intellectual and aesthetic figure central to the new plot, became a minor figure and foil to Maud in the published novel. Stuart, Helen's husband, whom the editor now feared would utter the poet's voice more than his own, entirely disappeared.

The following month, Brooks learned of her Guggenheim Fellowship, and in May she journeyed to New York to receive the $1,000 awarded by the American Academy of Arts and Letters. During her stay, she met Lawrence and left with her some new material for the novel. The editor was very pleased with the revision (EL/GB, May 21). She concurred with another reader who saw improvements toward a more relaxed style and diction. The story now began *in medias res*.

Only a few letters were exchanged between May 21, 1946, and January 28, 1947, when the editor wondered whether *American Family Brown* would be completed by the end of the year. The poet was having marital and financial difficulties at the time, as the editor guessed from Brooks's remark that she would have to support herself and her son (Feb. 8). The writer assured, however, that the novel would be ready in May. Her Guggenheim Fellowship was renewed in April; she wrote an excited and happy letter on April 21, announcing completion of the work that morning.

The final consensus on *American Family Brown* ran against it, mainly as being artificial. On October 20, Lawrence wrote a very regretful letter informing Brooks that the manuscript was being returned. The poet replied bravely that she would not be discouraged. Several months later, true to her word, she submitted another manuscript. This time, however, it was poetry, "Hester Allen," which became *Annie Allen*. The prose work was not mentioned again in the correspondence until January 14, 1949, when Brooks turned in her final manuscript of *Annie Allen*. Excited about doing *American Family Brown* from a new point of view, she expected Lawrence to be less than overjoyed at the news. On March 3, in a letter regarding the final manuscript of *Annie Allen*, the editor asked if Brooks were still interested in doing *American Family Brown* as verse. The poet replied that she was, indeed, still interested. In October 1950, Brooks revealed her plans for new works. One was a book of fifty long poems, entitled "Eminent Bronzevillians," deliberately reminiscent of Lytton Strachey's *Eminent Victorians*. Thus the Bronzeville themes persisted, and would continue.

By April 1951 the poet and her son had moved from a temporary stay with her parents to a new apartment at 32 West 70 Street in Chicago, where the family was reunited. She informed Lawrence that her "illness" since her February visit to New York had been confirmed as a symptom of pregnancy. Nora Blakely was born on September 8 of that year. At the time, Brooks was thirty-four—the number of chapters eventually to comprise *Maud Martha*.

The publishing tale of *American Family Brown* was not resumed until January 21, 1952, when a new work of fiction, "Bronzevillians," was sent to Harper's. The poet suggested photographs (and enclosed samples) to be taken by a young Bronzeville photographer, Gerald Cogbill, for inclusion in the volume. Brooks considered the tone warmer than that of *Annie Allen*, and saw it as nearly another book of poems. Lawrence found the manuscript quite absorbing but not yet a finished product (Feb. 26). She was unhappy with the title "Bronzevillians" and was returning both manuscript and pictures.

Brooks submitted *The Maud Martha Story*, her revision of "Bronzevillians," nearly seven months later. Her noteworthy covering letter of September 15 describes her main transition from the *American Family Brown* manuscript. It was Evelina whom she had favored all along. So she decided to build the novel around her, renaming it significantly, she felt, "Maud Martha." The new name had clarified the character for Brooks. Lawrence pleasurably anticipated reading the manuscript.

On October 17 the editor wrote a long letter of over three pages giving a detailed criticism of the book. Although the critique represented readings by four editors, Lawrence's own assurance in assessing prose shows clearly. She warmly accepted *Maud Martha* for Harper's with an offer of a $500 advance against royalties. The criticisms were directed toward fuller characterization of Maud Martha and keeping the point of view hers. It was proposed that the unpleasant experiences with whites be balanced by a positive encounter to justify the hopefulness she retains. Brooks replied forthwith that the editorial criticisms were helpful and revisions would take about a month. She agreed with Lawrence's reservations about "the literary club," omitted from the final manuscript. The editor submitted the contract for *The Maud Martha Story* on October 28 with advice not to rush the work and a suggestion on filling in later details about Maud Martha's family.

On December 31, Brooks resubmitted *Maud Martha*; a covering letter explained her revisions. Mainly striving to unify the viewpoint, she had nevertheless kept to the understating of detail that supported her impressionism. Lawrence was delighted with the changes (Jan. 23, 1953) but hoped for elaboration on Maud's relationship with her husband. The next month, despite reservations about possible stereotyping of whites, she affirmed that the book would soon be typeset. In a letter dated the same day (Feb. 14), Brooks wrote that she was contemplating buying a house, a longtime dream, the same house in which she lives today.

Lawrence did not expect the novel to be appreciated by a wide audience (March 2). The reviews, however, in Chicago papers (*Tribune, Sun-Times, Daily News*), the *New York Times*, and in California were overwhelmingly good. The literary editor of the *Chicago Daily News*, Van Allen Bradley, and of the *Sun-Times*,

Herman Kogan, telephoned her their highest praise. Langston Hughes sent his laudatory *Defender* review. On November 2, Brooks wrote her first letter to Lawrence from her new home, a small, five-room cottage.

The editor visited Brooks in Chicago on March 9, 1954, and the next day wrote her a letter in which "The Life of Lincoln West" is first mentioned. She hoped that the poet's future work would have a universal perspective.

While one may categorize *Maud Martha* as a Bildungsroman, like Jean Toomer's *Cane* it is unique. It covers more time and is more experimental than, say, Betty Smith's *A Tree Grows in Brooklyn*, a book which the poet told me she "intensely enjoyed and admired." Sherwood Anderson's *Winesburg, Ohio*, also much favored, and Hemingway's *In Our Time* are episodic precursors. Together with the latter's *style indirect libre*, both books point to the main approach in *Maud Martha*.

Brooks's vignetting technique has been identified frequently as "impressionistic." Although *Maud Martha* is impressionistic in certain chapters (most notably in the opening "description of Maud Martha" and in "spring landscape: detail") that seem to intersperse the work with prose poems, its moral, psychological, and realistic focusing elude this classification. Nor is its emotional surface raw enough to be expressionistic. Features of the narrative combine, moreover, to suggest the distant yet benign presence of Henry James, whom Brooks favors highly.[2] Maud functions as a unifying consciousness, as discussed in James's prefaces, the "fine central intelligence," in R. P. Blackmur's phrase (James, xviii). One remembers, also, the novelist's thesis of giving "a direct impression of life," and his description, in the preface to *The Ambassadors*, of "the process of vision" as seeing "the precious moral of everything" (James, 308), precisely Maud Martha's natural tendency. In fact, her original reading matter in "the young couple at home" was Henry James, but the selection was criticized as improbable (EL/GB, Oct. 17, 1952). *Of Human Bondage*, a good but less subtle choice, misses a fine point of the characterization.

Another significant comparison and contrast may be made with Gertrude Stein's *Three Lives*, particularly the "Melanctha"

section dealing with the unhappy young black woman.[3] Both
Stein and Brooks poetically compress content—Stein, to portray
consciousness; Brooks, to express character and feeling. Yet
Stein's achievement, despite her compassion, is more stylistic
and linguistic than humane. Style tends to blur differences among
the simple lives and mentalities of the three protagonists. Melanctha's friend, "the sullen, childish, cowardly, black Rosie" (85),
"was careless and was lazy. . . . Rose had the simple, promiscuous
unmorality of the black people" (86). "Melanctha Herbert was a
graceful, pale yellow, intelligent, attractive negress. She had not
been raised like Rose by white folks but then she had been half
made with real white blood" (86). Stein was not singling out blacks
(cf. "thrifty german Anna" and Lena's "german patience"). Her
stereotyping issued from the social Darwinism then popular.
Notwithstanding, such fallacies mar their literary context.

Brooks refers to *Maud Martha* as an autobiographical novel, a
fiction based upon and elaborating sundry facts of her life. This is a
summary of her random observations (*RPO*, 190-93): "spring
landscape: detail" melds impressions of her own schooldays with
those of Henry Jr. as she sat in Washington Park, awaiting his
dismissal from kindergarten. "[D]eath of Grandmother" refers to
the death of an aunt. "[Y]ou're being so good, so kind" depicts the
visit of a white schoolmate. She likes "at the Regal" very much.
"Tim" tangentially depicts her Uncle Ernest. "[H]ome" describes
the Brooks family's struggle with mortgage payments. Although
"Helen's" character is a fiction, Emmanuel and Maud (Brooks) are
real. "[F]irst beau" and "second beau" are inspired by William
(Bill) Couch, not really a beau but the "Adonis" of Brooks's milieu
and a member of Inez Stark's poetry workshop (see epigraph to
"gay chaps at the bar"). Prominent at the University of the District
of Columbia, Couch is editor of *New Black Playwrights*. "Maud
Martha and New York," eighteen-year-old Maud's recurrent fantasy visit which shows her imagination, artistic tastes, and the
penetration of white bourgeois values, makes no mention of
Harlem. In "low yellow," Paul primarily recalls "Virgil J——, who
used to live with his grandmother and brother on the second floor
of my family home long long long ago, when we were both
fifteen." "[A] birth" refers to the impromptu delivery of Henry Jr.
in the kitchenette at 623 East 63 Street (cf. Maud, "triumphant" at

her successful delivery, and Brooks's own satisfaction). "[A]t the Burns-Coopers'," a "much-juggled" account, builds on the author's brief service as a housemaid. The "tree leaves leaving trees" episode refers to herself and Henry Jr.

Transition from "Evelina" to "Maud Martha" involved focusing of character and subtle aesthetic judgments. First, the name "Evelina" is more local—Southern and black in association. It may even recall Fanny Burney's principled heroine in *Evelina, or A Young Lady's Entrance into the World*, and the song "Evelina" in the Harold Arlen and E. Y. Harburg feminist musical comedy adaptation *Bloomer Girl* (1947). More pertinent for Brooks, it evokes "Eveline" in Joyce's *Dubliners*, the home-bound heroine who could not follow her romantic dream. The musicality of "Evelina," however, conveys yielding rather than strength, while the alliteration in "Maud Martha" firms the image and broadens the social connotations.

Although Maud grows up accepting her prescribed role as a woman, her name indicates conflicts in disposition and circumstance. "Maud," as noted in the discussion of "Sadie and Maud," derives from the name "Magdalene," the devout converted adulteress in the New Testament. The ambivalence recalls Tennyson's "Maud," grappling with passion and duty. Maud in Brooks's earlier poem is a restricted personality. While Maud Martha partly shares this quality, her wholesome libido animates the life which the "thin brown mouse" of the first poem rejects. Martha in the New Testament, the sister of Mary, symbol of Christian faith, was also a doer and a worrier. Collocation of the names "Maud" and "Martha," therefore, suggests the conflict between self-assertion and self-restraint, the desire for freedom and the personal, familial, and social responsibilities—and the economics—that constrain the young woman.

Discrimination, both white and black, by society and by family, conditions Maud Martha's relationship with her husband and braces the narrative framework. Painful incident and withheld approval are the established contours of her environment. Against these negative aspects, however, positive ones reflect Brooks's own experiences during the time of composition. Henry Jr., born in 1940, was a child when the novel was being written; Nora was an infant, born two years before the book was published.

The poet's own life-nourishing qualities define her heroine. Angers recede; rage glimmers and gleams; but sanity lights the path. This is not yet the "essential sanity, black and electric," called for in "In the Mecca." Black, certainly, but the current is of low voltage here. Within the context of the early fifties, time of the "silent generation," the Dr. Spock era of the child-centered household, the novel reveals an archetypal, postwar, bourgeois concern with home and family, and aversion to politics.

The opening chapter describes seven-year-old "Maudie," as Brooks thought of her, in her own terms of appetite and affection. We enter immediately a world of sense impressions: taste, color, flowers, the sky, images of Brooks herself who "dreamed a lot" on the top step of her back porch. Sensitive, intelligent, caring, Maud loves dandelions because "it was comforting to find that what was common could also be a flower." Affection is "the dearest wish of the heart of Maud Martha Brown." Her older sister, Helen, aged nine, dainty and fair, has love from the entire family, including her brother; Maud makes an early connection between appearance and social value.

"[S]pring landscape: detail," with exquisite pointillism, creates a background of children moving past buildings and "keep off the grass" signs over the seedling grass, children perceived as multicolored bits of clothing carried by "jerky little stems of brown or yellow or brown-black, . . . Past the tiny lives the children blew." Inside and outside the classroom, Maud summons vitality and hope. Yet in emulating the perceived virtues of her parents' marriage, her desire for love results in paradox. Her seeming compensatory moral and intellectual vigor combines with physical disadvantage to alienate her from the family and deny her the very love she needs. Even as a grown woman in "Mother comes to call," she relearns her inability to earn love by being studious and good. By this time, however, she has gained ego-strength, accepting that her parents' values will never correspond with hers.

"[D]eath of Grandmother" fixes an important moment in Maud's consciousness and prefigures her adult confrontation in "Maud Martha's tumor." Comic, grotesque, and noble aspects of the dying woman imprint Maud's hospital visit; she controls her fear of the strange-looking invalid by attempts at conversation.

Repelled by the unfamiliar odor of death, Maud recognizes Gramma's new, queenly status, she "who, lying locked in boards with her 'hawhs,' yet towered, triumphed over them." Realities of hospital life, vain cries for the bedpan and attention, the sick who feel for each other, awareness of leave-taking—these fill Maud with compassion and grief, becoming near-introjection of Gramma's own dignity in her hard dying.

In a later chapter, "Tim," Maud's paternal uncle, dies and is viewed in his casket, where he looks like "a gray clay doll." Gray recurs in the novel, and elsewhere in Brooks, as the symbol of death and/or despair (see, for example, "The Last Quatrain" in *The Bean Eaters*). Maud attends to values even more than to her own physical demise. She wonders whether "the world was any better off for his having lived." Incipient skepticism touches her own faith as she turns from God's possible opinion of Tim's life to what Tim might have thought. Aunt Nannie, his widow, powders her face before the funeral because Uncle Tim, oily-nosed himself, had hated a shiny nose in others. The chapter closes with Maud's impressions of the ceremony. She realizes that the hymn, "We Shall Understand It By and By," makes little sense because "by and by" is too late. The sentiment echoes the "Now" of "Appendix to The Anniad" and "Exhaust the little moment" of "The Womanhood."

Racial and interracial themes are deftly handled, the tact ranging from amused insight to irony and controlled rage. In chapter 5, "you're being so good, so kind," a white schoolmate calls. In convoluted acceptance of black and white stereotypes, Maud has carefully opened the windows to dissipate any offensive odor on the premises. She feels she incarnates the whole "colored" race being judged by the entire "Caucasian plan." Fearing and welcoming the visit, she disapproves of her own gratitude which had made the occasion momentous.

The bitter recollection of Emmanuel's offer of a ride in his wagon (in "Helen"), his words to Maud—"I don't mean you, you old black gal"—and Helen's acceptance focus the "black-and-tan" motif. Similarities with Annie of "The Anniad" have been justly pointed out: both Annie and Maud are rejected by their lovers because of socially valued lightness and appearance in general.[4] Additionally, Annie functions within the larger context of war's psychic erosions and the fallacy of misplaced romanticism. Maud experiences some disillusion but maintains the optimism of a relatively comic view of life, as opposed to Annie's somewhat tragic one.

"[L]ow yellow" defines Maud's abject satisfaction that her "low-toned yellow" fiancé has chosen her dark, unattractive self because she is "sweet" and "good," Maud still trying to earn love. Their marriage soon founders upon intellectual and sexual differences. Maud submerges her cultural interests in bourgeois aspirations. Like the young Annie Allen, she romanticizes Paul's shortcomings, translates his frugality into a pioneer virtue she can admire in them both. Seeking a moral and secular faith, she imagines herself "dying for her man." Much later, she sees him as crude and superficial. "Clowning" to get her attention as they return from a musicale (remember the dignified Negroes who "would not clown" in "I love those little booths at Benvenuti's"), refusing to borrow a book from the library, looking only to see whether there was an author named "Bastard" in the author index (which there was), waiting until Christmas morning to buy a tree inexpensively, exchanging Maud's richness of family life and its holiday memories for one in which she struggles to establish traditions. Especially after the birth of her daughter Paulette, Paul becomes a man who "could eat from a splintery board, he could eat from the earth."

Segregation makes for a painfully self-conscious visit to the movie in "we're the only colored people here." But the black-and-tan dilemma more cruelly afflicts Maud at the Annual Dawn Ball of the Foxy Cats Club, a group of pleasure-seekers. Pregnant, watching Paul dance with the redhead, she realizes that her color will always be "like a wall. He has to jump over it in order to meet and touch what I've got for him. . . . He gets awful tired of all that jumping." After the birth of Paulette, at which Mrs. Brown plays impromptu midwife, Maud jubilantly advances toward maturity. Reference to the new grandmother as "Belva" instead of "Mama" equalizes mother and daughter. Maud's full married name appears for the first time: "Maud Martha Brown Phillips." The child's beauty is a welcome surprise. Later, drinking wine with "Paul in the 011 Club," Maud thinks, "The baby was getting darker all the time!" as if listing another failure Paul might escape

by joining the military service. This is the first citing of the war,
and the issue remains personal.

Maud's ambivalence, her inward struggles between realism
and romanticism, passivity and rebellion, domesticity and culture, determine the narrative sequence. The pattern, usually
alternating between lyrical and descriptive modes, maintains the
pace and tension from one vignette to the next. For example,
"first beau," symbolically unnamed, awakens Maud's sexual desires (no longer dream-disguised, as in the Freudian "love and
gorillas"). His lyrical portrait echoes the young Annie Allen's
gallant paladin ideal, one who has ways with "a Woman." This
episode follows the "Helen" chapter's psychological realism contrasting the sisters, with Helen sensually fluffing on "Golden
Peacock" powder (gold, the recurrent, illusive symbol in Brooks,
acquires from "Peacock" connotations of arrogance and pride) and
assuring Maud, "You'll never get a boy friend . . . if you don't stop
reading those books." And following the impressionistic "first
beau," "second beau" realistically presents Maud's romanticized
identification with David McKempster and his intellectual yearnings. The two beaux illustrate Maud's conflicting wishes at eighteen for domesticity, affection, and the intellectual good life.

Both Maud and David are misfits; he reappears as a parvenu
in "an encounter," years after Maud has entered motherhood. In
their chance meeting, he disillusions the young woman by his
white-imbued academic and social pretensions; she has already
discarded her illusions about marriage. Brooks's symbolic eloquence of detail sparks the Jungly Hovel campus scene. Maud
(who has attended a lecture at the college), David, and his two
white friends (an engaged couple whose company he prefers to
Maud's), await their order. In the ironic closing sentence, a wait-
ress brings "coffee, four lumps of sugar wrapped in pink paper, hot
mince pie." Pink, in context, suggests affectation and David's
white orientation. "Hot mince pie" is another white cultural
touch. Its chopped and mixed ingredients, their individuality
further surrendered in baking, connote David's assimilationism.

Contemplative "posts" follows the traumas of "a birth." The
quietly lyrical passage sets forth the virtues of a plain marriage, an
order of constancy in nature underlying a "system of change."
Maud supposes that the search for a secure relationship may be

essential. "Leaning was a work," she concludes. But the truce represents also a defeat for the independent self. "[T]radition and Maud Martha," however, succeeds "posts" with Maud's congestive dissatisfactions.

By antithesis and comparison, Brooks defines character and growth. "[K]itchenette folks," whose modest circumstances precede "encounter," inscribes Maud's social eclecticism and breadth of interest. It presents alternate views of marriage. The lively account memorably sketches neighbors such as the doorkey child Clement Lewy, who bravely takes care of himself while his mother, "gray"-looking, deserted by his father, works as a housemaid (anticipating Maud's employment in "at the Burns-Coopers'"); and the "Woman of Breeding," reclusive Miss Snow, who serves herself afternoon tea. Mostly hard-working and appealing, the neighbors reflect Maud herself.

Augmenting the tensions of the "encounter," "the self-solace" beauty salon episode permits Maud's cumulative angers to surface. The white cosmetics saleswoman, who comments unthinkingly that she "works like a nigger to make a few pennies," activates Maud's political consciousness, prefigured at seventeen in "Helen." There the "untamableness" of her hair (cf. "Taming all that anger down" in "The Anniad") offends her father's sense of order and sets her apart even more.

"[M]illinery," in which Maud refuses to buy the suddenly discount-priced hat, is reinforced by "at the Burns-Coopers'," where the heroine, responding staunchly to financial difficulties, accepts a position as maid. The employer's stringent demands echo in her mother-in-law, an imperious woman "with hair of a mighty white." Maud gains insight into the daily indignities Paul suffers on his job. He, too, has an officious "Boss" who views him stereotypically as a child. In a positive act of refusal, confirming that of "millinery," Maud decides not to return. She asserts her humanity: "one was a human being." She has progressed from acceptance of color stratifications—in family, school, marriage, and society—to rebellion.

Maud loves her father, whose imperfect acceptance repeats itself in her relationship with Paul. In "love and gorillas," she rejoices at Papa's return after his argument with her mother; in "home," when he arrives with a crucial mortgage loan, the welcome points up Maud's affection and their basic family solidarity. Papa's "dear little staccato walk" seems as evocative as the hands of Theodore Roethke's father in "My Papa's Waltz," or the mother's "small, poised feet" on the piano pedals as recollected by D. H. Lawrence in "Piano." In "Helen," a touching passage describes the homely, beloved house, cherished so deeply by Maud and her father; its kitchen chairs that "cried when people sat in them," inviting parallel with Maud herself: she who is not beautiful but serviceable, like the house, and who, like the chairs, also cried, alone in the pantry, when feeling abused.

Maud's relationship with her mother remains unresolved. In "a birth," annoyance at Mrs. Brown's obtrusive concern with appreciation gives way to the thought that it might be "as hard to watch suffering as to bear it." Still, Maud must retain the old hurt. In "Mother comes to call," despite wartime austerity, she enter-tains her visitor with the elegance available for "Tea," the cere-mony recalling the "Woman of Breeding" in "kitchenette folks." Dignity and decorum preside over the relationship (witness the formality of "call" in the chapter title). It is Mama who brings tidings of Helen's forthcoming, security-inspired marriage to the family doctor. Mama's pride in the match and disapproval of Paul (she brings food gifts, of which only one pecan is for him) contrast with Maud's disapproval of the union. And when Maud wistfully observes how siblings can differ in appearance and charm, Mrs. Brown, missing the cue, assures her that she is "wonderful" and makes "the best cocoa in the family." Though subdued, the con-flict suggests the daughter's continuing development.

In the penultimate chapter, "tree leaves leaving trees," the chiasmus of the title conveys joining and continuity, which persist in tension with losses, change, and growth, themes of the painful visit to Santa Claus. Anticipation fills the childlike listing in the introductory paragraph (with only two commas in the verbless sentence) of twenty-nine different toys for sale in the department store. In a stunning rejection of her blackness, Santa ignores Paulette. Maud's rage distinguishes her from Helen, who would have dismissed the matter, and Paul, who would have been angry momentarily. With this insight, Maud steps importantly toward self-identity, even though "those scraps of baffled hate" remain.

Maud insists to Paulette that Santa really loves her; she wants her daughter to share the beauty of her own childhood faith. The mother's silent cry "Keep her that land of blue!" recalls Langston Hughes's injunction "Hold fast to dreams."[5] Her plea is for the Romantic imagination and for the sustaining early sense of a world where love overcomes evil. Her idealism rejects her own mother's materialism.

Maud's ability to give love; her maturing perception of herself in relation to others (parents, husband, child); her merging of affectionate, intellectual, and artistic impulses within an increasingly vital, moral synthesis: these become beauties of the novel. In "at the Regal," Maud aestheticizes her morality with one "bit of art": "What she wanted was to donate to the world a good Maud Martha." Coming to terms with a sense of alienation and diminished worth, she evolves her personal meaning of "goodness." In the black singer's performance, she perceives discontinuity between art and life. Her gradual countering with existential values mildly rebukes aestheticism.[6] Reverence for life in "Maud Martha spares the mouse," restated pragmatically by "brotherly love," where Maud eviscerates a chicken, defines her achievement. Sparing the mouse, Maud discovers, "I am good," and reaffirms both precedence of life over art and life *as* art. "In the center of that simple restraint was—creation."

"[B]rotherly love" expresses the parallel antiwar theme. Nostalgia for "the happy, happy days" of her childhood mounts against her grotesque, butcher-knife struggle with the anonymous chicken, then combines into meditation on killing in war. Chickens, Brooks's recurrent image of the sacrificial victim (cf. "Sunday chicken," *Annie Allen*), will be safe in the world when people become familiar with them as individual creatures possessed of dignity. We infer an analogy with black-white relations. "What was unreal to you, you could deal with violently" also anticipates the lynching reference in the final chapter.

For Maud, life becomes humanistic faith and its joy. Reprieved from her contemplation of death in "Maud Martha's tumor," her equanimity comprises strength and a measure of weariness with a life she first judges as not "bad" and then "interesting." Yet her resilience as she rushes home bespeaks the author's own adaptive stamina.

In the last chapter, "back from the wars!" (again lyrical, following the Santa Claus incident), Maud's brother Harry has safely returned. Aware of her youthful vigor and hopes, she raises the shade to let in the morning light of reality. "What, *what* am I to do with all of this life?" she muses, expressing the essence of youth, its seeming endlessness. Racial troubles persist. Although the Negro press largely mirrors the white, carrying on its front pages lovely, pale, elegant women, inside, like the recessed anger in Maud herself, there are stories of Southern lynchings. Contemplating nature, however, reveals her own truth: "the basic equanimity of the least and commonest flower" would return in the spring. This Wordsworthian "natural piety" reverts to chapter 1. As the weather bids her "bon voyage," in the first passage written for the novel, Maud embarks upon another journey, expecting a second child.

Maud Martha abides for Brooks, who has planned a sequel— again largely autobiographical. In one version (Hull) the heroine will have three children, become widowed, fall in love at fifty or thereafter, and visit Africa—and all the while her feminist awareness deepens.

This little-appreciated masterpiece of classic simplicity and poetic precision, through an epiphanic mode, weaves dream and reality, philosophy and episode, individual psychology and social milieu. *Maud Martha* has a special significance in Brooks's development of breadth: the ability to project various characters and moods, to sustain a narrative, to balance the sequential with the episodic—all of which look ahead to her major work, *In the Mecca*. Themes of black-and-tan and black-and-white, of love and death, present from *Bronzeville* onward, lattice the personal narrative within the social frame. Her heroine's dilemma typifies the pre-women's liberation either-or choice between domestic duties and self-fulfillment, where attempts at flight were contained within the flock. Maud has learned to adapt, while maintaining the ego-strength that permits change and preserves dreams. One suspects from the novel that her passivity will continue to lift. Although her rationalizing sometimes works against her, it also bolsters her life-assertiveness. A frayed but tenacious idealism and anger spark Maud's consciousness and activist potential.

Like her heroine, Brooks moves on affirmatively to the statements of *The Bean Eaters* and toward prophetic and heroic utterance. What we hear in *Maud Martha*, nevertheless, is the sense of dignity which makes that latent voice elsewhere audible.

Bronzeville Boys and Girls

Bronzeville Boys and Girls,[7] a book of thirty-four poems dedicated to the poet's children, Henry Jr. and Nora, was handled as a juvenile and involved a minimal amount of correspondence. It does not figure in the correspondence between Brooks and Lawrence, although it was originally submitted to the editor on December 28, 1954, and was warmly acknowledged a week later. The publication date was October 3, 1956. While the charm and warmth of this little gem, illustrated by Ronni Solbert, suggest the virtues of Robert Louis Stevenson's *A Child's Garden of Verses*, its discussion is further warranted.

First, the book extends Bronzeville, the black ghetto that becomes Brooks's microcosm of national life. Second, it deepens the personal and familial context of *Maud Martha*, as if the Brown family and Maud's own life-serving qualities had borne dozens of distinctly rendered and endearing children: fixed in the urban scene but dreaming wider landscapes, immersed in their friends and games and families, and emerging as children anywhere. Maud herself might say with "Beulah at Church": "It feels good to be good." There is elegance and poverty, the mimicry of a grownup world, and the special terrain of the very young. Like *A Child's Garden*, it encompasses the wonder of growth and the love that encourages it. Brooks is more exemplary, however, than the English poet. She acknowledges no cruel children but implies cruelty, the indifference that sanctions poverty and compels children to be prematurely involved in adult problems. "Otto," who did not get the Christmas presents he had hoped for, insists, "My Dad must never know I care / It's hard enough for him to bear." Sensitivity to needs of grownups also appears in "Jim":

> There never was a nicer boy
> Than Mrs. Jackson's Jim.
> The sun should drop its greatest gold
> On him. [p. 34]

The dropping of "On him" to a separate line reinforces the injunction. Jim sacrifices his baseball game to nurse his mother without permitting her to see his disappointment. In Bronzeville, the gap between the world of children and that of adults narrows toward greater interdependence than in *A Child's Garden*. No nurse mediates between parents and children. The difference is partly one of social class: in Stevenson, upper middle or lower upper; in Brooks, working and modestly middle class.

Stevenson's imagination peoples his near-solitary life with travel and magic, observations of nature and human detail. The first person singular gives a full vision enriched by an extraordinary sensibility. The precocity of Brooks's children is social: they have real identities and relate to friends and family. Names fill the book: in the thirty-four poems, thirty-seven different children are the subjects. Their names, which appear in the fully capped poem titles, typify those in Bronzeville and elsewhere: Mexie and Bridie, Val, Timmie and Towanda, Narcissa, Andre, Keziah, Charles, Cynthia, John, Paulette, Rudolph, Eppie, Ella, Dave, Luther and Breck, Michael, Eldora, Beulah, Skipper, Robert, Lyle, Nora, Mirthine, Maurice, De Koven, Gertrude, Marie Lucille, Cheryl, Jim, Eunice, Vern, Otto, Tommy, and Willie. Others are named in the poems, including a dog (Rover) and a cat (Mootsie). And there is a real-life heroine to dream on. Gertrude says: "When I hear Marian Anderson sing / I am a STUFFless kind of thing." The children themselves have glimmerings of heroic qualities, as do Otto and Mrs. Jackson's Jim, mentioned above. The specificity helps to create a real world that may be entered by many doors. Some of the children speak in their own voices; some poems are narrated in second or third person. Metrical variety, also true of Stevenson, adapts to the content, although in both books tetrameter, ballad stanza, and couplets predominate.

A child's linguistic audacity skips through poems like "Cynthia in the Snow":

> It SUSHES.
> It hushes
> The loudness in the road.
> It flitter-twitters,
> And laughs away from me.

It laughs a lovely whiteness
And whitely whirs away,
To be
Some otherwhere,
Still white as milk or shirts.
So beautiful it hurts.[8]

Here, in little, we find the strengths of Brooks's work. She can feel by way of the child's sensibility. She almost verbalizes the snow. Onomatopoeia can disclose relationships that may become, at their extreme register, animistic. We recognize—unless we have lost all our childlike intuiting—that snow "sushes." Whether or not this is a converging of "slush" (possibly of Scandinavian origin) with "shush" or "hush," the question persists: why these particular sounds?[9]

Brooks is always sensitive to prosodic features of language. "Flitter-twitter" seems nearly tactile and helps define the snow's delicate motion; "whitely" and "otherwhere" are locutions a child might use. "Whitely" follows "whiteness" and precedes "white," identified with milk or shirts, necessities and goodnesses. Their whiteness partakes of the larger reality and value of whiteness, also powerful. The underlying irony: a gentle whiteness that uses its mild power to quell "the loudness in the road." "Loudness" suggests technology and traffic and is not a good in this quiet world. The color white, though racially problematic, is not spoiled thereby for the child. Often a benign element in Nature, snow covers all and suggests fresh beginnings. The lines themselves flutter down the page in slightly irregular lengths. The basic trimeter line (after initial emphasis by stress and contraction of the first two lines) breaks strategically at the eighth line, indicating a shift, a moving away of the snow to "otherwhere." We hear the alliteration, rhyme, slant rhyme, and assonance.

Other poems describe a tea party; the defensive reactions of a child excluded from an adult party; the freedom (and license) invited by festivities attending the relatives' Sunday visit; "Narcissa," whose solitary world is imaginatively enriched by metamorphoses; "Andre" dreaming he can choose his parents and choosing his own; "Keziah" hiding in her secret place; "Charles," who goes "inside" himself when he is sick; "John, Who Is Poor," living with his widowed mother, his friends encouraged by the poet to share food with him; "Paulette" wanting to run with squirrels and ants, not "To be a lady"; "Rudolph," who is tired of the city, wanting to push away buildings and spread his arms in the country; "Eppie" seeking to establish her identity in the form of "something / That's perfectly her own."

Despite or even because of their urban environment, the children react strongly to natural phenomena: "Ella" runs out in winter without her coat to see the clouds, and "Michael Is Afraid of the Storm." "De Koven" looks at the "dancy little thing" and concludes, "You are a rascal, star!" because he cannot grasp it and keep it with him to shine always. "Tommy" wonders at the seed he has planted which pops out of the ground. Paradoxes of the adult world abound in miniature: "Beulah at Church," clean and sin-free, enjoying her peaceable "goodness"; "Luther and Breck," fighting dragons and playing at being knights, bravely battling to do good. A stranger, such as "Eldora, Who Is Rich," can turn out amiably like the other children, or he/she can be different, like "Robert, Who Is Often a Stranger to Himself" when he looks into the mirror. The children love their pets. "Skipper" tries to save his goldfish (unlike careless Sally in "the ballad of the light-eyed little girl"); Cheryl admires her cat, Mootsie, "living her lovely little life / With scarcely any sound"; "Vern" walks with his comforting puppy after being scolded. Moving is an ever-present tragedy. "Maurice" feels important about moving until he realizes he will lose his friends. "Lyle," who has had to move seven times, personifies the enviable tree.

Outside of their warm relationships with one another, the most significant values for the children are familial. For "Eunice in the Evening," the best thing about the dining room is "Everybody's There!" The concluding poem, "The Admiration of Willie," lauds parental capabilities. Their wisdom extends from tying ties and baking cakes to providing medicine, helping at play, and "Kissing children into bed / After their prayers are said." Beauty for the children of Bronzeville chiefly means human relationships. The rare traces of nature inspire appreciation and wonder. Affection—like Tommy watering and caring for the seed—nourishes growth and mutes the harshness of the adult world. The poverty of Bronzeville is economic, never emotional or spiritual. In feelings, the children are indeed rich. Their sturdy qualities, retained in adulthood, will have the heroic capacity to grow and function there. And though parents are not physically present in most of the poems, they are the strength of warmth and closeness from which the marvelous children of Bronzeville have been drawn.

5

The Bean Eaters

"Bronzeville Men and Women," soon to become *The Bean Eaters*,[1] was submitted to Elizabeth Lawrence on December 21, 1958, together with another partial manuscript, a novel, "In the Mecca." The editor immediately acknowledged the manuscripts and, six weeks later, conveyed the joint editorial decision (EL/GB, Feb. 9, 1959). She enthusiastically accepted *The Bean Eaters* for publication. Among the poems, she singled out for special praise "A Bronzeville Mother . . ." and "The Chicago *Defender* Sends a Man to Little Rock." But there were reservations about "The Contemplation of Suicide," which had been rejected for *Annie Allen*, and "The Ghost at the Quincy Club." Lawrence hoped for more poems than the twenty-eight planned. As for the novel, she had doubts and was returning it. She felt that the poet's talent hampered her in the looser structures of prose.

Brooks graciously accepted criticism of the novel (GB/EL, Feb. 16). She hoped to write a good one in the future, preferably in verse. Elated at the poet's positive response, Lawrence immediately encouraged her to proceed. *Poetry* magazine took several poems for their September issue, including "The Bean Eaters," "Old Mary," "We Real Cool," and "Strong Men Riding Horses." Of the poems Lawrence had sent to *Harper's*, the magazine selected "The Explorer" and "For Clarice. . . ." On March 28, Brooks sent fourteen new poems; twelve of them appear in the final version. Uncertain about "The Ballad of Rudolph Reed," she felt sure of "The Ghost at the Quincy Club." And did Lawrence like the title

"The Bean Eaters" for the volume? Lawrence did, and would report after the manuscript had had several readings.

Editorial reactions were favorable. One omission was accepted out of eleven suggested by a reader, the same one who suggested beginning with "The Explorer" rather than "A Bronzeville Mother," the poet's choice. But Lawrence was firmly committed to nearly all the poems and found support in other readers. On May 15, she sent a memo to the Harper editors, requesting publication of *The Bean Eaters* with a first printing of 2,500 copies and an advance of $100 upon signature. In July, Lawrence visited Brooks in Chicago and was happy to learn that the poet was considering a verse biography of Phillis Wheatley.

Several months later, on November 21, 1959, the poet's father, David Anderson Brooks, died. The bereaved daughter wrote a deeply grieving letter in which she enclosed an elegy to replace the dedication (GB/EL, Dec. 2). The editor confirmed the change in a handwritten note. Bound proofs were sent to Rolfe Humphries and Peter Viereck, among others, and their warm replies previewed the public reception. A typical reaction by white critics to the political content was that of Harvey Curtis Webster.[2] In his very favorable review, he observed that "her best social poems yet" were in *The Bean Eaters*, but he preferred those in which race was "an accident" and craftsmanship more easily visible.

Having once agreed in an interview that "to be Black is political,"[3] Brooks added in a marginal comment on this manuscript, "Of course, to be *any*thing in this world as it is 'socially' constructed, is 'political.' Whites, too, and all other distinctions, operate politically as to offense, defense, and response—even when they don't know it." Race relations, war, poverty—three salient problems of American life—continue to animate her work in *The Bean Eaters*, but with a difference. Though she is not the "Teller" she becomes in *In the Mecca* (despite foreshadowings like "Leftist Orator . . ."), her book marks an important step toward the role in two ways: first, the increased specificity regarding political events; and second, the increased irregularity (or freeing) of the meter while shifting formal weights from the sonnet to the ballad. The form registers the content, and the content expresses activism, the quest for leadership, the emergence of folk heroes.

Although war was an almost constant national presence—
Korean peace in exchange for the beginning of American inter-
vention in Vietnam—the struggle for civil rights defined the
fifties. The historic Supreme Court decision Brown vs. Board of
Education of Topeka, Kansas (1954) catalyzed the desegregation of
public schools. In September 1957, Governor Orval Faubus, in an
act epitomizing segregation, ordered the National Guard to the
all-white Central High School of Little Rock, Arkansas, to prevent
the entry of nine black students. Faubus met with President
Eisenhower; their disagreement resulted in a federal court order
to remove the Guardsmen. Amid national publicity, the black
children entered the school but were ordered to withdraw by
public officials claiming to anticipate mob action. Eisenhower
sent federal troops in confrontation the next day, September 24.
The children returned, and integration was begun. Lynching as
an excrescence of Southern white supremacy was epitomized by
the murder of Emmett Till. His death and the trial of his alleged
murderers drew national attention. Till became archetypal of
martyred black youth.[4] He figures substantially in Brooks's volume.

   The Bean Eaters departs structurally from its predecessors. A
collection rather than a sequence, decentralized and seemingly
free-ranging, it actually clusters about several topics. Of the
thirty-five poems (excluding the first), roughly one-third can be
identified as distinctly political. These include the most significant in terms of length. The political character of *The Bean Eaters*,
often worried over by critics as "forsaking lyricism for polemics"
(*RPO*, 165), is reinforced in several ways. Class consciousness
frames several poems; bourgeois affluence, power, and racism
coalesce in others. Maud Martha's "baffled hate" surfaces caus-
tically. The black-and-tan motif, notable in earlier volumes, re-
gresses into one piece. Major attention targets white discrimination against blacks.

   In "Ballad of Pearl May Lee," Sammy's taste for "pink and
white honey" shares blame with the lynchers; no such diffusion
faces "A Bronzeville Mother." While killing may be merciful or
thoughtless or even practical in earlier volumes, there victims
confront other victims, including themselves. "The Ballad of
Rudolph Reed," however, clearly embodies a new defiance, ni-

hilistic, victim against oppressor. Blood imagery in *The Bean Eaters* should be noted, saliently in "A Bronzeville Mother" and "Rudolph Reed," and as it radically transforms in later works.

The Bean Eaters carries the heroic sound in tones of firm assessment. The word "clarify" is crucial here. Brooks sees her present and future work as "clarifying, not simple." And clarifying involves audience rapport. The task is served by music: the ballad, favored early, and jazz, more active, replacing the blues. The sonnet, reduced here to two poems, is usually more congenial to meditative works, like "Gay Chaps at the Bar" and "the children of the poor," though the latter bears heroic features. Several poems manifest such heroic-style traits as alliteration, compounding, epithet, and metonymy.

Along with specific issues and class consciousness, gender in *The Bean Eaters* also tempers the heroic role. Men have demanded some form of heroic from *Bronzeville* on. But women undergo a subtle metamorphosis and heroic definition throughout the books, with a transition apparent here. Though Brooks's women exhibit courage, strength is usually based on their roles as wives and mothers. She still feels, one must note, that "black men *need* their women beside them, supporting them in these tempestuous days" (*RPO*, 179). The support depends, however, upon reciprocity.

Visual inscriptions of heroic should be noted. For the first time in an adult work (including the chapter titles of *Maud Martha*), all poem titles in *The Bean Eaters* take initial capitalization. Despite its conventional aspect, the practice serves to differentiate, emphasize, and evaluate. It can convey a more objective tone, while lower case tends toward the subjective and introspective. Capitals, an element of the later heroic style, appear more frequently and serve several purposes. It is as if, having been deflected from using italics in *Maud Martha*, Brooks achieves special emphasis more adequately by this means.

Regarding the poem categories, "Political (Current)" includes current urgencies and events; "Political (General)" covers broader reference, attending class consciousness and the image of women. "A Penitent . . . ," for example, a religious poem, is arbitrarily grouped here because of its feminist perspective. Despite religious themes in "The Chicago *Defender*" and "In Emanuel's

Nightmare," their immediate content is political. "Political (Current)" pieces look toward the dramaturgy of *In the Mecca* and the "verse journalism" of "In Montgomery." Regarding her "Poet's Premise," Brooks observes to Paul M. Angle: " 'Vivify the contemporary fact,' said Whitman. I like to vivify the universal fact, when it occurs to me. But the universal wears contemporary clothing very well" (*RPO*, 146). The third category, "Miscellaneous," identifies several new themes and continuities. Nearly all are tinged with political nuances. Aging, for example, could merit a political heading. "We Real Cool" and "Kid Bruin," for that matter, also share a political cast. Poems about romance, children, philosophy, fame, faith, and nature will be grouped separately.

The dedicatory poem, "In Honor of David Anderson Brooks, My Father / July 30, 1883–November 21, 1959," introduces a paradigm of the volume's major theme: caritas, private and public. "A dryness is upon the house / My father loved and tended" it begins. Now freed into the universal, he "Translates to public Love / Old private charity," becoming the meanings and virtues of his family life. The words "Love," "Goodness," "Gentleness," and "Dignity," referring to him, are capitalized, the device familiar to Romantic hypostatizing. The ballad foreshadows the book's heroic use of the form.

Political (Current)

> "A Bronzeville Mother Loiters in Mississippi.
> Meanwhile, a Mississippi Mother Burns Bacon."

The two sentences read like a newspaper headline. "Loiters" ironically suggests a legal aspect and racial denigration. Details of the case will show how a first-rate talent can shape the power of indignation into poetry.[5]

Emmett Louis Till, a fourteen-year-old boy from Chicago, accompanied by his mother, was a guest of his uncle, Moses Till, in Greenwood, Mississippi. Upon visiting the store of Roy Bryant (twenty-four) in Money, Mississippi, on a friend's dare he allegedly made advances toward Mrs. Bryant. The woman claimed this had been done by "a Negro with a Northern brogue," not identified as Till, and that he "wolf-whistled" at her as a friend pulled him out of the store. Northern newspapers subsequently referred to the trial as the "wolf-whistle" case. Witnesses testified that Bryant and a half-brother, J. W. Milam ("Big Fella"), had kidnapped Till from his uncle's cabin on August 28, 1955, and taken him to a barn, where they heard screams. The badly mutilated and decomposed body was found in the Tallahatchie River on August 31. Bryant and Milam admitted that they had abducted Till, but insisted they had let him go. The jury's acquittal verdict was based on a defense contention that the body could not be identified. The governor of Illinois, William G. Stratton, requested a federal investigation which the attorney general, Herbert Brownell, Jr., denied.

Brooks's poem about the murder dramatizes its consequences in the lives of those directly responsible. The 138 lines represent the longest sustained effort since "The Anniad" with its 301. Both poems transmute reality into ironic myth, but there the parallel ends. "The Anniad" composes strict rhyme and meter within a seven-line stanza. The later poem employs free verse with stanzas of varying lengths. The bridge of ironic distance, lenient though it was in "The Anniad," is detonated here. The inverted romantic lexicon becomes a debasing technique; generic naming foregrounds the topic. The acquitted husband is the Fine Prince; the child lynch victim, the Dark Villain; the wife is the "maid mild." Suggestion of an unwritten, tragic ballad haunts the opening lines ("From the first it had been like a / Ballad. It had the beat inevitable. It had the blood") and the closing stanza. The stratagem poses the wife's romantic misconceptions against the poem's real mythos. By the third stanza, via *style indirect libre*, Brooks has clearly stepped into the psyche of the white Mississippi mother, who has imagined herself a rescued maiden in a romantic tale.

The scene opens on the wife's meditation. It is her husband's first morning home after his acquittal; she is preparing the family breakfast. The absent ballad stanza, the form of the poems she had "never quite / Understood" in school, is "A wilderness cut up, and tied in little bunches," an imagery of the victim. The form itself functions as an icon of brevity and truncation, to be realized in the next poem.

Distracted by her thoughts, the woman burns the bacon, hides it in the garbage can, and draws "more strips from the meat case" ("strip" suggesting the verb and "stripe" or lash). The ordinary gestures, burning the bacon and replacing the meat, are charged with dramatic tension by the opening lines and the fear implied by hiding evidence. In the context of murder, the bacon incident represents casual destruction and affluence or power. A poor family would probably have to eat the burned bacon or do without it in the first place. The burning suggests violence, even lynching (cf. "The Chicago *Defender*," below). The wife, "a milk-white maid," bakes sour-milk biscuits, her color joined with the taste (sour) of what she makes. She sets out her "new quince preserve" (cf. "The Ghost at the Quincy Club"). Quince is hard-fleshed and acid, companion to the sour milk in the biscuits. Like a bride, she is proving her domesticity, meriting the deed.

But she continues distracted. The Dark Villain was only a child, after all, his murder a grotesque gallantry. Losing control, she knows that "her composition / Had disintegrated." "Composition" summons the decomposed body of Till, referred to as a "blackish child of fourteen." Indeterminacy of the adjective emphasizes both the state of his corpse and his humanity. (See discussion of the "brownish" children in "The Chicago *Defender*.") The woman's moral decomposition parallels Till's physical mutilation, his decomposition in the river. It also suggests the decadence of society, a decline symbolized and accelerated by the fight against integration.

The wife applies makeup with a kind of desperation; she is about to be judged: "Had she been worth It?" Her physical beauty highlights the ugly deed. Seated, the husband contemplates his hands. He grumbles about Northern papers' "meddling headlines. / With their pepper-words, 'bestiality,' and 'barbarism,' and / 'Shocking.' " Angry with the notoriety, he is nevertheless pleased at his power to "show" Northern intruders and the dead boy's "snappy-eyed" mother that "Nothing could stop Mississippi," the sentiment repeated four lines later.

The older baby asks for molasses (" 'lasses on my jam," the elision and references as possible sexual foreshadowing), whereupon the younger baby throws the pitcher at his brother's face. The father, "The Fine Prince," slaps "The small and smiling

criminal." The description projects the motif of perpetuated violence, and suggests Cain and Abel.

The wife imagines blood on the baby's cheek, the blood of the
murdered boy transferred to her son. The meaning of the deed
touches her at last through her own child, extending the Cain and
Abel analogy. Fearful, she leaves the table. Her husband follows
to the window. As he places his hands upon her, she imagines her
shoulders covered with blood, a blood that seeps and spreads
"over all of Earth and Mars." The husband utters amorous inten-
tions, but the wife "heard no hoof-beat of the horse and saw no
flash of the shining steel." When he kisses her, she reacts to the
redness of his mouth. The "courtroom Coca-Cola / The courtroom
beer and hate and sweat and drone" overcome her. She desper-
ately wants to escape her husband's mouth and the "Decapitated
exclamation points in that Other Woman's eyes," a reference to
Mrs. Till. The wife feels hatred for her husband, a "glorious
flower" whose perfume was "Bigger than all magnolias." The
magnolia, symbolic of Southern romance and chivalry, is diminished in the wife's new consciousness. The Southern code has
been overtaken by "the last bleak news of the ballad. / The rest of
the rugged music. / The last quatrain," the closing stanza.

The "bleak news" announces a powerful paradox: the wife's
blossoming hatred and the grief of the dead boy's mother. In a
kind of dialectic, the white woman comes to mourn and reject a
false romantic posture, while the black mother, mourning her lost
son, is immortalized with him in the next poem.

"The Last Quatrain of the Ballad of Emmett Till," which
focuses on Till's mother, bears a complex relation to "A Bronzeville
Mother." Transition from free verse to the somewhat irregularly
metered and slant-rhymed "quatrain" in eight lines, augmented
by rhyme, yet broken as verse, connects the two poems, as with
"The Anniad" and "Appendix to The Anniad," but in reverse. The
"Appendix" steps down into reality from the mock heroic and
mythic. "The Last Quatrain," on the other hand, lifts the narrative
from a mockery of heroic into myth. Its restraint realizes the noble
synthesis portended by the previous poem.

Blood imagery inheres in the "red room." And while the milk-
white maid's color sours into sour-milk biscuits, the mother's
coffee remains plainly dark, symbolizing the austere dignity of her

sorrow. Like the white mother, she too is pretty. Her color of "pulled taffy" also suggests her son, both his color and child's taste for candy. "She kisses her killed boy / And she is sorry." The litotes, emerging from the stark ending of the preceding poem, is empowered by contrast with its dominant tone.

"Chaos in windy grays / through a red prairie," literal references to Chicago, "the Windy City," and the Illinois prairie, raise the narrative toward classical apotheosis in nature. The red room of mourning and the blood that the white mother sees move on to the dessicated landscape. Winds of change and death, in Brooks's symbolic gray of despair and annihilation, blow through the moral aridity. Liquid images in the two poems are apocalyptic, non-regenerative, or sorrowing: blood, souring milk, black coffee. The prairie is reddened with pain and anger radiating from Mississippi. Nor is the redemptive association of water permitted; the river is not mentioned. This signal omission, together with the image of the violence-nurtured prairie, confirms the genius of the work.

A relevant footnote: the poet's own son, Henry Jr., was also a Chicago teenager, also fourteen when Emmett Till's body was taken from the Tallahatchie River.

"The Chicago *Defender* Sends a Man to Little Rock / Fall, 1957" is a poem Brooks no longer especially favors, mainly because of its last line which, by 1969, she would have dropped. The flaw, however, does not detract from the poem's urgency and complexity, its technical and developmental importance. Considerably shorter than "A Bronzeville Mother," its sixty lines begin in tetrameter, both rhymed and slant rhymed. Rhyming tercets (beginning *a a a b b b b c c c d d d e f f f e*) in meter and style vary the ballad or hymn stanza; they continue with irregular lines that break into couplets, tercets, and individual verses that rhyme or slant rhyme with previous or succeeding ones.

The rhyme of the first three lines (*bear, hair, repair*) repeats crucially at lines 46-48 (*dare, chair, everywhere*) and slant rhymes with the last two lines (*deplored, Lord*), connecting and weighting their meanings. The tetrameter of lines 1-18 echoes in lines 46-60. The resulting tripartite order enhances the Trinitarian motif. Linear total of the tetrameter lines is thirty-three. The number recurs in religious literature; one thinks of the thirty--

three cantos of the *Purgatorio* and the *Paradiso* in the *Divina Commedia*. More important here, as John T. Shawcross points out, the figure represents the age of Jesus at his crucifixion, and is the product of three times eleven, the number symbolic of the Resurrection.[6]

Formal tensions (meter; stanzaic patterns; rhymes) work effectively. "The Chicago *Defender*" is a deeply religious poem about school integration; from title to imagery to scansion and rhyme, a Christian symbolism prevails. The suggestion of hymn stanza at the beginning is caustic, yet ambiguous, for "the people," depicted as churchgoers, bearing "Babes" and singing hymns, might well include both black and white. Although the narrative images feature whites, ambiguity—culminating in the black and white religious images—is a thematic strategy. Implied reformation of the Mississippi mother parallels the potential regeneration and rapprochement in the *Defender* poem. The dual reading gives the work its special power and makes the final equivalency between the Lord and the black children as lynch victims structurally inevitable. One stanzaic form (hymn) may also connote the singing of angels, pertinent to the sacred theme and the reporter's identity.

The title is symbolic and ironic. The *Defender* was one of the first black daily newspapers to be established in this century. Founded in 1905 by Robert S. Abbot, the son of a Georgia slave, it shared the leadership assumed by the Negro press at the death of Booker T. Washington in 1915.[1] During World War I it urged Negroes to ignore Southern white promises and come North as they had done in the "Great Migration." Both Gwendolyn Brooks and Willard Motley, author of *Knock on Any Door*, had their first significant publishing experiences with the newspaper.

The *Defender* (mildly invoking the phrase "of the faith") is represented by the godlike "Editor" who indirectly pronounces one word in the poem: "Why." In context, the solitary word suggests the Gospel of John: "In the beginning was the Word, and the Word was with God, and the Word was God." Thus, to some extent, the "Man" from the *Defender* is a heavenly messenger. "Man," however, has several interpretations. Though the *Defender* would probably send a black man, the word is ambiguous and generic. In Black English, "the man" refers to a white man or authority figure. The indefinite article, however, suggests a black man, if "man" is defined as "a word brought into popular use by black males to counteract the degrading effects of being addressed by whites as 'boy' " (Major, 80). Sending a white man would have been practical in terms of mobility. The daily, in fact, was one of the first black newspapers to hire a white reporter when, in 1945, it employed Earl Conrad, coauthor with Haywood Patterson of *Scottsboro Boy.*

On the religious level, "Man" suggests Jesus Christ, the Word of God made flesh. But the reference to "Babes" at the beginning, and the collocation of black schoolchildren with Jesus as lynch-victim at the end give the reporter a heraldic status, similar to that of the angels heralding the birth of Christ. The reporter as herald will understand the news he gathers only in the course of the poem. A bitter irony emerges so that the real news is not factual. The Editor's deeper question, unanswered, implies a spiritual answer.

"Little Rock" in the title invokes the rock of faith, the theological emblem of St. Peter. Thus Little Rock suggests the little faith of the people. Also recall that Peter denied Jesus three times. Presented from the reporter's viewpoint, the poem begins with quiet observations:

> In Little Rock the people bear
> Babes, and comb and part their hair
> And watch the want ads, put repair
> To roof and latch. While wheat toast burns
> A woman waters multiferns.

"Babes," importantly generic, suggests the Babe in the manger. "Wheat toast" burns as the bacon burned in Mississippi ("A Bronzeville Mother"), again suggesting violence in the common order of things. Whole wheat bread is naturally brown or "brownish," the color of the black schoolchildren who will be persecuted. And they are morally whole. The men of the town, however, are morally deficient (and average) in their "half-havings," depicted in the imagery and narrative.

Careless of the toast, the woman waters "multiferns," a Brooks compound that connotes abundance, even affluence. The toast is replaceable (expendable, burnable), like the Mississippi bacon. Nature, along with human life, receives merely polite attention, although nature seems to have the edge. The fern itself grows in swamps, implying a moral swamp, and represents a halfway stage in the evolution of plant-life from water to earth.

The churchgoing people of Little Rock "sing / Sunday hymns like anything." Their devotion and hypocrisy involve "Sunday pomp and polishing." They *seem* mild, eating Lorna Doones (a kind of communion) and drinking lemon tea on Sunday afternoons. These foods connote restraint and English decorum. Social forms contrast with violence. Etiquette precedes ethics.

By Christmas, the townspeople will make a holiday of "laugh and tinsel," glossing over the present conflict. They play baseball, the all-American game. They like "Barcarolle" (Boat Song), Offenbach's "O, night of love" duet from *Tales of Hoffman* (sung by Giulietta, the beautiful courtesan, and Nicklausse, Hoffman's friend and disguised Muse). Baseball images of players "Batting the hotness or clawing the suffering dust" convey disharmony with nature, violence, and the suffering dust of humanity—dust being symbolic of the "brownish" boys and girls in the poem. Music and baseball are interwoven: a concert takes place on "The special twilight green"—twilight games inferred. Violence of the sport spills over into the Open Air Concert where "Beethoven is brutal or whispers to lady-like air." "Johann troubles to lean / To tell them what to mean," however, seems excessive.

Stanza 7 begins:

> There is love, too, in Little Rock. Soft women softly
> Opening themselves in kindness,
> Or, pitying one's blindness,
> Awaiting one's pleasure
> In azure
> Glory with anguished rose at the root. . . .

The love is counterfeit (like Giulietta's for Hoffmann), offered for sale by prostitutes. Most of the other botanical symbols appear in everyday life: the multiferns, the "suffering dust," "the special twilight green" where the concert is played on grass denied enough light (spiritual light, Jesus as the light of the world) to grow, a color between light and dark, neither good nor evil, something like the people themselves. This stanza intensifies the terrible ironies by collocating religious symbols in the brothel: caritas housed in the heaven ("azure") of carnal delight. (In heraldry, azure is represented by horizontal lines, which may suggest the recumbent women.) The rose symbol of heavenly love toward which Beatrice led Dante turns anguished here, the pun invoking "rose" of the Ascension. Physiological "Glory" roots in sorrow as analogue to Christian martyrdom.

The prostitutes are victims, like the sinner Mary Magdalene, to whom Jesus offered forgiveness and who became his follower. The parallel continues, adding a significant ambiguity.

> To wash away old semi-discomfitures.
> They re-teach purple and unsullen blue.
> The wispy soils go. And uncertain
> Half-havings have they clarified to sures.

The ellipsis after "root" can signify a break, returning to the citizens, continued as "they" in stanza 8. Thus the people feel a lack that they and their clergy fill with righteous certainty. But "They" interpreted in this stanza as the prostitutes is still collocated with the townsfolk stanzas and yields a deeper meaning.

The Gospels tell how Mary Magdalene wept over Jesus, bathed his feet in her tears and ointment, and dried them with her hair. Thus the root of faith can be discovered at the feet of the Messiah, from whose life and teachings one can learn how to "re-teach purple" (the endurance of suffering) and "unsullen blue" (the traditional color of hope in Christian symbolism). Purple is also the color of a regular festal day, so that both Passion and meaningful celebration may be learned anew. Blue represents the color of the Virgin; thus "unsullen" implies "unsullied." Furthermore, "unsullen" is not melancholy (like the blues) or unsociable (the root of "sullen" is the Latin *solus*, alone). "The wispy soils" are the peccadilloes or minor sins of the patrons.

The prostitutes, like the townspeople and clergy, are not agents of genuine penitence. "Wisp" invokes "will-o-the-wisp," the ignis fatuus or false light that appears over marshy grounds (where the multiferns may grow), a light that misleads travelers.

The commonality of sin, coloring images of everyday life—their half-lit "twilight green"—continues in the "semi- discomfitures," the petty frustrations and half-havings falsely "clarified" (made light, illuminated) to "sures." Neither brothel nor town can offer moral certitude.

The reporter/messenger observes the people's friendly tolerance of each other. Puzzled, his preconceptions ("the hate-I-had") dissolving, he exclaims:

> The biggest News I do not dare
> Telegraph to the Editor's chair:
> "They are like people everywhere." [ll. 46-48]

This is the most appalling—yet hopeful—news of all. But the Editor would want to know "Why," a question involving the entire social structure. For if the people were not singularly evil, then the evil, like the good, would not be localized. The poem itself becomes the answer.

The stanza preceding the closing three lines describes the black students' reception by whites who "are hurling spittle, rock, / Garbage and fruit." The "Little Rock" of little faith objectifies into the small rocks thrown at the children. The "bright madonnas" (mothers of the Babes in l. 2), an acerbic allusion, join the angry white men: "And I saw coiling storm a-writhe / On bright madonnas. And a scythe / Of men harassing brownish girls." The "coiling storm," the white women's anger, suggests the coiling of a rope or snake, the latter image encountered in "The Anniad" where the serpentine "gold shriek" is described, "Coiling oil upon her ways" (st. 21). But the coiling storm further evokes a tornado or whirlwind, applicable to the black mothers' rage for their children and also to Babes of Little Rock who are being abused. The whirlwind image, of especial importance in the later Brooks, will reappear in "Riders to the Blood-red Wrath" and "The Second Sermon on the Warpland." Anger, then, becomes a complex, antithetical image, to be resolved in the black children's suffering and the synthesis offered by the poem's final line. The men, on the other hand, are clearly part of the "scythe" or semicircle of hate. The word summons the steel of the National Guardsmen's rifles as they barred the children from entering

Central High School before the federal court order to leave. The scythe is also emblematic of death, which threatens the schoolchildren.

The last three lines, "I saw a bleeding brownish boy. . . . / The lariat lynch-wish I deplored. / The loveliest lynchee was our Lord" are printed as separate stanzas, underscoring the Trinitarian motif of the rhyme. "Brownish" evokes the color of toast and the suffering dust, reminding of the "blackish" boy Emmett Till; the generic racial images stress humanity. The poet's justifiable reservations about the last line call for revision, not exclusion. The lynch imagery from the previous stanza, as it leads the figures of the black children into the Christ analogy and reverts to the "Babes" at the beginning, transfigures the children's image into a religious one. The "re-teaching" attempted in brothel and town instances the pastoral role embodied in Jesus and expressed by the black schoolchildren. They will genuinely "re-teach purple and unsullen blue," redeeming life through their suffering and impeccable spirit.

It is the black children, therefore, who become the Babes of Little Rock. The phrase "the loveliest lynchee," whatever its aesthetic and, in the poet's current view, political and religious defects, expresses a concept vital to the poem's integrity. Like rebellious Ireland in Yeats's "Easter 1916," Little Rock is a place where a terrible beauty is born. The grotesque Nativity scene at Central High School conveys a special grace and awe in this eminent poetic achievement.

"The Ballad of Rudolph Reed" again plies the form to tell a story with a strong moral or social theme. For the first time, however, the regular stanza serves the heroic concept, as it did partially in the previous poem. Rudolph Reed takes nihilistic action. While political solidarity compels social change, the latter ultimately rests upon the conscience of one who, as Herman Melville observed of Nathaniel Hawthorne, can say "No! in thunder."

The poem comprises sixteen ballad stanzas in tetrameter and trimeter and varies strong rhythms with some syncopation and inventive terminal rhyme and half-rhyme schemes. "Rudolph

Reed" is a strong, alliterative name; the first line describes the man's character as much as his color.[8]

> Rudolph Reed was oaken.
> His wife was oaken too.
> And his two good girls and his good little man
> Oakened as they grew.

The paradox between "Reed" and "oak" is obvious. The resilient reed combines its flexibility with the oak. Color and character join in a double image of strength and endurance, physical and moral.

Reed's wife and children support his desire to buy a house in a white neighborhood (cf. Maud Martha's family closeness, her father's economic struggle to keep their house, and the attitudes toward color). Few would care to undertake the ordeal of moving into "a street of bitter white." Reed "was oakener / Than others in the nation." Dignified, restrained in the style of the noble hero, he does not curse when rocks are thrown at his window on successive nights. The third night (the legendary number popular in folk ballads and tales) a rock crashes through the window and hits his daughter, Mabel, a name that means "lovable." The sight of his daughter's blood running from her forehead maddens Reed. He presses his wife's hand, then runs out into the street with a thirty-four and a butcher knife. He "hurts" four white men and is shot to death. His neighbors kick his corpse as they call him "Nigger."

In the last scene, Mabel whimpers and reproaches herself while her mother, in the manner of folk ballad understatement, stoically changes the bandage. The woman's determined attitude augurs a future of struggle, her strength partly introjected from the dead Rudolph Reed and more potent than the rocks that have been thrown.

Political (General)

In this category, class demarcations satirize the bourgeoisie and demonstrate social change accompanying decay of the white upper class. Black-white conflict intensifies. Black-and-tan interaction, though restricted to one poem, persists. The antiwar theme continues. As in "The Chicago *Defender*," capitalizations convey a biblical quality. In fact, a high correlation obtains throughout *The Bean Eaters* between capitalization and the sermonic or polemic.

Just as Brooks attends to precision of language, she selects and deploys her titles. In "The Lovers of the Poor," the first verse begins "arrive" (suggesting the French *arriviste*, social-climber), enjambing the title with the first line. Lower cased and paragraph indented, the verb's drop from the title and its lack of capitalization diminish the self-important visitors. Later, capitalization is used for emphasis, symbolism, and to satirize the uncharitable impressions and inflated personages of "The Ladies from the Ladies' Betterment League."

The rhymed and slant-rhymed, basically iambic pentameter of "The Lovers of the Poor" blocks its verse paragraphs. Forgoing stanzaic spacing, Brooks acknowledges the discursive needs of its ninety-nine lines. Alliteration strengthens the tone. The faint-hearted "Lovers of the Poor" are alarmed and finally routed ("Oh Squalor!") by the poverty, "The stench; the urine, cabbage, and dead beans" massed unremittingly against their copiously itemized affluence. Their guild gives money to the poor if they are "worthy," "beautiful," and "Perhaps not too swarthy." Verbs like "cutting" and "stab" tellingly apply to the women's office.

The corrosive narrative is burdened at times by heavy sarcasm and caricature. Nevertheless, Brooks's responses take a major step toward the dramatic realism of "In the Mecca," the "third person subjective" satire of "Riot" (chapter 8), and the verse journalism of "In Montgomery." While she suspends, until the penultimate stanza, information on the number of visitors (two), her tour de force/farce conveys the sense of an entire ruling elite.

"A Man of the Middle Class," a socially critical piece, differs from "The Lovers of the Poor" in several ways. Formally, the structure is stanzaic rather than verse paragraph. The basically pentameter verses vary and occasionally reduce line length for emphasis. More important, Brooks exchanges meditative irony for satirical polemics. "I have loved directions" (wry postscript to Rupert Brooke's "The Great Lover"), the middle-aged subject admits. But the conventional, materialistic, and authoritarian patterns he follows cannot direct him in "this outrageous air."

Naïve regarding the forces controlling him, like the periodic military conflict ("strident Aprils," reminiscent of Eliot's "cruellest month"; "Bugle Calls"), he accepts them. He cannot respect himself except to note, "I'm semi-splendid within what I've defended," his possessions and status. His elegant wife is a culturemonger. Suspecting he has missed authentic existence, disturbed by "Giants" whose wealth does not keep them from suicide ("Oh methinks / I've answers such as have / The executives I copied long ago"), he imparts Hamlet's tragic indecision. Brooks accepts a reader's impression of racial anonymity "as a mark of the poem's success." In a recent interview, she cites the man's having "defected his essential blackness . . . so that he can identify more with the larger culture."[9]

In thirteen lines (possibly connoting a failed sonnet, that symbol of order), "The Ghost at the Quincy Club" epitomizes social change. The old Chicago mansion that has become the modest black "Quincy Club" (*RPO*, 69) implies the decline of white landed aristocracy (Southern inferred) symbolized by the ghost: "Some gentle Gentile girl / Wafts down our Quincy Hall." Highly allusive in American history, "Quincy" also summons "quince," the hard, acid flesh of the applelike fruit from which marmalade, jelly, and preserves are made.

The upper-class, "gentle" girl, of gentle or noble birth, is called "Gentile" in a double irony. She is Christian, part of a race or clan (in the Latin meaning), and distinguished from Jewish, the implication being, from the point of view of the seemingly non-Gentile speaker, that the Jews, historically a mistreated minority, have bested their oppressors. The "Jews" in the poem are actually the lower socioeconomic classes with their "raucous Howdys," the "dark folk, drinking beer." The blacks have taken over the old mansion and substituted genuine warmth and proletarian beer for tea and "gentle" forms. They ignore spectres of the past. Only the narrator/observer attends to the ghost. The concluding couplet, "Where Tea and Father were (each clear / And lemony) are dark folk, drinking beer," hints that the racial purity ("clear") was not only lemony in its bleaching property, but also tinged with yellow, the lemon's color, which refers to interracial offspring, as well. These were not uncommon in the master-slave relationship.

The poet's formal strategy sets the first stanza, haunted by girl and mansion, into trimeter, with rhyme and a varied refrain. The sestet carries the three beats of a waltz into the nostalgia of a folk ballad. The next five lines, mostly pentameter, irregularly confront past with present. In the closing couplet, Tea and Father, ceremony and authority—the past (tetrameter)—accede to the altered, expansive present (pentameter).

With tough political irony, "Leftist Orator in Washington Park Pleasantly Punishes the Gropers" heralds the later Brooks's prophetic voice, clued in the title's highly symbolic figures and insistent alliteration. For the "Orator," public speaker distinguished for style and power, is the Teller, anticipated in *Annie Allen*. A prophet, he announces, "I foretell" (l. 6). In law, the orator is the plaintiff. The Orator, a man of power who can punish, charges the consciousness of his listeners. Oxymoronic "Pleasantly Punishes" suggests the ironic mask that Brooks/Orator will cast off in the poem, which begins: "Poor Pale-eyed, thrice-gulping Amazed. / It is white and rushed here, this is a crazy snow." "Thrice-gulping" may signify conventional, thoughtless "gulping" of the Eucharist by professed Christians. The "Pale-eyed" whites swallow belief without chewing or understanding its meaning.

The Orator, politely "afraid" that the night wind of change and judgment will not falter, with seeming mildness rebukes the whites. Frightened and aimless because they have no convictions, they feign ignorance, shun involvement. In the last line, "Because there will be No Thing for which you fall," a secondary meaning of "fall" is the slang for "love," evoking caritas or belief. The verb "fall" strikes hard. It culminates the apocalyptic suggestions of violence, hanging, and the demise of the whites, their involuntary gaping and forced vision contrasted with the voluntary gulping in the first line. The last four lines beginning with "Because" have a legalistic tone, like a brief read by the Orator-plaintiff against the defendant whites, self-incriminated by their apathy. "No Thing" suggests annihilation of the materialistic white world.

The poem's three stanzas describe the present, the coming apocalypse, and its nihilistic epilogue. A muted Trinitarian reference complements the diminishing realities (belief; the physical end of the white world) by reduction of stanzaic length: 5, 4, 2. If the Orator in the first may be analogue for the Father, the second suggests the Passion of the Son (the executed whites), and the third, the Holy Ghost, which becomes here "nothing." The meter and rhyme are irregular, but rhyme, alliteration, and strong stress predominate; within the metrical variety, spondee and anapest convey the Orator's forceful message and the rush of events. The last lines, a rhymed couplet prophetically ending "you fall," confirm the irony of the poem's first word. For the Orator has not pitied the "Poor Pale-eyed." Like an implacable judge or deity, he foretells their doom.

Writing of "Bronzeville Man with a Belt in the Back," Brooks observes that the man's coat, a popular style years ago, makes him feel "dapper and equal to the Fight that he must constantly wage, when he puts on such a suit" (*RPO*, 155). "In such an armor he may rise and raid," the poem begins. Within the decorum of mainly iambic pentameter and intricate rhyming, the "Bronzeville Man" becomes prototype of the Bronzevillian: clothing, his armor; nonchalance, his sword. "In such an armor he cannot be slain," the poem ends, repeating the introductory phrase like a shield. The need for such armor implies criticism of society that often diverts dissent into statements of fashion. The Bronzeville Everyman, potentially heroic, distorts his courage and excellence. Unsmiling, his coolness, like that of the pool players in "We Real Cool," defends his vulnerability.

What of the Bronzeville Everywoman? Brooks has always given respectful attention to members of her sex. In *The Bean Eaters*, one appreciates the range of sensibility that attention records. Past themes remain, like the black-and-tan motif of "Jessie Mitchell's Mother"; yet the heroic vision widens to include the maternal, politicized, and prophetic aspects of women's roles. Brooks taps her own deepening resources: wife, mother, and national figure affected by the Civil Rights Movement of the fifties and sixties.

Confrontation sparks the black-and-tan dilemma of "Jessie Mitchell's Mother," in which Brooks veers sharply from Maud Martha's tolerance. A hard-edged significance encrusts the older, yellow woman's confinement to bed, where she reluctantly submits to her daughter's ministrations. Even the poem title subordinates her. Mrs. Mitchell remembers "Her exquisite yellow youth" and foresees a traditionally inferior and poverty-ridden status for her dark-skinned daughter. But it was an irrelevant youth, an irrelevant life we see through her daughter's consciousness of "the stretched yellow rag," the sweet, "jelly-hearted" woman with "a brain of jelly." Though the mother will take her satisfaction with light skin to the grave, her daughter's strength, self-respect, and contempt for the old, white-inspired values will survive. Mrs. Mitchell's vision of a difficult future for her daughter rationalizes jealousy of the latter's youth; anger toward poor men who inflict lives of hardship and constant childbearing upon their women; a displaced black self-hate inflicted by the white culture; and the valuing of fair skin, which gives her a false sense of superiority. Tensions between the women inform tension between free and metrical verse, mainly hexameter. Finally, as Mrs. Mitchell "Refueled / Triumphant long-exhaled breaths. / Her exquisite yellow youth. . .," the long line breaks, and free verse wins out.

A haunting paradox lies in this strong work. Although Mrs. Mitchell is having a baby, all the mother images, particularly "ballooning body" and "stretched yellow rag," convey illness, age, and approaching death. A balloon is filled with air or gas, and a stretched rag is hardly an image of fruition. Even Jessie's question, "Are you better, mother, do you think it will come today?" after thinking that "Only a habit would cry if she should die," suggests illness or dying more than birth. Hostility and strength of the daughter's verticality and mobility and the feeble yet sly antipathy of the horizontal mother; new ways of Blackness symbolically prevailing over the *exhaled* (however "Triumphant"), not inhaled or life-inspired breaths, further accentuate the scene as termination. Indeed, although new consciousness has emerged from the old and is represented in Jessie's pride and defiance of her mother's depressed, almost vindictive expectations, no real health exudes from Mrs. Mitchell. Thus the conflation of childbed and illness (cf. Big Bessie's "beautiful disease," chapter 6) indicates debility of the old ways.

In "Mrs. Small," Brooks's *style indirect libre* projects the sensibility of a middle-aged woman trapped in daily domestic chores. Mrs. Small is caught between the economic pressures of white culture, symbolized by the insurance salesman who often figures as a predator among black people, and the male chauvinism of her husband joined to the demands of her ten children. She must deal with the insurance man and meet the payments.

Mrs. Small expresses her submerged rage by accidentally splattering two drops of hot coffee on the man's shirt. Chiasmus and repetition of "Pocketbook. Pot. / Pot. Pocketbook" and images of "the little plump tan woman / With the half-open mouth and the half-mad eyes / And the smile half-human," standing in the middle of her floor and proffering a steaming pot to the collector as she recalls her husband's praise of her brew depict vividly her dilemma, centrality, and fidelity to her role. Her color also stands midway between black and white. Small, like her name, indomitable, like the half-politically awakened common people and women she represents, she attends to "her part / Of the world's business."

"Bronzeville Woman in a Red Hat" registers passionate feelings in the color itself. One recalls that Brooks had worked briefly as a maid. The subhead, "Hires Out to Mrs. Miles," indicates both occupation of the employee and status of the housewife, implying the distance (miles) between them.

The poet's heavily sarcastic voice refers to the worker as a "slave." The poem satirizes the white woman's repugnance when her child is kissed by the black woman and kisses her in return. Mrs. Miles translates natural acceptance into "unnatural" animal wildness. For her, "nature" perversely roots in convention and prejudice. A two-part work, the poem's closing quatrain's *a b b a*, outer rhymes containing the inner two, suggests the reciprocated embrace. Division of the piece paradoxically indicates both separation (color, class) and, in the second part, pairing by natural affection. The child's response to the black woman (emergency replacement for an underpaid Irishwoman) conveys some optimism. Generic names ("child," "big black woman," "Bronzeville Woman," etc.) signal allegory. As in "Jessie Mitchell's Mother," the young offer hope for improving society.

"A Penitent Considers Another Coming of Mary," dedicated to the Reverend Theodore Richardson, pastor of Brooks's church, the Metropolitan Community Church of Chicago, furthers the heroic conception of women, specifically through the maternal role. "If Mary came again," she would forgive the world and furnish it with another Saviour, "ratify a modern hay, / And put her Baby there." (Cf. "In Emanuel's Nightmare," below.) Language of the ballad is utterly precise: Mary would "ratify" or give formal approval to such an event, as she had done once before (Luke 1:38). Her will here negates the traditional image of passivity. Despite the military air of the world that violates the Judeo-Christian injunction not to kill, Mary would not withhold her support.

Saliently feminist as well as humanist, the poem focuses on the Mother, not the Son, in the Second Coming. "Baby" reinforces the humanist aspect, instead of the conventional "Babe." (Cf. "The Chicago *Defender*.") This is a human mother, ready to assume her heroic/divine role as a duty. Her fortitude recalls the Bronzeville women, Brooks's own "Duty-loving Mother," and Brooks herself.

"In Emanuel's Nightmare: Another Coming of Christ / (Speaks, Among Spirit Questioners, of Marvelous Spirit Affairs.)" may be deemed a male response to "A Penitent." A religious antiwar poem, in closing the volume it bears a special weight. The subhead indicates that Emanuel is, at least partly, a spirit; his name in Hebrew means "God with us." Emanuel dreams on earth where, having won the Great War-Naming Contest, he regrets the folly of his pride. Although war terrifies the people, it does not invoke Judgment Day, "For we are here." So they continue warring against their "Fellow Man" as solutions ("Doors") to their problems. "Doors," richly resonant, anticipates Christianity as "the door" (John 10:9; see also "Malcolm X" and "The Wall," chapter 7).

A dramatic monologue, the form used elsewhere in Brooks and favored by her admired Robert Frost, the poem's mainly blank verse carries a like sense of psychological inquiry. Beautiful lyrical passages refer to Jesus (pronoun references initially capped) and his divine birth: "Yet no parturient creature ever knew / That naturalness, that hurtlessness, that ease" (ll. 29-30). Just as Mary ("A Penitent") would repeat her choice of a heroic role, Emanuel dreams that in another coming of Christ, "to clean the earth / Of the dirtiness of war," his reception would again be negative. Instead of accepting another crucifixion, however, Christ himself would be disheartened by the people's rejection of peace. Weeping "the tears of men," he would return home.[10]

Notwithstanding a diffusion of effect, this ambitious work shows the poet's dramatic grasp of character and incident. Her own voice breaks through at times, as if Emanuel's persona hampered her. The poem marks the end of such conflict, which no longer appears in succeeding works.

Miscellaneous

These poems, scattered throughout the volume, cluster around four main subjects: aging, romance, philosophy, and children, with single poems on fame, nature, and faith, the last also treated in several pieces above.

The title poem, "The Bean Eaters," irregularly metered and rhymed, describes an "old yellow pair" who are "Mostly Good." They continue the routines of their lives, strong in mutual affection and shared memories. Because they are indigent, their conventional lives have neither troubled nor impressed the world. In subdued tone, they echo the endurance of Mrs. Small. Their reward for a "good" life is an old age of poverty, symbolized by the beans they can afford. Their fate implicitly rebukes a youth-obsessed society that neither esteems nor intelligently employs its elderly.

"Old Mary," a cameo portrait of fortitude, declares, "My last defense / Is the present tense." The verb proclaims that her limited present gives her a kind of immortality. Complementing Old Mary's vigor, "The Crazy Woman" chooses to sing in November "a song of gray," recurrent hue of death and decay. Singing her ballad, flaunting conventional censure, she will not submit to an ageist pattern. "Crazy Woman" is capitalized as concept and person. Through her persona, the poet rejoices in a determined spirit that will praise life to the end.

"A Sunset of the City" compassionately depicts an aging woman alone. Emotionally dependent, facing empty later years, suicide enters her thoughts. Her monologue laments that children, husband, lovers, all view her as a relic of the past. "My daughters and sons have put me away with marbles and dolls" suggests the urban erosion of family life. "Indrying" flowers of "summer-gone" illustrates Brooks's compounding technique.

"On the Occasion of the Open-Air Formation / of the Olde

Tymers' Walking and Nature Club" observes, with gentle amusement, the attempt of old people to recapture their childhood
closeness to nature. Stately iambic pentameter and the title's
antiquated spelling wryly comment on the proposed romp in the
woods. The poet identifies with the old people ("we merry girls
and men"), who may falter.

A lively strand of continuity from earlier volumes explores the
romantic terrain. "My Little 'Bout-town Gal" is an amusing ballad
in Calypso rhythm about two lovers who cheat on each other. "A
Lovely Love," its antithesis, crafts a lyrical Petrarchan/Shake-
spearean sonnet variation of deep feeling. The birth of love in
shabby surroundings is imaged in the Nativity. The lovers must
hide in alleys and halls. There is no proper place for them, just as
there was no proper place at the inn for Mary and Joseph, who
stayed in the barn. The poem begins, "Let it be alleys. Let it be a
hall / Whose janitor javelins epithet and thought." The javelin
image fits the chronology of reference. An elegant diction and
stately meter, together with the Nativity allusions, elevate the
action. The last line, "Definitionless in this strict atmosphere," its
first word connoting the ineffable mystery, completes the Nativity
reference. "Definitionless," also limitless, is literally down or
away from the finite, paradoxically restricted by physical location
and, pertinently, the confines of the sonnet form. Thus the infin-
ite within the finite is expressed through love.

Turning from sincerity to fatuousness, Brooks chides, "For
Clarice It Is Terrible Because with This He Takes Away All the
Popular Songs and the Moonlights and Still Night Hushes and the
Movies with Star-eyed Girls and Simpering Males."[11] This little
editorial on false sentiment and values recalls the mock-heroic
approach to Annie Allen's early romanticizing. The poet's impatience also etches "Callie Ford." More intelligent than Clarice
and equipped with Annie Allen's defensive irony, Callie imagines
both the experience of love and its ending. Her name wryly
suggests, among other meanings, the call of natural beauty and
the house plant "calla." ("Calla" and "Calliope" derive from the
Greek *kallos*, beauty.) "Ford" produces an image of shallow waters, representing Callie's somewhat shallow feelings in the
poem.

"Priscilla Assails the Sepulchre of Love," a finely wrought ballad, studies the self-restraint that may "assail" the death of love. "Priscilla," the name of a ruffled curtain, also refers to a prophet associated with Montanus, who claimed inspiration by the Holy Spirit or Paraclete. Later followers, their sect proscribed by Justinian, locked themselves in their churches and set them afire. Priscilla dares not "unlock" her eyes (in Christian symbolism, the windows of the soul), which would reveal her passion. Since her lover wants "no sort of gift outright," an allusion to Robert Frost's "The Gift Outright," where the gift to the country is one's whole life, she defends against rejection by suiting his restricted needs. Negatives, especially mounted in stanza 2, deftly express emotional barriers in the relationship.

Circumspect, the philosophical poems reflect metaphysical and moral concerns of daily life. "The Explorer" follows the dedication. Irregularly rhymed and metered, its tone recalls Eliot. "Somehow to find a still spot in the noise" renews the quest for "the still point of the turning world" in *Burnt Norton* or the Wordsworthian lament that "the world is too much with us." The "spiraling" human voices are those Prufrock fears will drown us. The Explorer "feared most of all the choices." "There were no bourns. / There were no quiet rooms." "Bourns" invokes the "bourne" in Hamlet's soliloquy. Considering the volume's dynamic, political character, this piece inadequately serves as introduction. (See related correspondence, page 101, above.)

"Strong Men, Riding Horses," male companion piece to "For Clarice," looks ahead to the later style of capitalization ("Strong Men," "Rough Man," "Challenger"), epithet ("Desert-eyed")—used here for Romantic irony—and compounding ("To word-wall off"). Again chiding the fictive movie ideal, the poem explores interactions of myth and reality. Although the speaker, like "The Explorer," is fearful, he is more self-aware ("I am not brave at all") and less apologetic. Appraising his life gives him a kind of strength the "Strong Men" cannot achieve.

"The Artists' and Models' Ball," a sestet in blank verse with some slant rhyme, notes the wonder of the commonplace and its mutability. As a costume ball, its marvels are visible. But daily matters and, by inference, the humans conducting them, are even

more extraordinary in their transience. The theme of wonder in
everyday existence complements Brooks's concept of the heroic
potential in the Bronzeville Everyman. The poem is dedicated to
Frank Shepherd, a Chicago photographer who was director of the
South Side Community Art Center at the time.

"The Contemplation of Suicide: / The Temptation of Timothy"
is the only poem on suicide among Brooks's published works,
excepting mention in "A Sunset of the City" and "A Man of the
Middle Class." Rejected for the *Annie Allen* volume, where it
would have had companion poems about death, here it is unique.
Brooks begins at a distance with the indefinite third person, then
closes in with first person quotation. The poem quietly inverts the
theme from meditation on death to acceptance of life. The name
"Timothy" means "honoring God," in Greek. For the poet, honoring God means respecting the life force in daily existence.

Widely varying verse length (increased by justified margins)
and irregular rhyme express the mood of the poem. The urgent
sweep of the verses allows, in their several rhythms, a fluid
restlessness of thought. The long, stress-packed lines expand the
conceptual space and time (cf. Milton's *Paradise Lost*, Book II, l.
621). Alliteration and assonance propel the imagery. Beginning,
"One poises, poses, at track, or range, or river," the poem finds
Timothy examining his life and deeming it worthless; he has come
to a "foppish end." The first stanza presents his despair; the
second begins "Then," as if following a hypothetical "if," and
concludes with life as a given, a natural value that "relates / Its
common cliché." The chicken ("chicken reeks or squalls") recurs
as the image of innocent sacrifice.

"The Egg Boiler," a Shakespearean sonnet, ironically glorifies
the aesthetics of utility, "the mundane," as described in Brooks's
comments on the poem (*RPO*, 186). The man presents a narrowly
utilitarian view of life and art.[12] "Being you, you cut your poetry
from wood. / The boiling of an egg is heavy art." The poem begins
ingenuously and contrasts the other poets ("We fools") who cut
their poetry from air. The latter recall Yeats who, when asked how
he had written his poetry, replied that he had made it "out of a
mouthful of air." Air signifies a "weightlessness" or lightness so
heavy with meaning (as opposed to the "heavy art" of egg boiling)
that it sometimes is "much to bear."

Yet there is respect for the matter of existence. The egg carries a potential for life, and so pertains both to the making of art and to its content. Wood has a potential to boil the egg, as well as a sturdiness and a utility that can also relate to the making of a poem. It is the conventional, ethereal "poetic" images, "Night color, wind soprano and such stuff," however, that Brooks wafts here through the deprecating sensibility of the subject. "You watch us, eat your egg, and laugh aloud," she concludes. The egg, instead of hatching ideas and life, is consumed. The Egg Boiler has transformed latent life, and therefore art, into an object useful to himself. For him the creative act is primarily self-nourishing. In "We fools" we again encounter Brooks's ironic extravagance. The Egg Boiler, as prototype, marks the obverse of "the young Dante" in Pound's "The Study in Aesthetics," who admires, for its own sake, the beauty of sardines being packed for market.[13]

The three poems on children represent diverse strands in the poet's development. "Pete at the Zoo," a ballad, mirrors Brooks's deep sensitivity to children, their needs for security, imagination, and freedom, and their ability to identify with other creatures. "Naomi" shows the adolescent impatience with unimaginative grownups that nagged Annie Allen's childhood. She would seek the meaning of life outside the material setting of her conventional existence. Naomi, in Hebrew, means "my sweetness," and implies here a search for the speaker's own self or "sweetness." The biblical Naomi (from the Book of Ruth) was the mother-in-law whom Ruth would not abandon. In the poem, Naomi's alienation promotes her developing selfhood.

One of the most interesting pieces technically is probably the most widely known of Brooks's works: "We Real Cool." Along with "the preacher: ruminates behind the sermon," it was banned in a 1974 West Virginia public school dispute and in Nebraska, allegedly for use of the word "jazz." Erroneously interpreted as a sexual reference, which it has acquired, the word has an obscure etymology, possibly African via French. Brooks's usage pertains to "having fun."

In both the Stavros interview and her notes to the poems (*RPO*) she describes the soft reading of the line-terminal *We*, "tiny, wispy, weakly argumentative 'Kilroy-is-here' announcements." The pause at the end of the line, she explains, signifies the reflection upon "*validity*, the self-questioning and uncertainty of the speakers" (155-56, 185). Hearing Brooks read the verses, however, reveals them as breath pauses which incur a syncopation, reinforced by alliteration and epistrophe. This is the peculiar and subtle brilliance of the poem. The subhead "The Pool Players. Seven at the Golden Shovel," implies the jazzy or modish predilections of the protagonists. Seven, a number favored in gambling, connotes the element of chance in their lives, the lack of planning. Gold is the recurrent image of illusion; "the Golden Shovel" is clarified by the last line. The poem's eight lines are these:

> We real cool. We
> Left school. We
>
> Lurk late. We
> Strike straight. We
>
> Sing sin. We
> Thin gin. We
>
> Jazz June. We
> Die soon. [14]

Typographically, Brooks handles the diminished and tentative status of the boys in two ways: by enjambment, which truncates the thought (at "we")), and by linear brevity, the narrow field of vision and short breath required by the lines. The capitalized *We*s are also balanced by the capitalization at line initial. The eye is trapped between the capitals just as the pool players are trapped in their lives. Pairing of the short lines, in addition to the paired stresses, rhymes, and *We*s, conveys both the closeness and the narrowness of the group. The eye hops down from couplet to couplet without going far left or right horizontally. The hopping itself suggests the pronounced rhythm in the poem's diction. Verbal as well as phonic repetition at the end of each line impedes any sense of continuity or development in the teenagers' lives. The only line that does not end in "We" is the last line, referring to death. While the poem abounds in rhyme, internal and terminal, the *We*s rhyme only with each other, just as the adolescents relate only among themselves. The trail of *Wes* faintly suggests the nursery rhyme "This little piggy went to market." The fourth piggy, one remembers, had no roast beef, and the fifth cried "Wee, wee, wee, wee, wee" all the way home.

Indeed, these are children who have no roast beef or much of anything else except their peer-group sense of stylish behavior. The coolness of the players is the crux of their personalities, the key to their lives and to the poem. Despite presentation in the voice of the gang, this is a maternal poem, gently scolding yet deeply sorrowing for the hopelessness of the boys. While "Old Mary" vigorously defends herself by immersion in the vital present, the pool players defend themselves against defeat, despair, and indifference by rejecting social norms. Their "coolness" of alienation responds by dropping out, drinking, debauching, dying. It is this wasteful aggression against the self, this fragile wall of bravado that the poet mourns.

The three remaining poems are slight in relation to Brooks's other works, but they serve to widen her lens. One subject, fame, is new; faith, prominent in *A Street in Bronzeville* and *Annie Allen*, is restricted to one poem here although religion, subordinate to politics, appears elsewhere in the volume; nature, never a strong interest, is attended in one poem and noted in "The Olde Tymers." Fame, a part of the poet's life for years, filters through a social consciousness. Faith in God recedes as Brooks turns to the individual's faith in self, her people's selfhood merging into racial pride. Concern with nature, often minimal for an urban poet whose landscapes are human, is complicated by the black experience in the United States. In 1969, acknowledging the controversy among black poets over the propriety of nature as a subject, Brooks observed that all subjects merited poetic attention. However, "A black poet may be involved in a concern for trees, if only because when he looks at one he thinks of how his ancestors have been lynched thereon" (*RPO*, 166). Such equivocal reference shapes the black experience into a naturally complex vision, a synthesis of opposites and contrasts. Blacks pay a terrible price for this enrichment, this ground of serious literature.

The title, "Kid Bruin" and the subhead, "Arranges Another Title Defense," announce the subject as a young black (or "brown," in Danish; also a bear) pugilist, embattled like his people. He must use the weapons literally at hand, his fists (bare) as compared with the dapper "Bronzeville Man with a Belt in the Back." The first lines, "I rode into the golden yell / Of the hollow land of fame," with their faintly equestrian image, summon a major figure in Brooks: the gallant, romantic hero (or mock hero, like the "paladin" of "The Anniad") and his role as fighter in the struggle of everyday life. (See also "Riders to the Blood-red Wrath," chapter 6.) The trial is social as well as economic and political. The poem criticizes indirectly the society that offers a poor man this brutal, destructive channel for success ("Bruin" aurally yokes "brutal" and "ruin"). The youth pursues the rainbow into the "hollow land," morally empty, like fame itself, and presumably populated by hollow men, more deceitful than Eliotic. Conversely, the rainbow is a biblical symbol of hope ("God gave Noah the rainbow sign," in the words of the Negro spiritual). In the hollow land, it is supposedly unknown, evanescent, possibly mythical. Integration, anticipated like colors coexisting in the rainbow (before Jesse Jackson's "Rainbow Coalition"), proves chimerical as the permanence of fame.

Gold as illusion attaches to the rainbow, conventionally imagined with a pot of gold at the end. Gold also appears as a pejorative symbol in Hughes. (His poem "Revolution," for example, exhorts the "Mob" to "split his golden throat," referring to the enslaving white capitalist "of iron and steel and gold" [GMR, 6].) The ballad form reinforces the sense of a mythic folk figure. Kid Bruin's lament holds special meaning for common people who similarly aspire and who, usually on lesser levels, are also disappointed.

"Jack" represents a significant reduction of concern with religious belief per se in Brooks's poetry, as her religious motives become increasingly politicized. The skepticism of earlier volumes was an engaged skepticism, a wrestling with conscience about something that deeply mattered. Here attention shrinks to a man who "is not a spendthrift of faith." His belief—divine or humanistic—is lean, contingent, pragmatic. "He spends a wariness of faith." Like a cautious investor, Jack will commit himself only to the degree of profitable return. Minimal expectations that insure him against disappointments also contract feelings and spirit into his "skinny eye" and "store" of belief. The name "Jack" denotes one of the common people, Everyman; it also denotes the game of jacks, where a number of objects are picked up from a progressively diminishing store; it is a coarse, cheap, medieval garment worn for defense; and, in the vernacular, it can mean money. All of these meanings apply.

"Bessie of Bronzeville Visits Mary and Norman at a Beachhouse in New Buffalo" is the only poem in the volume that celebrates nature for its own sake. Its additional interest lies in oblique class confrontation and the psychic metamorphosis of Bessie, for whom the lake changes into a sea. She romanticizes in the style of "Big Bessie" and Annie Allen. Despite skillful formal structure (mainly iambic pentameter), the direction toward irony seems uncertain.

The Bean Eaters marks Brooks's ascent to the foothills of her grand heroic style. Fom the new level, we see the power of skill and commitment combining with her narrative gift. We note the inclusion of more types of characters, white as well as black; the use of satire along with irony; and projection into white consciousness. We observe the precision that extends to titles, the increasing freedom of linear length, the adaptations of conventional form, and the artistry of joining random, slant, internal, and full rhyme. While romantic love crumples with a wry, post-Annie Allen disenchantment, passion centers on ethics, politics, and politicized religion. The topical poem surges dominant, sounding the righteous thunder of the Civil Rights Movement.[15]

6

Selected Poems

The year of *The Bean Eaters* brought financial hardship to the Brooks/Blakely household. Henry Blakely was poorly employed and poorly paid most of the year. *The Bean Eaters* was not reprinted and went out of print in 1963, as had *Annie Allen* and *Maud Martha* in 1954 and *A Street in Bronzeville* in 1957. The poet considered doing a verse biography of Phillis Wheatley, which did not materialize. A volume of selected poems, first proposed to Harper's in January 1961, was then discouraged as premature. Brooks had been working on *In the Mecca* as a novel; the editor's response dissuaded her from continuing it in prose.

January 1962 was the time of Brooks's controversy with WNEW over "of De Witt Williams on his way to Lincoln Cemetery." This was the same station that had broadcast her reading of the poem, among others, in the forties. Oscar Brown, Jr., had set it to music as "Elegy for A Plain Black Boy" (Columbia recording), in which the phrase "a plain black boy" occurred in the refrain. The song was banned by the New York station and one in Los Angeles, partly because its political tone supposedly lessened its entertainment value; mostly for its use of the phrase which, it was thought, might offend Negroes. Brooks wrote an eloquent "defense" of the song, the poem, and the word "black," which had not yet come into vogue ("A DEFENSE OF 'ELEGY,' " included with GB/Herbert Marks, Feb. 1, 1962). She vigorously justified her language regarding "the life and death of a pitiful yet proud and lip-out-thrusting, chest-announcing youth." Her defense is not only interesting for promoting the word "black," which she had employed twenty years before. It also features the compounding technique that characterizes her heroic style. The ban, nevertheless, was not lifted at the time. So much for the politics of language.

Brooks continued to work on *In the Mecca* as verse, but knew that she would need at least a year to finish it. She again requested that, meanwhile, a volume of selected poems be issued, especially since it was difficult to locate copies of the earlier volumes in demand but out of print (GB/EL, Aug. 22). Lawrence replied affirmatively a week later, pleased that Brooks was working on poetry and certain that *Selected Poems*[1] could be ready for fall 1963, if gathered early enough.

The Harvey Curtis Webster review article[2] on Brooks confirmed Lawrence's resolve to bring out the book. His critical appraisal, reprinted in the *Chicago Daily News*, compared Brooks with Langston Hughes, Countee Cullen, and Margaret Walker. In her "ability to see through the temporal," she equalled Richard Wright, James Baldwin, and Ralph Ellison. Heartened, the poet included in *Selected Poems* those which had been singled out for special praise. Together with her other choices, she mailed them to Lawrence on February 4, 1963. The dedication read, "To Bob and Alice Cromie / and to the memory of Frank Brown," author of *Trumbull Park,* who had died the year before.

The title of the volume troubled Brooks. Appreciating its dignity, she still preferred "Contemporary Fact," a quotation from Walt Whitman, who advised writers to "vivify the contemporary fact" (GB/EL, Feb. 28; *RPO*, 146). Nor did she care for "Addenda" as a heading for the new poems. Lawrence expressed a preference for *Selected Poems* and offered "New Poems" as a substitute for "Addenda."

Limited space required exclusions. "Matthew Cole," a new poem, "Riders to the Blood-red Wrath," five from "A Catch of Shy Fish," and "To a Winter Squirrel" were among those suggested as unequal in quality to the collection (EL/GB, March 18). Brooks quickly agreed to some omissions, but asserted her liking for "Matthew Cole" (omitted) and insisted that "Riders" be kept; it was. Instead of "the ballad of the light-eyed little girl" and "We Real Cool," two of six omissions proposed by Harper's a month later, the poet, stressing that the two were technically unique, suggested "the funeral," "the soft man," "obituary for a living lady," and "my own sweet good," all of which were excluded.

Selected Poems was ready in August and pleased both the poet and the editor as a distinguished volume. Critically acclaimed, it underwent several printings in hardbound and paperback editions. It was to be the final Brooks work edited by Lawrence, who had been hospitalized with pneumonia early in the year. One of the last letters the editor received at Harper's from Brooks, written New Year's Day 1964, included a clipping from the *Chicago Sun-Times*, Sunday, December 29, 1963, her elegy "The Assassination of John F. Kennedy," comprising three slant-rhymed quatrains.

On June 25, 1964, Brooks wrote to Pat McNees, Lawrence's new secretary, informing her of extensive speaking, reading, and teaching engagements throughout the country, and inquiring whether Harper's would be interested in a book about her childhood and youth, as suggested by William Targ at Putnam's. Lawrence replied on June 30 that the project sounded interesting, particularly with her background in predominantly white neighborhoods. (Brooks notes that Lawrence was incorrect. She had *always* lived in black neighborhoods.) Lawrence also informed the poet of her forthcoming retirement to her house in Connecticut. It was the valedictory letter as Brooks's editor at Harper and Row.

Just as Brooks wished later to include *In the Mecca* in her omnibus volume, so did she seek to update the current volume by adding new poems. Let it be noted that the selections made from published works do not seem to follow any pattern, nor do the omissions, regarding subject matter or style. Of the three books represented, eleven plus the "Hattie Scott" five are excluded from *A Street in Bronzeville*; seven from *Annie Allen*; fifteen from *The Bean Eaters*. There are many regrettable omissions among both the long and the short poems, the former including "Ballad of Pearl May Lee" and "Queen of the Blues"; the latter including "Matthew Cole," "the birth in a narrow room," "The Ghost at the Quincy Club," and "The Egg Boiler," any of which might have been substituted for "My Little 'Bout-town Gal.'" The volume, however, presents much of Brook's best work up to the time. "The Ballad of Rudolph Reed" ends the selections; "Riders to the Blood-red Wrath," her longest effort since "A Bronzeville Mother" and "The Lovers of the Poor," begins the "New Poems."

"Riders to the Blood-red Wrath" is a tribute to the Freedom Riders and, as the poet notes in her stanza-by-stanza commentary (*RPO*, 187-89), to "their fellows the sit-ins, the wade-ins, read-ins, pray-ins, vote-ins, and all related strugglers for what is reliably right" (187). The Freedom Riders were black and white, Northern as well as Southern. In May 1961, five and a half years after Rosa Parks sat in the white section of her bus and inaugurated the Montgomery Bus Boycott of 1955-56, they joined the fight of Southern blacks to integrate public transportation. The Freedom Riders followed the sit-ins of 1960, and continued the fight for integration and civil rights by legal means.

The poem title alludes to John M. Synge's one-act play *Riders to the Sea* (1904), in which a mother loses her sixth and last son to the sea. Struggle against the environment is natural and fatalistic in Synge, man-made and vulnerable in Brooks. The "Blood-red Wrath" implies a revolutionary animus, yet it also conveys the wrath of God. "To" suggests "toward" and "in keeping with." The title invokes the vision of St. John the Divine, the Second Coming in which the Lord, "Faithful and True," is clothed with "a vesture dipped in blood" (Rev. 19:11-13). Seated upon a white horse, "in righteousness he doth judge and make war."

This poem demonstrates, at a critical juncture, what the poet was gaining and what she eventually would discard. It is a poem of great stature, rhetorical, written mainly in iambic pentameter with irregular rhyme and slant rhyme, its twelve stanzas of varying lengths. An elegant diction articulates the theme of necessary struggle. The poetic voice is sober, at times a trifle self-conscious. The Freedom Rider's persona removes it from the direct statement typical of later work. The voice is reined in, like the charger, appropriately restrained because of the legalistic framework. By the end of the poem, tension and control become so intense that the underlying threat of violence seems more rhetorical than real. In this voice, Brooks speaks out of general rather than specific identity with the group. And at this point we understand that depersonalizing is the very process of the work: the Rider must disappear into guile and animated principle.[3]

The Rider is a powerful central image, already encountered ironically in the paladin of "The Anniad" and the prizefighter, "Kid Bruin," positively in the armored "Bronzeville Man with a Belt in the Back," somewhat negatively in "Strong Men, Riding Horses," and quite negatively in "A Bronzeville Mother." The knight/prince/rider metaphor represents, even when distorted, the heroic possibility in ordinary life, basic to Brooks's canon. Placement after "Rudolph Reed" emphasizes this theme.

Transition from old to new is bridged also by the imagery of violence in both poems, especially the blood imagery. While little Mabel's blood is shed in "Rudolph Reed," in the new poem "the National Anthem vampires at the blood" and the Rider remembers his African royal heritage, his right "To flay my lions, eat blood with a spoon," suggestive of the lion-hunting Masai warriors (moran), who drink ox blood.[4] Working within a structure both democratic and Christian is the proposed solution, reminiscent of "The Chicago *Defender*." Typical features from the early work are symbolism, allusiveness, and the terse brilliance and occasional abstruseness of "The Anniad." Brooks tightly controls the line and employs the alliteration characteristic of later work. The device of a persona, like that of the "Leftist Orator" in *The Bean Eaters*, will also be discarded with *In the Mecca*.

Beginning "My proper prudence toward his proper probe/ Astonished their ancestral seemliness," and noting that "They" are "the 'segregationists,' etc." (*RPO*, 187), Brooks sets a formal tone, replete with legal-sounding phraseology like "howas" and "waiving all witness." The first stanza, twenty lines long, gives the social and legal context of the narrative. The Freedom Riders, apart from their physical bravery, were testing and probing the state laws for constitutionality. No widespread rioting occurred, as did later in the decade. The poem's decorum reflects the attempt to use "proper" channels in dealing with established authority. The charger, identified by the poet as "the feelings that I rode" (*RPO*, 187), is reined. The Rider has "channeled the fit fume / Of his most splendid honorable jazz." There is irony in reclaiming the equestrian as a heroic figure, reminiscent of Wallace Stevens's essay "The Noble Rider and the Sound of Words."[5] For the "rider" in the South too often has come to be associated with the Ku Klux Klan.

The "honorable jazz" of the horse is the new black music of liberation, "discordances" orchestrated into a developing art of the spirit. This spirit confronts the rulers who represent the past, confounds them and their "demi-art" of "rotted flowers / Framed in maimed velvet," a reference to the early American custom of framing flowers pressed against a background of velvet that is also crushed or "maimed." Recall the image of rotting flowers in "throwing out the flowers" (*Annie Allen*), the poignant need to dispose of them, just as one must clean the roasting pan of the duck fat. Temporal exigency, a key to Brooks, is ignored by rulers who, like the rotted flowers, are trapped in their own decay. Besides the flowers, waived witnesses include "dimnesses / From which extrude beloved and pennant arms / Of a renegade death," with punning on both "waived" and "arms." Violence—the embrace of death, himself a renegade or rebel; his pennant arms, corporal and seductive emblems of combat (pennant suggesting flag, obliquely connecting with the American flag, and implying allegiance to past order as well as to the present "renegade")— these merely begin to examine the poetic subleties.

In the second stanza, "The National Anthem vampires at the blood" dramatizes a contrast with the "honorable jazz" of the charger. Depersonalizing the Rider into a braying uniform makes him a charger who must, nevertheless, speak in "a little voice," recalling God's "still small voice" to Elijah after the wind, the earthquake, and the fire (1 Kings 19:11-12). The small voice suggests the appeal being made to conscience. The Rider must restrain his "unedited" scream and hide his pain. "I / Have sewn my guns inside my burning lips."

The third stanza continues the symbolic refining, which reveals the horse as "My Revolution." But the masculine terminology breeds "his twin the mare." Brooks's own explication of stanza 3 identifies the mare as "a softer horse . . . a soft mask" that "does the official talking" and elicits the segregationist acts of sedition or transgression against God's law (*RPO*, 188). It seems equally valid to accept the mare as the female Revolutionary. Valiant women like Rosa Parks played a crucial role, notably in the

Montgomery Bus Boycott. Freedom Riders themselves, they, too, sallied into "a firm skirmish which / Has tickled out the enemy's sedition." "Tickle" suggests an accounting reminder; the "enemy," the Establishment, again exposes its "sedition," reminiscent of its Confederate past. Physical "tickling" underscores the tactics of provocation.

The fourth stanza introduces the important whirlwind image, presaged by the "coiling storm" of "The Chicago *Defender.*"

> They do not see how deftly I endure.
> Deep down the whirlwind of good rage I store
> Commemorations in an utter thrall.
> Although I need not eat them any more.

In both "Riders" and, later, "The Second Sermon on the Warpland," the whirlwind adds a religious connotation to the political one. The first poem weights the religious ("good" rage, though pious, may be vengeful, like prophetic Amos in "In the Mecca"); the second weights the political and social. The whirlwind recalls the prophet Elijah taken up to heaven by God (2 Kings 2:1-11). More aptly, it summons Ezekiel's vision of God in a whirlwind (Ezek. 1:4). The prophet was sent "to the children of Israel, to a rebellious nation that hath rebelled against me" (Ezek. 2:3).

A double irony obtains. Brooks comments that the gentle folk—the segregationists—confronted by the "mild" façade of the revolutionary Rider, respond by committing "crimes against God himself" (*RPO*, 188). Supposedly imbued with biblical teaching, the former rebels face a religious revolutionary who tests their beliefs. The "whirlwind of good rage" is the repository for "Commemorations," the memorializing of slavery (literally, enslaved memorials) and what need no longer be "eaten" or suffered.

Stanza 5, historical, recalls the royal African heritage: its power, pride, unity with nature, and freedom. The "I" who remembers evolves not just temporally but racially as a people who, once free, are trying to regain autonomy. This point is central to understanding the growing racial pride, both impulse and product of the Civil Rights Movement, augmented by contact with emerging African nations, splendidly visible at the United Nations in regal native dress. The interest in Africa became very keen among black people in the sixties. The poet herself describes in her autobiography the almost unbearable excitement of her first visit to the continent in 1971.

Stanzas 6 and 7 recall the slave trade: "blazing dementias," the horror of blacks thrown like "Black pudding" into holds, the racially destructive slavery in the United States. In stanza 8 the Calvary image, notable in "The Chicago *Defender*," is invoked and compressed into ironic statement, ground into "a little light lorgnette / Most sly: to read man's inhumanity." The affected lorgnette reverses the oppressor's pretensions, yet the reading matter includes conflicts in China, India, Israel, Europe. The Rider, having assumed the historical stature of his origins, now takes a spiritual perspective. "And I remark my Matter is not all." He sees the global context of cruelty. Nevertheless, "Behind my exposé" he will "formalize" his pity and live in reverence for life. Journalistic images revert to the "Chicago *Defender*"; headline-terse observations on foreign violence and injustice look ahead to "In the Mecca." Brooks textures the voice: subjective, objective, angry, sympathetic, sermonic, pragmatic, principled; a voice that renders the protean response required of black civil rights workers at the time.

The Rider upholds both the Judeo-Christian tradition and American democratic ideals. "Democracy and Christianity / Recommence with me" (st. 10). Renewal parallels regaining of freedom for blacks, the subject of stanzas 5 through 8. Black freedom, therefore, will be the instrument spiritually regenerating national life. This confirms the thought of Du Bois and more recent scholars such as Bennett, who see the Negro as repository of American idealism.

Undaunted in his ride toward a "continuing Calvary," the Rider merges with historical process (st. 11). He rides into "wrath, wraith and menagerie," the anger, apotheosis, and jail comprising his destiny. The "I" of historical process, however, joined by "My fellow, and those canny consorts," suggests that the Southern blacks have been joined by Northern sympathizers. Transition from first person singular to plural in the following stanza implies companions who, within the religious context, become Apostles. The struggle, a "contretemps-for-love," associates with caritas and accords the poem's twelve-stanza division an apostolic connotation. "Contretemps," a French words, is *le mot juste* here. Musically it refers to syncopation and relates to the "honorable jazz" of the charger. Joining the defensive lorgnette, another French word, this linguistic play catches the absurdity and intensifies the paradox of the stranger-citizen claiming his native rights.

Stanza 12, the concluding couplet, admits the possibility of failure: "To fail, to flourish, to wither or to win. / We lurch, distribute, we extend, begin." The sentiment parallels Alfred Tennyson's in "Ulysses": "To strive, to seek, to find, and not to yield." Brooks's version is tougher semantically and aurally, despite its appeal to emotion and idealism. Tennyson, as in "In Memoriam," converges upon will to combat skepticism and accepts faith as a practical necessity. Brooks's faith, even when steeped in religion, attends the improvement of daily life, the necessity of struggle, the trust in possibility.

The poet summarizes her current disapproval of the poem's restraint and the integration it idealizes: "What changes twelve years have secured, in self and society. I could not write—in 1972—this poem as it stands" (*RPO*, 189).

The remaining five pieces, miscellaneous, bridge the social activism of "Riders" to the personalism of "A Catch of Shy Fish." "The Empty Woman" and "To Be In Love" approach two kinds of emptiness. The first uses realistic irony; the second, the romantic irony of Annie Allen and "Callie Ford." "The Empty Woman," childless, adorns herself and likes cats and pigeons. She indulges her nieces and nephews, for whom she apparently envies her sisters. We are nevertheless uncertain why she "hated" her siblings (the verb implies motivation stronger than envy), or whether she gives toys instead of more practical items merely to satisfy her ego. The mothers, who care for the children all year long, can scarcely afford any luxuries for themselves or their offspring. Yet effective social contrast depends upon establishing the reader's attitude toward "The Empty Woman." Linked rhyme and irregularly metered tercets that suggest terza rima do express her obsessive nature, her compulsion to give what she will give, her ineluctable concern with the children. The triadic form bespeaks the family ties: woman, sisters, children.

"To Be in Love" complements "The Empty Woman"'s familial

love and hate with a rather acerbic vision of romantic love. This lyric starts with a couplet (the couple) stating what it is to be in love, moves to a single-line stanza indicating the satisfied self, expands to the third stanza of eight lines describing the joy of being together, breaks to a couplet, in which the pain of having implies the pain of losing, increases to a tercet suggesting difficult communication as an obtrusive presence, moves on to a quatrain for the actual departure, and concludes with a series of six couplets in which the absent lover is replaced by pain, memory, the "golden hurt." True appraisal comes "To see fall down, the Column of Gold, / Into the commonest ash." Gold again symbolizes illusion. Ironic tone and second person distancing do not diminish sympathy for the woman whose romance, partly because she fears to announce her love, has been fruitless. (Cf. "Priscilla Assails the Sepulchre of Love.")

The next two pieces, encomiums to a white and a black poet, reveal Brooks's own dual allegiance to craft and social commitment and define the qualities of her own work. Frost and Hughes shared, moreover, a devotion to writing of common people in accessible language. Brooks wrote "Of Robert Frost" for a tribute to him by the *Beloit Poetry Journal* (Chapbook No. 5). In six epigrammatic lines (3, 1, 2) of free verse, with some slant rhyme and careful internal assonance, she inscribes Frost's elemental strength ("a little lightning in his eyes / Iron at the mouth") and judicious austerity. Frost's poetry (to which some of Brooks's earlier work may be compared, "Matthew Cole," for example), projects location and identity, "the common blood" and "Some specialness within." This recognition of essences becomes a high order of literary criticism.

"Langston Hughes" pleased the subject (LH/EL, June 13, 1963). Immediately we note his liveliness: From the title our eyes jump to "is merry glory" indented below it, then down to "Is saltatory," left-aligned like the rest of the poem. The tersely rhyming couplets, though irregularly metered, stress a pairing motif. Brooks met Hughes in Chicago. While she matured as a writer, their friendship grew. One of her most memorable parties was given in his honor "at 623 East 63rd Street, our most exciting kitchenette" (*RPO*, 69; "when you have forgotten Sunday: the love story," chapter 3).

The Hughes poem illustrates a continuing dialogue with the heroic. Alliteration is pronounced; metonymy, even more so. Concluding stanza 3 informs:

> In the breath
> Of the holocaust he
> Is helmsman, hatchet, headlight.

"Holocaust," an apocalyptic image for the Black situation, relates to "the whirlwind of good rage" in the "Riders" poem. The poet esteems Hughes as a luminous guide, one determined that the American dream apply to all people. He "Has a long reach," says Brooks in stanza 2, after which the lines jaggedly broaden toward the bottom of the page like gestures of extension or perhaps a hand. Indeed, the imagery here is largely kinetic: Hughes, "saltatory," "grips" his right to freedom, sheds "muscular tears," "Holds horticulture," and is "restless in the exotic time" of "the Compression." Note the last word—associating ahead with "holocaust"—for its capitalization and symbolism allied with the figures Brooks favors increasingly. "Exotic time" is not merely strange or different; it is the time of blacks who have been introduced from outside as slaves and remain, by treatment and status, unwelcome strangers in their own country.

By holding "horticulture," Hughes affirms art as organic growth and implies a kinship between the practical and the decorative. He does so "In the eye of the vulture," a bird of prey like the eagle, emblem of the United States. Hughes grows his useful art within sight, within the very body politic of hostile forces that have weakened creativity (the "Infirm profession" of "horticulture") and life itself. "Compression," an antithetical image of extreme density, refers to black unity, pressure, and revolt, while it connotes their repression, and thus conveys conflict and holocaust. Compression also denotes an important poetic element distinguishing this poem and the previous one, so that the destructive (and purifying) fire becomes associated with creativity. Thus Compression also relates Hughes to Frost. The coupling of apocalyptic and symbolic horticultural imagery, intimated here, will resound fully in "The Second Sermon on the Warpland."

"A Catch of Shy Fish"

This group of eight poems, mostly short, ranges from four to twenty lines. In the style of *Bronzeville* and *Annie Allen*, individual poem titles are lower cased, suggesting both the contemplative and the common experiences they address. Brooks sees the "Shy Fish" as blacks who are powerless in the socioracial structure, "hard to 'net down'—hard to 'net *up*.' " Neither easily caught nor understood, they retain an innocence which makes them prey to the unprincipled fishermen of this world. No protagonist or situation is identified specifically as black, however. The allegory and typology, individually set, apply to all shy fish who populate the seas of existence.

Beyond its fishing associations, "catch" denotes music (cf. Eliot's usage of "Four Quartets"). At times ludicrous or coarse, a "catch" is a round for three or more unaccompanied voices. It is written out as one continuous melody, taken up in turn by each succeeding singer. "Catch" may refer to a concealed difficulty designed to trick the unwary. All of these meanings apply to the poems. Their thematic orchestration presents ways of coping with life. The participants display a modest but persistent valor, even when it is misplaced. Innocence bobs about them as they attempt to be true to themselves. This innocence, to a degree, makes them "fish" in the traditional Christian sense, which points toward their redemption and their self-entrapment. The net, unseen except in "old tennis player," is also that of universal love, Brooks's major theme of caritas, and recalls the invitation by Jesus to Peter and Andrew, "Come ye after me, and I will make you to become fishers of men" (Mark 1:17). But the fish are shy of the net, not wishing to be caught or directed by external or mysterious forces, social or spiritual. Thus they are also "shy" in the way of inadequacy, by which they are, nevertheless, "caught." Their ties with the world are limited, personal. In a sense, the poems observe and meditate upon solitudes, the self trying to maintain and assess its length against potential, or striving toward its image of excellence. Solitude, then, becomes a place of quiet struggle and return.

The pieces measure isolation, defense, and discrete alliances against a charitable Christian referent, literally a "network." The first poem, "garbageman," basically poses the question: How shall (should) I live in the world? and asks whether light (reason, knowledge, belief) will be enough in itself. The remaining seven pieces are replies.

The most subtle dimension of these poems tests the reader's own responses. This aspect recalls the theme of Stanley Fish's *Surprised by Sin* (1967), that in *Paradise Lost* the poem assails the reader's own value system. Similarly, one's attitudes may obscure intention in the "Catch" poems. Is "weaponed woman," for instance, merely a strong, sensible type who deals with the world on its own contentious terms? Her deficiency may escape a reader who values pugnacity per se and shares the woman's image of existence. The "Catch" poems encourage a probing of values. Truths may be more relative than absolute, but they are there.

"[G]arbageman: the man with the orderly mind" is a poem about the quest for certainty, the confusion and inaction bred of too much knowledge. Their verses long and talky, rhythmically shifting, rhymed and slant rhymed, the two quatrains bear structural testimony to both the groping and the cause of failure. Following questions addressed to the garbageman, the last line, relatively brief and indented, casts its imperatives: "Dilute confusion. Find and explode our mist." The poem suggests that earnestness, even knowledge, will not suffice for present or future. One needs a spiritual garbageman who will clear the refuse of thought that impedes action. For confusion, recognizing its impotence, eventually "shuts down the shades" against life. The mist, however, is explosive with potential action. The respectful image of the garbageman—one thinks of Martin Luther King's last days in Memphis, Tennessee, where he went to lead the sanitationmen's strike—will recur with "The Second Sermon on the Warpland." In his humble occupation and integrity, the garbageman is Everyman from whom, ultimately, our answers must be forthcoming.

One answer in effect rejects the question. In "sick man looks at flowers," an old man controls his environment of misery by withdrawing into "the desert" of his bed and the "little isle" of his mind. With "eyes gone dead," his spirit nearly extinguished, he rejects the world that seems to offer him more suffering. The pentameter's attempt at complete control of the end-rhymes (*a b c b d e d*) and the enclosing rhyme of the tercet, itself reduced, project this image. Flowers, "this impudence of red," impinge, reminding the man that he shuts out beauty as well as pain. The speaker's shift from impersonal second person in the first stanza to first person in the last line is a large step for a small poem, but the insight is true. And the transition from copula (st. 1) to transitives (st. 2) sharpens the contrast.

The subjects of "old people working (garden, car)" have cultivated their small space in the world. The tightly made quatrain's technical interest is the marked caesuras of the first three lines and the structure as four sentence fragments. The pauses themselves seem short-winded, balancing tentative choices. Modestly, the workers affirm benevolent life, while brevity, phrases, fragments, participles, open-ended rhyme (*a b b c*), and somewhat regular meter together suggest restriction, continuity, shared chores, "A note of alliance" with living.

This benevolence escapes "weaponed woman," who finds life "a baffled vehicle / And baffling." She fights on her embattled turf, her "whirling-place," a compounding associated with Brooks's whirlwind image. Challenging the " 'When' and 'If' " of the future, she does "Rather Well." Capitalizations, hallmarks of the heroic voice, announce her possibilities. Two irregularly metered quatrains rhyme the second and third lines of each (double rhymed in the first stanza) with internal rhyme. The end-rhyme coupling makes a symbolic enclosure into which the woman's personality withdraws. The internal rhyme ("whirling-place" and "face") and repeated "she fights" add connections between the stanzas, reinforcing rhyme as an emblem of the woman's self-possession or self-protection and girded strength. These are her "weapons," like the "semi-folded arms" (a good pun) with which she fights.

While "weaponed woman" defines her own battleground, her male complement, "old tennis player," fights in an externally (socially) ordered space: the game and its rules. His poem, a gem of four lines, renders his persistence and small-scale engagement.

> Refuses
> To refuse the racket, to mutter No to the net.
> He leans to life, conspires to give and get
> Other serving yet.[6]

The man will not refuse the serve or the limited risk of involvement and failure that challenge all players and plays. Unlike the old people above, with their implied Christian doctrine that it is more blessed to give than to receive, his life is bound by quid pro quo. The player "conspires," nevertheless (not aspires), literally breathes with others, cooperates as well as competes. Position correct, ready, he leans into the net to return the ball.

"Refuses" represents the player, a solitary strength. Caesuras in lines 2 and 3 seem to mark an invisible net. The consonants *k* and *t* in "racket," "net," "get," "to," and "mutter," often unreleased in common American speech, are sharply plosive here, conveying the crackling impact of gut (nylon unlikely) against the ball. (In "get" we may even hear "gut" and, by association, "guts".) Combining with these sounds, the three terminal rhymes indicate a consistency of return. The last line contracts and with its last word sparely suggests the man persisting at the game, at life.

After these personal answers to "garbageman," Brooks submits an aesthetic one. "[A] surrealist and Omega," mock heroic in tone, describes a duel to maintain artistic integrity. The protagonist is based upon a "good black painter, Ernest Alexander, completely fond of and dedicated to himself" (*RPO*, 206). Brooks's reminiscence and her reproduction of the entire poem enable us to compare it with its inspiration. Alexander's self-absorption, she writes, endears him to friends, who are intrigued by his puzzling egoism. Though unlike the surrealist he is tall and long-legged, he too "zigzags" into a room. Regarding the crucial reference to "cash" (see excerpt, below), Brooks remarks significantly, "there was no 'cash' involved!—I merely wanted to alliterate."

Like "Kid Bruin," the poem deals with success. Both men are combative. In pugilistic terms, the surrealist figures hypothetically as "bantam," Kid Bruin literally as prizefighter. While the boxer finds disappointment in success, the surrealist avoids its pursuit, preferring personal standards, freedom, and illusions about himself and his work.

The twenty lines in five stanzas constitute the longest poem in the group. Expressed through the free verse and randomness of rhyme, imaginative play or "surrealism" imparts a sense of restless, desultory application. It also shapes the imagery, whose highly symbolic form relates to "The Anniad." There, too, we

encounter personalized food imagery ("Think of sweet and chocolate").

> Omega ran to witness him; beseeched;
> Brought caution and carnality and cash.
> She sauced him brownly, eating him
> Under her fancy's finest Worcestershire. (st. 1)

Although "witness" bears a religious connotation, Omega
psychologically devours the painter. For her, the surrealist is what
Thorstein Veblen called "conspicuous consumption." In her lexicon, the artist creates nothing useful unless it can be consumed
or exchanged for cash. She would buy him, corrupt him with
money. But he entertains no intrusions on his solipsism.
"Brownly" suggests his color, as well as the Worcestershire.
Omega bestows her fancy or capricious interest as an English
sauce, a second intimation—after her Greek name—of something
foreign imposed.

In line 19, the surrealist is called "A bantam beauty," small,
immature and/or young ("A god, a child"), perhaps even a small
talent. His description as "bantam" recalls the chicken/victim
image. The meanings of bantam include saucy, so that a subtle
punning ensues on "bantam" and Omega's saucing him. The artist
is "a god" as well as "a child," his innocence become devilish and
perverse, his work aspiring to "a careless, flailed-out bleakness"
that somehow reflects Omega. Seemingly, in trying to elude her,
the surrealist creates the very aridity she represents; he sacrifices
(as victim) the vitality of his art. "Child" and "bantam" imply limits
to his growth. As god, however, his work will survive.

While Omega hopes to persuade her lover to more salable
work, to do so would mean the end of him, just as her name stands
for the end. Omega is associated with sin and death in the
coupling of carnality and cash, recalling that "the wages of sin is
death" (Rom. 6:23). On one level she is Eve, tempting the surrealist Adam. His defensive, parodic Fall turns him into a rebellious little snake of "small strengths" and weakness, in keeping
with the reduced scale of the "Catch" poems. Though Omega's
aesthetic caution inverts Eve's intellectual audacity, both are
culpable as temptation. The name Omega also summons "I am

Alpha and Omega" in Revelation, which provides the Second Coming imagery of the poem. The child/god/serpent/rebel imagery for the artist, moreover, reminds us of Blake and the crucifixion of Orc, the child/god/rebel/Jesus symbol who, in Night VIII of *The Four Zoas*, diminishes to a serpent. Antithesis of Urizen (whose frozen, self-contained reason also resembles the painter), Orc combines with him into Satan as the culture dies.[7]

Tempting the surrealist, Omega "had no purple or pearl to hang/About the neck of one a-wild." Purple indicates royalty; pearl invokes both the "pearl of great price"—for which the merchantman sold all that he had (Matt. 12:45-46)—and purity, another attribute of the painter. Omega cannot bring him appreciation for the qualities she neither understands nor values. As an emblem of death, moreover, she functions outside a value system. The verb "to hang" acquires a sinister cast, especially after the eating imagery. Omega's accolades would be deadly, but the artist is "a-wild," and she cannot reach him.

Brooks humorously views him examining a "smear" of yellow in the corner of his canvas, where the painting is not right to his eye, not carelessly "bleak" enough. She mildly pokes fun at surrealism as representing detached art. At the opposite pole is "The Egg Boiler"; both extremes are deficient, in Brooks's view. The stunted art of the painter cannot grow without nurture from reality. Even the man's rage, strength, and weakness are miniatures. Though he will not capitulate to external pressures, his pyrrhic victory means "Loving his ownhood for all it was worth." "Ownhood" compares with "Selfhood" in Blake, the "egocentric life, or pride," which Frye identifies with narcissism as the primary sin of the Fall (282).

And so art per se fails as an answer. The quest continues with "Spaulding and Francois." This intriguing work concerns two men who are lovers. Speaking as the couple, Brooks sympathetically presents them confronting social norms. While they relate to the artistic focus of "a surrealist and Omega," their obsessions are mutually benign. The poet's immediate subject is discrimination against gay people.[8] Continuing to articulate the aesthetic, sexual, and moral concerns of the previous poem, instead of personifying social forces she generalizes the impinging environment (akin to Omega) as "the People," "moderate Christians." The men's names, German and French, symbolize friendship between two traditional enemies and convey, in the popular national stereotypes, a male-female opposition.

Spaulding and Francois are aesthetes who seek a dreamlike spirituality in an unsympathetic world. The object of their "art-loves," by which Brooks means their feelings for each other, extends to the delicate beauty in existence and the reality beyond it. Kin to the surrealist, whose art is similarly devoted to his own dreams and style of perception, the two men pursue "Things Ethereal," their private, quasi-religious vision. A mild humor tinges their description among cloudlets, cool silver, pine scent, and angels' eyes, especially in contrast to their opponents' rotting condition. But Brooks reserves censure for the leveling world that treats them as "exotics," behavior she finds intolerable in society's attitude toward blacks.

Little clouds (compatible with the small-scale imagery of the "Catch" poems) and the cool silver of their "dream" oppose the unmitigated sunshine in which, paradoxically, the "moderate Christians" rot. Because their Christianity is inadequate and hypocritical, the sun ("Son" implied) cannot sustain them. Sun becomes an antithetical image and takes on apocalyptic significance. The couple's moon imagery, inferred, counters that of the sunlit People. If the latter were sincere—to pursue the biblical analogues—the sun would not smite them by day, as the moon at night does not disturb Spaulding and Francois (see Psalms 121:6).

Easy, light, exploratory, especially in its first six lines, the free verse of the first stanza expresses the men's peaceful ambience in quiet copulas of the present tense. Then the solemn, formalistic quatrain strives toward regular meter.

> But the People
> Will not let us alone; will not credit, condone
> Art-loves that shun
> Them (moderate Christians rotting in the sun.)

The people will not forgive what they interpret as rejection. Enjambment foregrounds "Them" and its near rhyme "shun." Society treats nonconformity as a personal affront. Lacking both faith and charity, it neither believes nor forgives. The quatrain's three terminal rhymes, masculine, plus the leonine rhyme with "alone," weigh against "Heavy" compulsion of angels' eyes (and mainly feminine rhymes) in the first stanza. The admixture of free verse and rhyme will distinguish "In the Mecca."

From the premise of confusion in "garbageman," Brooks has surveyed isolation, egotism, personalism, aestheticism, sexual and material obsession as provisional answers. Finally she turns to "Big Bessie throws her son into the street," which closes the volume. It is a strong poem with tough advice from mother to son. In stanza 2, a couplet with double oxymoron, she addresses him: "Bright lameness from my beautiful disease,/You have your destiny to chip and eat." For Brooks, the woman's "beautiful disease" is pregnancy. Bessie throws her son ("a leftover!" from it, the poet notes) into the street. While she resembles Hera expelling Hephaestos from Heaven, as Shawcross observes, she is, nevertheless, a loving Hera. (In some accounts, the god was lame at birth; in others, he was made so by the act of Zeus, who hurled him from Olympus.) The analogy holds further: Hephaestos became a symbol of strength, tutelary of metals, forging, architecture, and art. "Chip" connotes shaping and also associates, in context, with chipped beef—smoked, dried, preserved nourishment. Although Bessie's son is "lame," he too can walk and acquire strength. In "the street" of life, he may discover his own resources and decipher his own destiny. He will overcome, at least partly, the defect he has already absorbed from his mother. His illness is "bright," both good and bad, like her disease (cf. "bright madonnas" in "The Chicago *Defender*").

While a disease may be infectious, the son's life affirms the positive ("bright") nature of pregnancy. Procreation itself, however, is not a solution. The noun's literal meaning recedes into a figurative one, supported by "beautiful." Crippling of the son results from a romanticized hopefulness, one that pregnancy usually connotes. Like the young Annie Allen, Bessie is afflicted with pernicious romanticizing. From this contagion she would safeguard her son.

Bessie's malady is further defined in stanza 3. She cautions:

Be precise.
With something better than candles in the eyes.
(Candles are not enough.)

Of transient duration and little heat, candles also connote the quest for truth, belief, certainty, collocated with the eye. Thus earnestness or light ("garbageman") cannot suffice. "At the root of the will, a wild inflammable stuff" (st. 4) is needed, the impulse to freedom and love, which leads to action. The adjective "inflammable" augments the verb "explode" in "garbageman," links with sun imagery in the poem and in "Spaulding and Francois," and associates with the light imagery of the "Catch" group. Action, then, becomes incandescence, like the "physical light" of the prophetic "Don Lee" stanza 41 ("In the Mecca") and "An Aspect of Love" (*Riot*). Brooks's fire imagery enters here a new phase. Antecedent burning images ("A Bronzeville Mother" and "The Chicago *Defender*") evoke martyred blacks; the present poem locates a curative fire in the will.

The name "Big Bessie" sounds powerful. She is the only "big" figure in the "Catch" group, an attribute which, along with the poem's terminal placement, marks her importance. Hers is also the second longest poem in the group. Even though Bessie's name implies strength, her illness has been debilitating; nor does elegant sensibility weaken her advice.

Prosodic structure mirrors the mother's special shielding and conflict, and epitomizes Brooks's growing versatility. Of the twelve lines, grouped 3, 2, 3, 1, 2, 1, stanza 1 is in free verse; 2 is a closed heroic couplet; 3's middle line is in pentameter; 4 is a single pentameter line; 5, a closed heroic couplet; and 6 is in dimeter. Stanzas of equal length protectively bracket the two couplets addressed to the son, while metrical irregularity struggles toward freedom. The stanzas progress from present to future like a series of openings toward experience. At the bottom of the page, the last line and last imperative, "Go down the street," stands alone, as the son must.

Bessie feels and hears rather than sees the external world. Her personified day has a "sunny face and temper"; "The winter trees / are musical." Her subjectiveness and internalizing of nature relate her to Bessie of Bronzeville, as well as to Annie Allen. In trying to be a good mother, however, she bravely faces her deficiencies. If her son is to become a "New pioneer," perhaps realizing the heroic potential of Everyman, he must discover and nurture within himself that enduring strength "at the root of the will." Like Lambert Strether's advice in *The Ambassadors,* and Brooks's own, forthcoming in "The Second Sermon on the Warpland," the command is "Live!"

The beauty of the "Catch" poems radiates from their microcosmic vitality and quiet power. Their compression weights the semantic pressure upon each word. Their world is detailed in irony, wit, imagination, and is distilled with revelatory precision. The poetic voice is a force under great discipline, projecting a series of related "short subjects" upon a screen. In the next volume, the film will become a feature, the sound amplified and orchestrated. Brooks is already a Teller here, despite the initial assignment of the role to the garbageman.

Except for Big Bessie, the "Catch" people are small, like most of their poems. More acquainted with losses than with gains, they typify humanity. As firmly as they are able, they hold on, exemplifying the uncommon within the common, which "could also be a flower." Brooks moves through the poems like a searchlight, training its beams on one reductive attitude, then another, illuminating a vital synthesis. Her persona is Big Bessie, who will reappear in "The Second Sermon" with her feet hurting, perhaps from marching in a civil rights protest and from the menial tasks as servant or factory worker Brooks imagines for her. Brooks/Big Bessie of the "Catch" poem maternally addresses all young people; later she will speak to young black people. "A Catch of Shy Fish" is a remarkable accomplishment, one of the poet's finest works.

Selected Poems recapitulates past growth and signals ahead. The new poems appear somwhat transitional, especially in their sustained usage of irony. Yet the heroic/political matrix of "Riders to the Blood-red Wrath" and the continued approach to a larger framework with "A Catch of Shy Fish" sound the deepest markings. Even so, the contours of Brooks's sensibility have not basically altered since *A Street in Bronzeville. Selected Poems* witnesses the rich texture in style and span of interest that materialized early; the full, steady vision of her "Astonished Eye" (in Kenneth Patchen's image); and the love and loving anger for her people that grew to blossom in the whirlwind.

7

In the Mecca

In the Mecca[1] was conceived about 1954 as a teen-age novel. It drew upon Brooks's early, firsthand experience in the Mecca Building as secretary to a patent-medicine purveyor. On December 21,1958, the poet submitted parts of two books: verse from "Bronzeville Men and Women" (later *The Bean Eaters*), and a novel, "In the Mecca." Lawrence didn't care for "Mecca" as a novel (EL/GB, Feb. 9). She felt Brooks's discipline in poetry to be a handicap in the larger, freer area of prose. The poet accepted the criticism, noting that she wanted to try writing a verse novel with historical background. The editor responded enthusiastically. In December 1961 she met with Brooks in Chicago and was given a completed version of "In the Mecca" as a novel. Still not favorably impressed, Lawrence suggested that the poet continue in the medium of poetry. On August 22, Brooks reported progress with a poem of "2,000 lines at least, thick with story and music and sound and fury and I hope idea and sense—based on life 'in the Mecca.'"

Writing for the young did not represent a passing interest. *Maud Martha, Bronzeville Boys and Girls*, and, later, *Aloneness, The Tiger Who Wore White Gloves*, and *Very Young Poets* reflect Brooks's welcomed role as mother and teacher. All these books, in fact, excepting *Maud Martha* (for Henry, Henry Jr., and Nora), are dedicated to her children. In 1954, when she began working on the young adult novel, Henry Jr. was fourteen and Nora was three. Brooks's alertness to the ideas and welfare of young people, expressed also through her poetry workshops and the bestowal of numerous literary prizes and other benefits, never diminished. The anthology *To Gwen With Love* (1971), mainly of poems by young black poets, witnesses the bond, "her most cherished award."[2]

While Brooks worked on the poetic conversion of "In the Mecca," *Selected Poems* was issued. Lecture and reading commitments throughout the United States became heavy. Upon retirement of Elizabeth Lawrence in 1964, Genevieve ("Gene") Young, who did not pretend to familiarity with poetry, became Brooks's editor. Brooks and Young enjoyed a warm and mutually respectful relationship throughout the production of *In the Mecca*. The poet had been planning to leave Harper's for some time because of her interest in the new black publishing companies, and did leave after Young's departure in 1970 to join J. B. Lippincott.

In 1964 the Illinois Bell Telephone Company commissioned Brooks to write a poem about Chicago. "I See Chicago," a strongly alliterative variation of a Petrarchan/Shakespearean sonnet, appeared in *Time* magazine under the puzzling caption "Vers Libre." The poet also completed a chapter of her autobiography. She continued to travel and write until 1966, when she suffered a mild heart attack, followed by influenza. After the illness, she labored assiduously on *In the Mecca* until, in January 1967, she anticipated completion by mid-year.

In the spring, the Second Fisk University Writers' Conference seeded a new psychopoetic awareness for Brooks. The new Black consciousness and its surging creativity; meeting Walter Bradford, the Blackstone Rangers, and the students she organized into a workshop—these register in the style and matter of *In the Mecca*. *Jump Bad*, Brooks's workshop anthology, is livened by Black speech, consciousness, and pride in African heritage. The poet also responded to her students' talent and thought with the second dedication of *In the Mecca*, "In Tribute," where their names appear.

On September 1, Brooks mailed the manuscript to Young and wrote her two days later, including a three-page revision. Editorial reaction was somewhat negative at Harper's; Lawrence's opinion was again solicited. She made known her reservations to Brooks, with hopes for a larger and more diversified volume, one that was less stylized in language (Oct. 4). In a letter to Young bearing the same date, Brooks agreed that ten poems should be added; an improvement, the new editor subsequently assured. In the November correspondence, Dudley Randall is mentioned as planning to print "The Wall" as a broadside, already having done so with "We Real Cool."

Brooks sent several new poems, including "Two Dedications," to Gene Young on November 8 and enclosed newspaper clippings of the events. The poet considered the works "art reports." The editor suggested, with the concurrence of Ann Harris, then poetry editor, that some newspaper account precede each poem. Brooks agreed in a telegram received at Harper's March 5, 1968; she carefully selected and edited the epigraphs which appear. As printed by Dudley Randall's Broadside Press (1967), "The Wall," without epigraph, shares the immediacy of a journalistic account.

In the Mecca was so well received in the summer of 1968 that by September a second printing was ordered and in November, a third. In February 1969, Brooks was nominated for a National Book Award; she has never received one. James N. Johnson warmly reviewed *In the Mecca,* stating, "No white poet of her quality is so undervalued, so unpardonably unread."[3]

By August 1969, Brooks had located her publishing allegiance in the black press. She informed her editor that Dudley Randall would publish her next book, *Riot,* and that she planned to do no further teaching. It interfered with her own writing and kept her in Chicago; she liked to travel. In June she sent the editor a photo of herself with her hair natural, the style she had adopted in February.

There was little personal correspondence with Harper's after the departure of Young in October. On December 14, 1970, the *New York Times* carried an article headlined "Yale Conference Studies Role of Black Woman," by Thomas A. Johnson, who stated that Brooks's future work would be published by Broadside Press. The last book published by Harper's, *The World of Gwendolyn Brooks,* involved a minimum of correspondence, that between Roslyn Targ, her first and last literary agent (they are no longer associated), and her last editor at Harper's, Ann Harris. At first the plan was to exclude *In the Mecca.* But Brooks firmly and correctly insisted that the omission would disregard her development and ignore her contemporary vitality.

Brooks notes that she and Harper's "parted company" with mutual respect and understanding. At all times, she avows, her former publisher has treated her with consideration, cooperation, and kindness.

"In the Mecca"

In the Mecca bears the spiritual imprint of the turbulent sixties. Added to the Civil Rights Movement, the mass politicizing of the decade mounted an enlarging opposition to the Vietnam War. Early in the period, widespread street demonstrations against nuclear testing helped expedite the 1963 Nuclear Test Ban Treaty. The year of Martin Luther King's "I Have a Dream" speech at the Lincoln Memorial (Aug. 28, 1963) saw the assassinations of President John F. Kennedy (Nov. 22) and Medgar Evers, the NAACP leader (June 13). Brooks wrote poems about both victims; the one for Evers appears in *In the Mecca*. Hazards to civil rights workers, both white and black, were tragically enacted in the murders of Michael Schwerner, Andrew Goodman, and James E. Chaney by members of the Ku Klux Klan in Philadelphia, Mississippi, June 22, 1964.

The assassination of Malcolm X on February 21, 1965, in Harlem held great meaning for the future of integration. The Black Muslim minister had turned away from separatism after his pilgrimage to Mecca in the spring of 1964. Dr. C. Eric Lincoln told the press that "for the Negroes in America, the death of Malcolm X is the most portentous event since the deportation of Marcus Garvey in the 1920s."[4] Brooks's poem "Malcolm X" significantly appears in "After Mecca."

Riots in Watts, the black ghetto in Los Angeles, August 11-16, 1965, resulted in the death of thirty-five people and considerable property damage, calling attention to the miserable economic conditions of the residents. Anti-Vietnam War protests increased in size and intensity throughout 1966 and 1967. Draft card burnings and antidraft demonstrations grew widespread. The black ghetto of Newark experienced a devastating riot in 1967. During this turbulence, Brooks attended the Fisk University Conference that impressed her so deeply. The following year, the murder of

Martin Luther King and ensuing urban riots, specifically those in Chicago, inspired *Riot*, her first volume with Broadside Press.

Two indications of the breadth, indeed, the poetic breath to which *In the Mecca* would expand greeted the reader of the 1968 volume. Reprinted in the omnibus, they constitute the jacket quotation from Brooks and the two sets of dedications. On May 31, 1968, Young sent the author a copy of the jacket material which had already gone to the printer, and assured that changes could still be made. Brooks wrote back immediately, relieved that she could alter her statement, and happily inscribed the final version on the letter itself in both ink and type: "I was to be a Watchful Eye; a Tuned Ear; a Super-Reporter." She was concerned that the semicolons and capitals be maintained. The statement confirms Brooks's own view of her work as quasi-divine reportage—close to the actual text of existence—a spiritual closeness indicated by the "Eye" of the soul as well as of the body, the "Ear" attuned to the urgencies of her people. The "Super-Reporter" relates to the "Teller" and to the prophetic voice.

Composition, Language, Themes, Images, Characters. Of the two portentous dedications, the first honors the memory of Langston Hughes, along with James Baldwin, LeRoi Jones (Amiri Baraka), and Mirron ("Mike") Alexandroff who, as president of Columbia College, Chicago, gave Brooks her first teaching job, a poetry workshop. The four-part epigraph, appearing between the two dedications, quotes author John Bartlow Martin; a Blackstone Ranger, Richard "Peanut" Washington; a Chicago political activist, Russ Meek; and "A Meccan," cited in Martin's article on the Mecca Building, "The Strangest Place in Chicago."[5]

"In the Mecca," the title poem, is by far Brooks's longest single work. Its 807 lines are divided into fifty-six stanzas of uneven length, ranging from one to fifty-three lines. The multiform verse is mostly free. Incantatory modes, parallel constructions evoke the chanted sermon (see discussion of "Sermon[s] on the Warpland"). Random, slant, and internal rhyme and varied metrical patterns enhance a formal freedom with counterparts in African polyrhythm. Some compounding, more alliteration, and rich imagery limn the highly figurative contours of the heroic style. The most apparent departure from the past, outside the variety of embedded forms, meets the eye at line initial. Brooks abandons conventional capitalization; words that begin sentences take capitals as they would in prose. Other capitals lend occasional emphasis, but mainly indicate the abundance of names—people, places, real and imaginary objects, ideas, items of dailiness, identities that crowd the life of the Mecca as its inhabitants crowd its apartments.

From time to time, the poet's voice modulates from objective narration to subjective, to *style indirect libre*, to protagonist-Teller. Yet the shifts cohere. Through Brooks's purposeful vision, the real and fictive worlds interact to present a social panorama. The dramatic poem "In the Mecca" exposes the detritus of a competitive system and comments indirectly upon American capitalism, the price of its success and failure. Brooks's black world mirrors the psychic isolation of its white environment. Like the pool players in "We Real Cool," embattled Mecca residents arm themselves with indifference.

The setting is the "great gray hulk of brick four stories high," as described by John Bartlow Martin in his article cited above. Built in 1891, it was "a splendid palace, a showplace of Chicago" with carpeted stairs and goldfish bowls in the lobby. By 1912, it housed the black elite. But the Depression of the thirties hastened its decline into a slum building with fire escapes cluttering the façade. The Mecca was the location for one of Brooks's earliest jobs, secretary to a patent-medicine man, mildly recalled by "Prophet Williams," who sells magic remedies in the poem. In 1941, the Illinois Institute of Technology bought the building and, despite opposition, tore it down nine years later to extend facilities on the site.[6] The Mecca Building was cleared as a slum.

The narrative framework is simple. Mrs. Sallie Smith goes home to the Mecca. A poor woman, mother of nine children, she works as a domestic. Filled with fantasies of reversing roles ("And that would be my baby . . . I my lady"), she "loves and loathes" her employer's pink "toy-child," who is indulged with the material things denied her own family. A good mother, she can afford only ham hocks, "six ruddy yams," and "cornbread made with water" to feed her brood. She is an expansive woman, suggested by the children's names, Yvonne, Melodie Mary, Cap, Casey, Thomas Earl, Tennessee, Emmett, Briggs, Pepita—a cosmopolitan mélange indicating both city life and a possible variety of fathers, none of them mentioned. Mrs. Sallie's introductory reverie ends with the narrator's comment, expendable, "What else is there to say but everything?" (unilinear st. 16). When she thinks of Pepita, the two sentences in bold-looking capitals are set off as a stanza: "SUDDENLY, COUNTING NOSES, MRS. SALLIE SEES NO PEPITA. WHERE PEPITA BE?" Typography stresses both grammar and emotion. A common Black English construction makes its first appearance in Brooks's work: "invariant *be*."

Noting first that the study of Black English was initiated by William A. Stewart's work from 1962 on, William Labov gives attention to the copula in his major study *Language in the Inner City.*[7] Labov sees BEV ("black English vernacular") as "a distant subsystem within the larger grammar of English" (63-64). What he calls "invariant *be*" or be_2, the use of *be* to indicate "'habitual' behavior: durative or iterative depending on the nature of the action" (51), is differentiated from be_1, "the ordinary finite *be* which alternates with *am, is, are,* etc." Disagreeing with Stewart and Dillard on a Creole origin for be_2, Labov observes: "The closest analogy is with the Anglo-Irish *be*, stemming from the Celtic "consuetudinal or habitual copula." Both Labov and Dillard argue convincingly for BEV as a coherent system which, as dialect in the former and language in the latter, displays the logical features of a bona fide grammatical structure, exemplified by Mrs. Sallie's speech.

Her frantic pilgrimage through the Mecca forms the action. In the course of Mrs. Sallie's search for her daughter, Brooks sketches a representative number of tenants and addresses a broad range of contemporary and philosophical subjects. The technique—flexible, cinematographic—cuts to vignettes, close-ups, and landscapes while moving the narrative.

The religious impulse of "In the Mecca" is cued by the homiletic epigraph set apart on the verso page preceding the poem: "Now the way of the Mecca was on this wise." This line was originally the last line of the poem and remained there as late as September 1967 in a revised fragment sent to Harper's (GB/GY,

Sept. 3, 1967). The transposition, of course, lends a biblical tone. A parable is forthcoming; the Mecca Building wil become a social paradigm.

The opening lines,

> Sit where the light corrupts your face.
> Miës Van der Rohe retires from grace
> And the fair fables fall.

invite a reverie of the past, nearly two decades before. Then the Miës Van der Rohe-designed Illinois Institute of Technology still faced the Mecca Building, which was already a roiling ghost of its splendor. The lines also connote the failure of religion, art, and politics in confronting American life.

Brooks packs her images with meaning: the revelatory light (natural and heavenly light, reason) that will become physical in the "Don Lee" section, is powerless to sanctify, being itself tainted. Modern art, expressed by Miës Van der Rohe, who has produced exemplary new architecture in Chicago, cannot save the Mecca. Indeed, modern art turns away. It would replace the building with a structure detached from the environment, like the surrealist's "careless flailed-out bleakness" in the "Catch" poem.

"Fair" mainly connotes beautiful or pleasing to the eye, light, just, so that the lovely fables of the American Dream are also fables of fairness. The collocation of "light," "face," and "fair" suggests some association with whiteness as skin color. Brooks says she did not intend "fair fables" as a reference to whiteness, however. An ironic semantic note is that "fair," usually associated with blondness and light skin among whites, carries, along with "light," a parallel regard for skin color among blacks, where the range of hue actually varies from white to brown and black. "Fair" is noteworthy in the "Amos" passage (st. 43), the prophetic denunciation of American society that must remove her "fair fine mask."

Immediately following, "The ballad of Edie Barrow" tells of a "fair" wealthy lover who will marry a "Gentile" girl "come fall, come falling of fall" while he retains his black mistress. Repetition of "fall" connects with the theme of a declining white culture. "Fall" also summons the fall from innocence in the Garden of

Eden, Edie's paradisaic innocence (like that of Annie Allen). Her treacherous lover destroys her ingenuous hopes, revealing them as "a fair fable."

The fall of the fables—tales of the American success system—accompanies the resonant image of the Mecca Building. In re-creating the demolished edifice, Brooks offers a new legend, infused with anger, compassion, despair, and hope, as she imbricates past, present, and future. The name "Mecca," that of the holy city to which Muslims turn in prayer, has acquired the connotation of a special focus or goal. Combining literal and figurative referents, the building achieves its bitter apotheosis as Brooks's central image. Its crumbling magnificence, housing the decay of religious, economic, and moral energy, becomes a power-ful symbol of deteriorated spiritual and economic health. Yet dialectical forces within the decay work toward regeneration.

Religion in the Mecca is a hodgepodge of cant, self-seeking, and the sale of indulgences; it represents and parodies what passes for religion in much of American society, as elsewhere. Alfred scores the betrayal of "trinities"; Jamaican Edward "thrice denies" his guilt (cf. "thrice-gulping" in "Leftist Orator"), recalling folk-tale numerology and Peter's denial of Jesus. Concern with religion permeates the narrative. "St. Julia Jones" prays with enthusiasm; Mrs. Sallie, "all innocent of saints and signatures," wryly observes her, "content to endorse / Lord as an incense and a vintage," no more vital than a nostalgic fragrance (though "vin-tage" subtly echoes "the grapes of wrath" in Julia Ward Howe's "Battle Hymn of the Republic"). Sallie herself retains the dignity and loving strength of a fundamental religiosity. From the outset, as she climbs the "sick and influential stair" of her environment, Brooks regards her with compassionate amusement as a "prudent partridge," a game bird who becomes "a fugitive attar and a district hymn." Both "attar" and "hymn," the floral and the relig-ious musical attributes (the former fleeting, mortal, the latter local and sacred), endow Sallie with a native, humanistic grace.

The critical stance toward formal religion scatters. It appears in the parodic usage of the Twenty-third Psalm in the "Loam Norton" stanza (26), its furious outcry against the suffering that Belsen and Dachau prisoners were permitted to endure. Like the allusion to the civil war in China (st. 10), where Melodie Mary, who likes roaches "and pities the gray rat," is only mildly touched by headlines about the foreign children, the concentration camp reference is vital to the scope of the poem. For the work reaches far beyond the Mecca into violence and absence of caritas in the world. This breadth lends aesthetic validity to the villain as a nonnative black man, "Jamaican Edward," since the conceptual framework moves beyond American society to the world of heroes, villains, and victims.[8] Moreover, the Anglo-Saxon name Edward means "guardian of property," here both destroyer and emblem of destructive materialism. Pepita, on the other hand, in Spanish means "a grain of pure gold" or the seed of a fruit.

Unhappy Thomas Earl clings to his life-asserting fantasy-identity with Johnny Appleseed in the midst of "hells and gruels," where the ground gives forth not increase in the spring but "gnarls and rust, / derangement and fever, or blare and clerical treasons" (st. 13). This is a time far removed from the renewal promised by religion and nature. Of Sallie's children, the poet asks, "What shall their redeemer be?" and answers, "Greens and hock of ham." Physical needs must precede spiritual ones. The children are hungry.

In the next passage, Alfred, teacher and intellectual, views "The faithless world! / betraying yet again / trinities!" (st. 15), a world without charity, offering no meaningful Christianity that will feed its hungry children. Prophet Williams, widower, lustful fraud, advertises his nostrums, potions, charms, and lucky numbers "in evey Colored journal in the world." People seek his magic to cope with problems, material needs, and desires. Yet Brooks views the Mecca residents compassionately. They move through "martyred halls"; their fate borders that of the concentration camp inmates of Belsen and Dachau in a deeply moving reflection by Loam Norton. His name denoting earth, he is one of the few caring individuals in the Mecca.

The martyr theme colors the blood imagery of the Loam Norton passage. The ghastly sacrament of concentration camp victims, like the blood of Chinese Civil War victims in the Melodie Mary stanza, later transforms into the blood of tormentors, when Amos and "Way-out Morgan" seek vengeance (sts. 43 and 50). The martyr theme recurs in burning images: "Insane Sophie," who sees fires running up and down a world aslant in a macabre dance; Sallie, who comforts herself with the thought that "Pepita's smart" while "Knowing the ham hocks are burning at the bottom of the pan" (st. 29). We have encountered the burning food image in "A Bronzeville Mother" and "The Chicago *Defender.*" Here again, the victim is a child, her martydom portended in the homely image of the burned dinner. ("Hocks" may further suggest Pepita's physical defect, discussed later.) Burned bacon and wheat toast in the previous poems similarly point to the near-casual violence in daily life. The innocent victim theme recurs in the now-familiar chicken image (Briggs is a gang member who must "choke the chickens" to prove his manhood), and the cockroach and insect images (cf. Melodie Mary, Great-Gram, and the discovery of Pepita).

Religion, martyrdom, innocence broadly subsume under caritas, observed as a major theme in Brooks. "How many care, Pepita?" becomes a rhetorical question. The difficult, circumscribed lives, "the hollowed, the scant, the / played-out deformities? the margins?" (st. 46) have little to offer of their spent selves. *Vogue* is a grotesque here. Darkara looks at its improbable world of haute couture. She studies a picture of playboy Laddie Sanford, who says, "I call it My Ocean. Of course it's the Atlantic" (st. 47). The self-indulgent rich are as detached emotionally as they are physically from the Meccas around them.

Like the depression and apathy discerned by Freud as anger deflected toward the self, indifference within the Mecca charts a survival tactic of oppressed people. Psychologically, loss of affect may signal its repression. Feelings make one vulnerable. The Mecca, so crammed with misery, injustice, poverty, and squalor, can lacerate the undefended heart into a screaming rage.

This rage, the extreme of and alternate to apathy/coolness, surges variously at three critical points: the descriptions of Amos, Way-out Morgan, and Don Lee. Amos, namesake of the prophet of a vengeful God, demands a blood bath, a "good rage" to wash America pure (st. 43). The "good rage" recalls "the whirlwind of good rage" in "Riders to the Blood-red Wrath." It relates to the Don Lee stanza (41)—which calls for "a new music screaming in the sun"—and to the Way-out Morgan stanza (50) summoning a terrible vengeance as he collects guns in his fourth-floor room. Rage also looks to the whirlwind image in "The Second Sermon on

the Warpland." Like Amos, who is weary of gradualism (" 'Takes
time,' grated the gradualist. / 'Starting from when?' asked
Amos"), these activists propose desperate remedies. The three
represent phases of rage: prophecy, destruction, and construction. "In the Mecca" moves from expression to interpretation; from questions to possibilities for action.

The Don Lee stanza, about two-thirds into the poem, together with stanza 54 near the end, forms the pivot of hope
countering Pepita's fate as the pivot of despair. It illustrates,
moreover, the alternating or antithetical structure of the poem.
And it gives insight into the important light imagery previously
discussed in "Big Bessie" and the "Catch" poems. Big Bessie does
not want her son to be misled by illusive "candles in the eyes."
Don Lee, however, becomes a symbol of positive action, desiring
"a physical light that waxes," one that grows from the efforts and
commitment of black people themselves. As the poem's blood
imagery turns from victim to oppressor, so does the light imagery
move from its revelatory function in the first line, "Sit where the
light corrupts your face," to the "least light" given off by the
environment as Sallie contemplates her shabby kitchen, toward
fulfillment as human energy. Removing her hat, Sallie confesses,
overwhelmed, "But all my lights are little!" (st. 7), ironic coupling
of small hopes and small children.

In contrast with Big Bessie and Sallie, Don Lee "is not candle-
lit" like the former or frustrated by the "least light" of the latter.
He calls vigorously for a new nation "under nothing" (partly
alluding to the Gettysburg Address and the revised Pledge of
Allegiance), as he "stands out in the auspices of fire / and rock and
jungle-flail" (st. 41). Evoking the prophetic image of Shadrach,
Meshach, and Abed-nego (Dan. 3:12-30), a human "physical light
that waxes" triumphs over the fiery furnace of political attack,
even as light turns to fire in the process of action. The new black,
embodied by Lee, will want a "new art and anthem . . . a new
music screaming in the sun," partly a reference to his *Don't Cry,
Scream* (1969). Light moves from fire to sun in a progression
toward the "new black sun" (*RPO*, 86) where Brooks will find her
"surprised queenhood" several years later. The light becomes
physical as it rises to consciousness. Guided truly from within,

people illuminate each other. This dynamic transformation of imagery is one of the technical splendors of the poem.

The Don Lee section is bracketed by stanzas on "Hyena," the self-engrossed debutante (39), death (40), and Alfred, the teacher/intellectual/failed artist (42). Directly preceding 39 and 40 is the tribute to Léopold Sédar Senghor, the poet who became the first president of the Independent Republic of Senegal in 1960. The escapist yearnings of Alfred contrast with Lee and with the ambition of prophetic Amos in the next section. Transitions are deftly graded.

The call for a "new art and anthem" recognizes that art in contemporary society cannot save the Mecca, nor can its detached contemplation. Art is a palliative, not a cure or an organic endeavor. Returning from work, Sallie surveys her kitchen, the antagonist she would conquer by decoration. The poet comments, "A pomade atop a sewage. An offense. / First comes correctness, *then* embellishment!" (st. 7). This states a moral concern with art in society, with the concept of beauty as a wholeness, "an essential sanity" called for near the end of the poem. The Mecca will not be improved by Darkara's imported *Vogue*, by Alfred's amiable dabbling in the arts, his reduction of literature to an obsession with language and his knowledge of Senghor. Reiteration that Alfred has not seen Pepita, though he can describe the Mecca and and praise the poet-president, emphasizes his well-meaning yet ineffectual nature, his inability to relate actively to his own environment.

The Senghor passage (st. 38) begins with Alfred "(who might have been a poet-king)" and dissolves into a description of the man who was both poet and political leader. (The fragment first appeared in *Negro Digest*, Sept. 1964). Pictured in Europe as "rootless and lonely," Senghor is still revered for representing an ideal: the artist as man-of-action, whose art expresses communal needs. Proximity of the important passage to Don Lee, the two bridged by relatively short, emotionally pacing stanzas (Hyena and death) joins historical and dramatic impact near the core of the narrative. Yet Senghor's wistful, exiled call for "negritude," filled with past achievement, cedes to the younger poet's rousing exhortation.

Contemporary world politics, which permit a Mecca at home and concentration camps abroad, cannot save the Mecca. Justice is fugitive. "The Law" visits reluctantly. The final insight, nevertheless, before the dreadful denouement, is given to Alfred in one of the poem's absolute passages. In stanza 54, Alfred, "lean," leans over the balcony and looks out over the wretchedness of the scene. Listening, he is aware that

> something, something in Mecca
> continues to call! Substanceless; yet like mountains,
> like rivers and oceans too; and like trees
> with wind whistling through them. And steadily
> an essential sanity, black and electric,
> builds to a reportage and redemption.
>> A hot estrangement.
>> A material collapse
> that is Construction.

The epiphanic moment recalls William Wordsworth on Mount Snowden (*The Prelude*, Book XIV), the sense of continuity with nature through which human life perceives the universal bond. "Substanceless" implies nonmaterial or spiritual, as in Wordsworth. For the latter, imagination combines with the Platonic hierarchy leading to intellectual love; in Brooks there is a similar emphasis on imagination as empathy, but the engagement is more immediately applicable to daily life. In a destructive environment, she suggests, black sanity will be curative, not by passive alienation but through a passionate "estrangement" from prevailing values. "Material collapse" will be the collapse of a materialistic society. Construction must involve essential change. In leaning toward Mecca, Alfred inclines toward a new ethos for an entire social order.

Compare the Alfred of this passage with his introduction at stanza 4, where we encounter his narrow (though benign) pedantry, minor lubricities, and occasional overindulgence in drinking. Alcohol induces a pseudo-mystical insight where "the Everything / is vaguely a part of One thing and the One thing / delightfully anonymous / and undiscoverable." The balcony episode, by contrast, occurs in a state of sobriety, in the sanctuary of consciousness. Alfred's development critically supports the theme of possible redemption, reminding that his Anglo-Saxon name, originally "elf-in-council," means "good counselor." He reinforces at stanza 48 the poet's appraisal of the Black situation in the Don Lee passage. His impotent intellectualism, limned in stanzas 4 and 38, undergoes modification with the insights of 48, where he turns away from Baudelaire, "Bob Browning," and Neruda, foreign white poets dealing with foreign matters, to the need for native "Giants over Steeples." (Cf. "'pygmies are pygmies still,'" chapter 3.) The giants are empowered, super- (as opposed to supra-) human beings who will rise above the very edifices of religion. Alfred acknowledges both "confusion and conclusion." Conclusion is not only the end of things but the *conclusion* to be drawn. Conclusions entail judgment and understanding. From this point Alfred can move to the moment on the balcony and the pinnacle of insight.

Despite the mild suggestion that Alfred turns toward Mecca as religion, plausible considering the shambles of organized (or disorganized) religion the poem portrays, Mecca remains basically the aspirations and potential of black people housed in the Mecca Building. The ambiguity, however, enriches the poem's texture, both in ironic and spiritual substance. Like the Mahayana Buddhist, however, who eschews Nirvana for the return to help his fellow creatures, Brooks drops from contemplative height to the body of Pepita and the ground of daily life.

Structure, Narrator, Forms. Although a work of such complexity cannot be reduced to simple patterns, it is helpful to view (and review) the structure in several ways. Partly, as noted above, it is a series of antithetical and graded movements. These alternate between a despairing past and present which interact with hope. They do so by means of the narrative, the narrator, and juxtaposition, by the tesselating of personae and poetic forms. Main characters appear early but the cast continually augments. We draw analogies with art and music: a mosaic of themes with variations, movement toward multi- and polyrhythm, the gradual revelation of tapestry by the shuttle.

Above all, "In the Mecca" is a dramatic quest of a parent for her child. The panorama eddying around her, Mrs. Sallie advances with the tragic aura of a Hecuba or Niobe. She begins with the problem of feeding her children and ends with the murder of one. From start to finish, she must address existential matters, basic and extreme. Thus the work moves dipodally between "How shall I live?" and "What shall I live by?" the two questions being related in the poem as they are in life. The economic, moral, and psychological function like agitated particles trapped in solution. Mrs. Sallie and her mission are the bestirring agents. The distraught mother, more catalyst than developing character, progresses mainly through degrees of alarm. Her reflection in stanza 18 (after noting the absence of Pepita), "I fear the end of Peace," merges with the poet-narrator in harsh irony. Sallie Smith, embattled and harried, has known no peace from the beginning.

The narrator is a strategic tour de force. Though Sallie is the dramatic agent, the poet addresses the reader and the characters. "Sit where the light corrupts your face" notifies us that the poet will participate in the action. At times observing, at times entering in *style indirect libre*, the narrator reacts to character and to plot. She functions as a Greek tragic chorus, embodying moral and social commentary, and acquires a personality. Her delineation advances the heroic dimensions she invokes in others. Moral and intellectual vigor refine the Don Lee section, where her praise enunciates her own ideals and native optimism.

Thus evolve another pair of foci: the drama unfolding around Mrs. Sallie and the poet's sensibility. This double perspective enables the latter to approach, embrace, and observe the former. The dynamics of the poem's hope-despair motifs, set constantly in tension, remain essentially connected. As medium of temporal connections, moreover, the narrator/interpreter joins past, present, and future.

Range and variety of characters in the Mecca bespeak a microcosm. This diversity, in turn, imprints the form. Free verse, metrical verse, random rhyme, slant rhyme, alliteration, the couplet, and the ballad accompany moods varying through sermonic, dramatic, and ironic, and objective and subjective narrative modes encompassing a spectrum of attitudes. Brooks's magisterial prosody summons historical figures from contemporary life, houses present action in a demolished edifice, and images the past in the "Great-great Gram" passage (st. 25, which recalls the system of slavery). Formally she utilizes and renovates the past, drawing it to the present. But her emphasis is contemporary, progressive.

Inclusion of the ballad at three points—in modified form describing Prophet Williams's wife, Ida (st. 3), the material aspirations of Emmett, Cap, and Casey (st. 22), and "The ballad of Edie Barrow" (st. 44), a tale of white betrayal of black love—should be noted. Disguised by block presentation, the poems provide the "clarifying" which Brooks will continue to pursue. In addition to linguistic paring, the ballad strips down narrative to heroic essentials, a prerequisite for mythologizing. Formal blending affects the poem as a whole and, like the poetic voice, serves to unify within diversity. If Brooks had employed the ballad in, say, the Senghor or Don Lee sections, the distinctive form coupled with the elevated subject matter might have detached either one from its context. What the poet has done, then, is meld the diverse elements into an organic entity. Her tact corresponds to the poem's underlying quest for social cohesion.

The ballad is further compatible with the narrative and journalistic modes and with parable ("Now the way of the Mecca was on this wise"). In Brooks's supple narration, personae speak directly or indirectly, as observed and interpreted. Old St. Julia Jones, Great-great Gram, Aunt Dill, Great-uncle Beer, and others tell their own tales through the omniscient observer, reporter, interpreter, prophet. As Brooks herself notes of the growing Black consciousness described in the Alfred balcony passage, there is a building toward "reportage and redemption." The bodily eye, ultimately, accommodates the deeper perceptions of the soul. "Ye shall know the truth, and the truth shall make you free" (John 8:32).

Dynamics of Narrative Sequence. In narrative sequence, the first stanza introduces the themes of failed art, religion, and politics, or Western ethos; the first sixteen stanzas (and, intermittently, the next fourteen, mainly through action) describe Sallie and her children, alternating with certain key neighbors. Superpious and, significantly, "old" St. Julia Jones and the cynical hypocrite Prophet Williams act as foils to the sincere religiosity and prophecy in the poem. They also permit announcement of

Sallie's skepticism and humanistic concern with her children's needs. Stanza 4 introduces two extremes: Hyena, the modish, hedonistic "debutante," and Alfred, the self-engrossed intellectual. They represent two aspects of disengagement from the scene, although Alfred will change. Selfishness in the poem associates with despair; caritas, communality, with hope and psychic health.

The children span egoism, sociability, antisociality. Youth makes them less responsible and defined, but we can see how they, too, will be ground into quotidian ferocities. Melodie Mary likes roaches but is emotionally removed from the children of China's civil war; Briggs belongs to a gang and learns violence (choking chickens); Thomas Earl fantasizes, his generous sympathies deflected by the environment; Tennessee is passive like his cat; Emmett, Cap, and Casey ("skin wiped over bones") are "redeemed" by food (ironically recalling Jesus' "Man shall not live by bread alone," Matt. 4:4 reference to Deuter. 8:3); Yvonne, in her teens, reflects upon her shared lover with a tough satisfaction that she will have her portion. Stanza 15 importantly precedes discovery of Pepita's disappearance. The passage presents Alfred's "faithless world" reflection and reverts to skepticism of the introductory stanzas. Thus weighted, the stanza ironically describes the indulged child of Sallie's rich employer. Wealth, like the egocentricity of Hyena and early Alfred, the religious fanaticism of St. Julia Jones, and the religious fraud of Prophet Williams, flaunts another extreme and contrast. Moving from Sallie to the others and back, Brooks's technique widens consciousness.

Stanza 17 acts as a stop of full tension. When Sallie asks, "WHERE PEPITA BE?" her terrified question casts the story into chiaroscuro. Stanza 18 refers to the child as

> our Woman with her terrible eye,
> with iron and feathers in her feet,
> with all her songs so lemon-sweet,
> with lightning and a candle too. . .

Stanza 30 will clarify that she is "halted." Within the elemental and human terms of her description, "candle" and "halt" relate her to Big Bessie's son in the "Catch" poems, the "bright lameness from my beautiful disease" of romantic illusion. The penultimate stanza will reveal Pepita's love of beauty, perhaps implicated in her death, and the "petals of a rose" which she once touched and for which her mother will try.

Highlighted by the ballad of adolescent wants (st. 22), the children's dreams intensify impressions of social evils grown immediately menacing. As the children acknowledge the unknown peril to their sister, they become "constrained." The word, appearing three times in stanzas 20 and 23, suggests force, the unnatural restraint involved in the murder itself. In stanza 23 the family is suddenly activated; the frieze of their emerging terror gives way to the charge "down the martyred halls." The adjective not only recognizes the martyr theme initially portended by the name "St. Julia Jones." It projects an associated guilt on to the external environment of the Mecca Building.

While the search for Pepita begins at stanza 23, Mrs. Sallie's pilgrimage actually begins in stanza 2, where she seeks rest at home, peace from her chores and anxieties. Economic struggle determines her life; survival and conflict rudely foreground the tragedy. Choked chickens (st. 11), Belsen and Dachau (st. 26), and burning ham hocks in the pan (st. 29) foreshadow the sacrifice. Directly follows the second description of Pepita: "the puny—the halted, glad-sad child" (st. 30). Particularly shocking at this point comes the reality of Pepita: an undernourished, lame little girl. The question of brute survival of the "fittest," subtly yet unmistakably raised, extends the urgency into an awesome, pernicious dimension. Suddenly the world seems threatening and cruel to the family. Succeeding stanzas on the police and Aunt Dill turn acerbic.

Summoned, the police dally and present "a lariat of questions," recalling the "lariat lynch-wish" and the "scythe / of men" in "The Chicago *Defender.*" Mrs. Sallie "wants her baby" in a screaming variation on the rhyme "And that would be my baby" in stanza 15. Aunt Dill (st. 36) dispenses solace as dour as her name, recounting a child's murder from the week before. Her account heightens tension and adds to the violent context. "The Law" (st. 37) searches in vain. At stanza 38 Alfred, whose moderate character eases transitions both in himself and the action, has not seen Pepita. But he can speak of Senghor, "the line of

Leopold." This crucial moment offers, at nearly the nadir of despair, a kind of hope, not personal, not even complete (Senghor is pictured in exile), but a generalized aspiration for all black people.

The abrupt shift to Hyena's self-indulgence (st. 39) underscores her dislike of "a puny and a putrid little child." Her lack of sympathy and her hostility parallel the next stanza's ultimate negative, uttered by the narrator, beginning, "Death is easy." Death and denial of caritas foreshadow the denouement. More immediately, they permit stunning contrast with the following Don Lee stanza's upward swing to a vigorous hopefulness. Stanza 42 contemplates Alfred musing over semantics. Action recoils from the constructive stance of 41 toward the prophesied violence of Amos (43). This shift partly anticipates the closing violence. At the same time, it offers a transforming potential, the blood bath that will regenerate the country.

There is a further, unmediated transition to "The ballad of Edie Barrow" (st. 44), the young black woman betrayed by a rich white man, "a Gentile boy." This lyrical interlude poises before the wider hope/despair oscillations in the last third of the poem. It illustrates white perfidy and the exploitation of blacks—and of women generally (the lover also manipulates his future bride)— by white society. At the same time, it broadens the work to include lyrical expression of a major theme.

"Gentile boy" lends typology to the action. The subtle parallel between blacks and Jews (cf. "The Ghost at the Quincy Club"), the latter already seen as concentration camp victims, etches the Mecca as an oppressive ghetto. Martin Luther King similarly utilized the parallel in one of his sermons, "The Death of Evil upon the Seashore," in alluding to the Supreme Court decision of Brown vs. Board of Education of Topeka, 1954. "A world-shaking decree by the nine justices of the Supreme Court," he stated, "opened the Red Sea and the forces of justice are moving to the other side."[9]

The cynicism of false Prophet Williams in stanza 45 acts as a foil to the sincerity of apocalyptic Amos in 43. Stanza 46 is introduced by a variety of minor characters who lead to the powerful description of insane Sophie. She sees "the fires run up" in a world askew. Violence and purgation forge her consciousness

which, in turn, expresses her mad environment. Besides epitomizing the burning and apocalyptic imagery, the Sophie passage
again instances the failed religion theme. Her "Mad life heralding
the blue heat of God / snickers in a corner of the west windowsill."
She resembles "Wezlyn, the wandering woman" in the stanza,
who prowls the halls of Mecca at night "in search of Lawrence and
Love," reiterating the failed art and caritas themes. (D. H. Lawrence's individualist solutions would little avail the socioeconomic
morass of the Mecca.) The "blue heat of God"—the pure flame of
religion and hope—burns closer to Sophie's madness and Amos's
apocalyptic cleansing than it does to organized religion. Sophie
knows she has failed herself, the love she has "promised Mother,"
and the world. She has the pristine insight that endows saints,
fools, and frequently the insane. The most withdrawn character,
she epitomizes both rejection and its consequences. In the west
windowsill, she snickers her commentary on the religious and
moral valetude of the West.

Stanza 47 veers from psychic atrocity to a listing of minor
figures who do not care, people like Darkara who studies *Vogue*.
Characters are deftly imaged; or else their vivid names ("Aunt
Tippie," "Zombie Bell") join others more amply cited ("Mr. Kelly
with long gray hair who begs / subtly from door to door"). Stanza
48 presents Alfred's growing consciousness, his turning away from
foreign poets toward the need for "Giants over Steeples" and "A
violent reverse." This new reaching braces the possibility of
changes invoked by Amos and Don Lee. Stanza 49 reverts to the
policemen as they question two sisters, whose caring limits itself
to Gustav Mahler (composer of "Kindertotenlieder" or "Songs on
the Death of Children") and tea. The next stanza portrays Way-out
Morgan. Vengeance-seeker, victim of white violence, Morgan
remembers his mob-raped Sister and murdered comrades. He
collects guns, preparing for "Ruin." This glimpse of havoc foreshadows Pepita's death and, like the Amos passage, further politicizes the action.

Stanza 51 retrenches to Marian's repressed violence. An unappreciated housewife, she sublimates her anger by fascination
with crime. The next stanza glances at meek, forgetful Pops
Pinkham. Aunt Dill (st. 53), revisited, collects items including
"bits of brass and marble," listed and held as lovingly as Way-out

Morgan hoards guns. Self-considered a "woman-in-love-with-God," she gives no real assistance to Sallie, whose anxiety (and the reader's) she intensifies. This postscript on inadequate religion precedes Alfred's introductory statement in stanza 54, "I hate it. Yet . . ." and his epiphanic moment on the balcony. His insight counters the shabbiness of conventional faith with the possibility of constructive belief. From this height, narrative plunges toward Pepita's body "lying in dust with roaches," finally discovered under the cot where her murderer sits as he is questioned by police. The swift antithetical movement locates the strongest dramatic impact.

Yet Brooks's magnificent tapestry has already lifted the child into mythos. "Hateful things sometimes befall the hateful / but the hateful are not rendered lovable thereby" understands without condoning the murderer. Caught with subtly webbed sounds, the closing stanza leaves epitaph and apotheosis:

> She whose little stomach fought the world had
> wriggled, like a robin!
> Odd were the little wrigglings
> and the chopped chirpings oddly rising.

Pepita's physical reality, a hunger bravely confronting life—and death—has been ended. But the robin also means spring and renewal, paradox of the heartbreaking lines. The feminine endings support the continuing movement. Although her frailty was mortally exploited, Pepita's inviolate spirit, become bird, will not be subdued. (The word "odd" will recur in "The Life of Lincoln West"; the two contexts bear comparison.) The small stanza reverts the panoramic scope to personal scale, while it expresses an altered reality, permanently rendered.

"In the Mecca" is a great work deserving the closest study. It takes strength from controlled, formal diversity, from the detailed presence of Mecca in the world and the pressures of life, and from the poet's urgency that fuses craft and intelligence to its dimensions. Particulars of black experience draw its themes into a universal vortex. As a black mother, Mrs. Sallie projects an identity of hope and sorrows. Above the rubble of the physical site, the poem creates a Mecca that is something past, something present, infusing both with meaning and hope, with fair black fables that may revive its shattered realities.

"After Mecca"

Eight poems, including one diptych and one triptych, follow "In the Mecca." The title, "After Mecca," restates the narrative tact, anticipating the questions "What happened afterwards?" and, more urgently, "What can be done?"

"To a Winter Squirrel" functions in the book as intermezzo. Beginning "This is the way God made you," its religious regard for nature links the theme and closing verses of "In the Mecca" and its ravished spring (Pepita as robin) with hopeful winter (the squirrel). Of the poem, first published in *Sisters Today* (Nov. 1965) and originally intended for "A Catch of Shy Fish," Brooks writes: "Years ago, when we were *poor*-poor, we would sometimes run out of coal. I would turn on the gas stove, sit down on a stool beside it, and prop my legs up on the lid. While thus hoisted, a book and a cup of tea forbade self-pity" (*RPO*, 184). "Merdice / of murdered heart and docked sarcastic soul," persona and subject of the poet-narrator, sits by her gas stove to keep warm and envies the freedom of a squirrel outside her window. "Merdice" offers many allusions, including "mer" ("sea" in French) and the life where her spirit is "docked," tied, or reduced; and "dice" or chance; also, the name suggests her "murdered heart." A "bolted nomad," she wants to travel, but life has fastened (or wrapped or swallowed) her with indigence. She would like to "bolt" or flee.

Conforming to her style in "In the Mecca," Brooks directly addresses the squirrel. Identifying with the animal extends Merdice past "the shellac of her look" as he becomes transcendent nature, "a mountain and a star, unbaffleable, / with sentient twitch and scurry." The last line expresses his action and graces him with feeling. Tension between inner and outer realities braces the poem's minimal outward movement: three progressively lengthening stanzas, in free verse with random rhyme intricately varied—full, slant, apocopated, to name several types. Paradoxes abound: the squirrel, naturally protected by his fur, in the cold; Merdice, cold behind glass, with insufficient heat.

Going out to the snow means warmth; remaining in chilly safety means becoming spiritually inert, like the woman's posture at the stove. Yet alliteration firms her image; the mountain and star metaphors hint at departure. A winter squirrel, moreover, implies retrieval and—evoking the Pepita quatrain—the coming seasonal change to spring.

Merdice's quiet window shatters with the next poem, "Boy Breaking Glass." First published in *Negro Digest* (1967), it is dedicated to Marc Crawford, a black writer and editor of *Time Capsule*, who suggested that Brooks write a poem about ghetto blacks surviving "inequity and white power" (*RPO*, 184-85). A boy also breaks glass in stanza 5 of "In the Mecca." This common vandalism, used to justify "functional" windowless, penitentiary-style architecture (including schools), is examined as an inverted act of creation, a *claiming* act of the dispossessed.[10]

From the first line, "Whose broken window is a cry of art," the cry *for* art deflects energy from the making to the unmaking of an object. "If not a note, a hole." The phrase recalls the concept of negative space interacting with the sculpture. It suggests the intimate relation between Being and Nothingness in Sartre, support of the latter by the former, and their joint presence as consciousness. The glass—transparent, fragile as human life, a medium for light and reality—is nearly interchangeable with the hole. The boy himself is somewhat metaphysical: "Nobody knew where I was and now I am no longer there" (st. 5). Freudian Eros/ Thanatos identities, the "cry" of anger that cries for help, and the need for art as communication further engage the poem.

At the beginning of stanza 2 the boy says, "I shall create!" Iambic pentameter dominance in the first stanza anticipates this reaching toward form, together with a subtle mingling of rhyme and slant rhyme. The poem seems freely structured while it strictly controls phonic affinities within the lines (assonance, alliteration, internal rhyme) and in the stanzaic groupings. Stanza lengths nearly balance: 6, 2, 2, 4, 1, 2, 2, 2, 6. Although the first and last stanzas are linear equals, the last moves quickly as the boy runs, and pauses in the last line to appraise him respectfully, "a hymn, a snare, and an exceeding sun." A shattered sonnet hints in the first fourteen lines; the single line follows like a break, a hole at the center. Brooks's verbal playfulness and irony spark the verses. Witness "The music is in minors" with assonance and irony evoking the minor key and the boy being a minor from a racial minority. The couplet, used in half the stanzas, presents the most interesting formal icon. Here is the boy's perverse quest for contact and communication, an "I-Thou," to use Martin Buber's image.

From the passive observer to the seeming nihilist, Brooks turns her attention to positive figures, two martyrs who, in a sense, fulfill the prophetic "martyred halls" and epiphany of "In the Mecca." "Medgar Evers" eulogizes the National Association for the Advancement of Colored People (NAACP) leader who, at thirty-seven, was assassinated in Jackson, Mississippi, on June 13, 1963. (Trial of the accused, Byron de la Beckwith, resulted in a hung jury.) Dedicated to Evers's brother Charles, the poem describes a man who inspired fear by advancing social change. The free verse employs rhyme and slant rhyme, mostly internal. The last element gives a rolling, inevitable quality to the reinforced sound and rhythms, particularly in the second stanza, which targets the past in a compact list of heroic-style epithets. (Compare "Moral rose" with "anguished rose" in "The Chicago *Defender*.") The poet herself was pleased with her image of Evers as he "leaned across tomorrow. People said that / he was holding clean globes in his hands." Connoting a world morally cleansed, it also suggests the balanced scales of justice and recalls the spiritual, "He's Got the Whole World in His Hands."

Brooks's fine tribute, "Malcolm X" (May 19, 1925-Feb. 31, 1965), sets him firmly in the pantheon of heroes. Like Medgar Evers, the Black Muslim leader was assassinated. The poem is dedicated to Dudley Randall, who not only esteems Malcolm but also shares his confidence in Black potential.[11] The five stanzas begin:

Original.
Ragged-round.
Rich-robust.

He had the hawk-man's eyes.
We gasped. We saw the maleness.
The maleness raking out and making guttural the air
and pushing us to walls.

Free verse, girded with assonance and consonance, reveals typically heroic features of compounding, alliteration, and spondaic or strong- stressing. Lines are spare and muscular; images project clearly, swiftly. Malcolm is an "original" sensibility and accomplishment, in leading Blackness to its own sources and heritage.

On the page, the poem takes the wedgelike shape of a bird, birds in flight, or a wing. "[T]he hawk-man's eyes," far-seeing, command a different vision from that of the eagle in the same family, emblem of the United States. A hawk, varieties of which are rufous-marked (Malcolm X was often called "Red" because of his reddish-brown hair),[12] pursues its prey by "raking," which also means to collect or gather laboriously. The "guttural" sound made by some hawks has no counterpart in English, but does in Arabic, spoken by many Muslims. The word thus associates with Malcolm's faith and his pilgrimage to Mecca in 1964, shortly before his death. The journey catalyzed his acceptance of racial brotherhood. "Walls" summons Mecca, a walled city, its enclosure of faith toward which Muslims pray; it also summons the "Wall of Respect" in Chicago, the wall of Black solidarity and consciousness, and a surrender (as in "up against the wall") to Malcolm's teachings. God or Jesus often has been portrayed in literature as predator/pursuer of the soul; witness Francis Thompson's "The Hound of Heaven," T. S. Eliot's "Christ the tiger" in "Gerontion," and Gerard Manley Hopkins's "The Windhover," which refers to a kestrel or sparrow hawk. Hopkins also compounds and alliterates freely, but usually in agitated rhythms of the devotional spirit. "We gasped" suggests taking in the spiritual air of "maleness" that propagates purposeful strength.

"He opened us— / who was a key, // who was a man" ends the poem with a reinforcing of "maleness" and the activist conception of Black manhood. (See the discussion of "boy" in *Beckonings*, chapter 9). Malcolm's "key" "opened us" to selfhood. "Key" suggests "us" as doors and the Christian "door."

For Brooks, art must join the political life-or-death struggle. "Two Dedications: I. The Chicago Picasso; II. The Wall," dramatic contrasts yet thematic supplements, oppose formal to popular art.[13] Both sections of the diptych treat art in its human environment, its functions, origins, and experience by an audience. The first subpoem, "The Chicago Picasso," written at the request of Mayor Daley (*RPO*, 147), refers to the gigantic steel sculpture he unveiled at the Civic Center on August 15, 1967. The event was accompanied by Seiji Ozawa leading the Chicago Symphony before an audience of 50,000. The structure, described in the *Chicago Sun-Times* as having the appearance of a bird and a woman (it does, to this viewer), was cheered upon sight. The abstracted newspaper quotations (one, the poet's dramatic observation) anticipate the "Super-Reporter," but the reflective, conversational approach steps away from the factual epigraph.

Brooks examines art's worthwhile demands: "Does man love Art? Man visits Art, but squirms. / Art hurts. Art urges voyages—." Capitalized "Art" (personified as a "requiring courtesan"), "Lion," "Flower," and the conventionally capitalized "Mona Lisa" become concepts. In the quatrain concluding the free-verse poem, Brooks invites us to "Observe the tall cold of a Flower," itself indifferent, "as meaningful and as meaningless" as our perceptions of it, in the way we would admire the made art object. Yet the Flower resembles other flowers "in the western field" or the western world. The passage recalls the child Maud Martha sitting on the back steps, cherishing the "everydayness" of dandelions and wishing for meadow lilies. The Flower summons also the peerless "lilies of the field" in the Sermon on the Mount (Matt. 6:28-29).

"The Wall" eulogizes "The Wall of Respect," dedicated on August 27, 1967, twelve days after the Chicago Picasso unveiling. Its epigraph relates it structurally to the first subpoem, while the poem, itself the event, previews the "verse journalism" of "In Montgomery." The epigraph, briefer than the first, also differs in being a comment (from *Ebony*) instead of simulated newspaper items. There is a roughly inverse relationship between the two elements of each subpoem, so that epigraph is to subpoem as subpoem is to epigraph, the differences themselves a kind of chiasmic yoking.

"The Wall" is inscribed to Edward Christmas, the black artist who painted Brooks's portrait on the Wall of Respect. Part of a slum building later demolished by the city, it bore a "mural communicating black dignity": heroic black figures from contemporary life, including art, religion, politics, and sports. The poem carries the equipment of Brooks's heroic style: alliteration, epithets, verbal compounding, perspicuous metaphor and metonymy, capitalization, and the vigorous, prophetic voice. "The Wall" creates a human tableau, without formal division between art and artist, as in the Picasso unveiling. "Worship" of the Wall suggests hieratic connections with the origins of art. The poet-protagonist, eyewitness, enters the scene.

When Brooks mounts the rattling wood to address the crowd, she becomes part of her poem and the heroine of it, subject and narrator in an unfolding historical dimension beyond first person (singular and plural) through description, into the augmented first person plural of the conclusion, "And we sing." She redeems Mrs. Sallie climbing "the sick and influential stair." Her audience shares in making the heroic moment and, therefore, the poem, effecting the familial merging proclaimed in Walter Bradford's introduction, "She / our Sister is." Cinematographic zooming in on various chromatic, aural, and kinesthetic densities portrays the scene. An exultant work, it gathers excitement and phonic energy into its cries of "Black Power."

"A drumdrumdrum. / Humbly we come." From the beginning, concrete images crowd the lines with action and texture. Val Gray Ward, the actress and organizer of Kuumba, her performance troupe; Phil Cohran, the musician; Walter Bradford; Brooks, standing on the wobbly platform, and the crowd from which she has emerged create a mutual commitment. Physical and moral ascendance meet in eloquent description of the Wall: "this serious Appointment / this still Wing / this Scald this Flute this heavy Light this Hinge." The eulogy, a verbal stream without commas, combines epithet, biblical metonymy, and realistic projection. "Scald" is an ancient Scandinavian poet or historiographer, a Norse reciter of heroic poems and eulogies, like the Anglo-Saxon "scop" of *Beowulf* and, in terms of the perspective here, especially apt. The word also means, of course, a burning, here administered rather than endured, the latter associated with Brooks's other burning images in previous volumes.

"[H]eavy Light" importantly modifies the usual concept of a weightless light that falls upon the earth. Heaviness connotes a material light, one deriving its substance from the earth and, finally, from human life. It is the spiritual light cast by good works, referred to by Jesus as the candle not placed under a bushel but on a candlestick, "and it giveth light to all that are in the house" (Matthew 5:15). The "Hinge" evokes Jesus' metonymic reference to himself as "the door" (John 10:9) and links with the "key" image in "Malcolm X." A hinge is the flexible piece on which the door turns; an obsolete meaning of hinge is the earth's axis.

And so the Wall's heroic figures take on a religious aura. The collocation of "Wing" and "Light" further defines the religious configuration. The "still Wing" is a pause in flight, a benediction. "Flute" interprets the art and artists celebrated. Music from the highly pitched wind instrument depends upon human breath, associated with spirit. "Flute" as a groove in a classical column picks up the other architectural connotations: "Appointment" (usually in plural as equipment for a hotel or a ship, besides its other pertinent associations), "Wing" (section), "Light" (window), and "Hinge." "The Wall" is part of a building; it becomes part of a spiritual architecture by and for black people. Art joins with politics, moderated through religious commitment. Figurative splendor lifts the narrative into sacramental anthem. As the poem becomes a struggling toward grace, it articulates all who "worship the Wall" in joyful respect and shared self-esteem.

What of the ghetto young people, those who are lost to this moment of affirmation? Brooks turns sharply to "The Blackstone Rangers," a triptych concerning the Chicago youth gang, whose members she had met through Walter Bradford. "I / As Seen by Disciples" tersely surveys the thirty young men from the negative viewpoint ("sores in the city") of another gang, implying social censure. Vexed by some who misread the passage as her own condemnation, Brooks insists that, in any reprinting, the entire poem be published as a unit since the other sections are clearly sympathetic (GB/GY, Nov. 1969). "II / The Leaders" and "III / Gang Girls / A Rangerette" depict thwarted potential, limited aspirations, the raw strength of the wayward "boy-men," and the affections of their girl-women. The few rhymes and slant rhymes scatter through these sections.

Heavy alliteration in "The Leaders" accompanies strong and copious stressing. Names like Gene (from "Eugene," well- or nobly bred) and "Geronimo" (namesake of the Apache chief, leader of a band of "hostiles" who terrorized New Mexico and

Arizona) emphasize leadership potential. Constructive energy and fellowship ("monstrous hand on monstrous hand") of "The Blackstone bitter bureaus" organize into "a monstrous pearl or grace" (pearl, symbol of purity, an abnormal growth, valuable, the "Blackstones"). The last of the three stanzas eulogizes the "descent"—richly connotative—of the failed heroes, their "unfashionable damnations," renewing the tragic theme of redemption. Though accompanying prominent and/or heroic black figures, the young men are still embraced as racial brethren whose "country is a Nation on no map."

The third section, beginning "Gang Girls are sweet exotics," presents Mary Ann, "rose in a whiskey glass" (cf. "anguished rose" in "The Chicago *Defender*" and "Moral rose" in "Medgar Evers"), "the Shakedancer's child" from a rooming-house. Conventionally feminine, her hopes limited to immediate pleasures, she recalls Maud Martha finally accepting that "Leaning was a work." Mary Ann similarly seeks "non-loneliness— / the rhymes of Leaning."

The three sections achieve a stepped entry. Ironic stance gives way to Super-Reportage, then to direct address and the imperatives (ironic here) that characterize the succeeding pieces. Mary Ann elicits the poem's warmest sympathies. One of the few significant events in her life, "Somebody Terribly Dying / under the philanthropy of robins" (youthful, recurrent spring), alludes to Pepita, even as it implies Mary herself. Thus Brooks further links the two sections of the book.

"After Mecca" closes with the First and Second "Sermon[s] on the Warpland." These poems of controlled power affirm Brooks's aim to "call" black people. Although she states this as a future objective, the beginning is clearly here.

The bond between art and the black church should be remarked at this point. Even though the church's relation to music is best known, literary ties were also developed, not only in the black sermon as a stylistic entity, but in the hospitality of black churches to artistic pursuits. Aesthetic life was not detached; it was integral to the spiritual life of the community, like the religious origins of drama.

James Weldon Johnson, in his preface to *God's Trombones*, a book of sermonic poems, describes the Negro preacher as orator and actor and detects the source of the sermon's poetic character: "He knew the secret of oratory, that at bottom it is a progression of rhythmic words more than it is anything else."[14] Henderson's "elegant Black linguistic gesture" Johnson finds in the preacher's eloquence, his love for "the sonorous, mouth-filling, ear-filling phrase because it gratified a highly developed sense of sound and rhythm in himself and his hearers" (Johnson, 19). The old-time preachers, Johnson notes, did not use dialect. Their sermons were "a fusion of Negro idioms with Bible English; and in this there may have been, after all, some kinship with the innate grandiloquence of their old African tongues" (18).

Bruce A. Rosenberg's valuable study *The Art of the American Folk Preacher* distinguishes the chanted sermon as "an art form worthy of study in its own right."[15] "Its oral style," he finds, "echoes *Beowulf* or the *Nibelungenlied,* but is usually not a conventional or sophisticated poetry" (p.5). The sermons quoted, however, show a unique poetic quality. Here is an excerpt from one given by the Reverend Rubin Lacy (1967), a brilliant black preacher:

> If the Lord is your shepherd preach on
> Preacher, preach on
> Singers, sing on
> You gonna get your reward
> God has given you that gift
> You sing on
> And God will give you your reward. [150]

The author discerns the chanted sermon as a variety of "spiritual" sermon whose practitioners, like Reverend Lacy, distinguish between their own largely spontaneous preaching and the "manuscript" sermons of the majority. Rosenberg's reference to *Beowulf,* moreover, invokes the identification made here of Anglo-Saxon and Homeric elements in Brooks's poetry, chiefly regarding alliteration, compounding, and epithet. The Sermons on the Warpland abound in repetition—parallel constructions like those he analyzes—along with the redundant phrasing, metaphors, and metonymy which characterize the Bible itself.

"The Sermon on the Warpland" carries an epigraph from Ron

Karenga, Black Nationalist organizer: "The fact that we are black is our ultimate reality." Brooks's majestic tempo of what Arnold would have appreciated as "high seriousness" paces her opening lines, "And several strengths from drowsiness campaigned / but spoke in Single Sermon on the warpland." She continues by quotation, merging with the composite voice of leadership and prophecy that utters a "Single Sermon." Besides unity, "Single" in its religious context connotes honesty and sincerity, memorable in the Sermon on the Mount: "The light of the body is the eye: if therefore thine eye be single, thy whole body shall be full of light" (Matt. 6:22). Capitalization of "Single Sermon" also marks the later style. The power which "from drowsiness campaigned," like a melding of voices at "The Wall" dedication, rouses to battle.

The title indicates themes and stylistic traits of the prophetic Brooks. Although "Sermon" is self-explanatory, "warpland" is complex. "Warp" plus "land" forms a warped land.[16] Compounding, however, involves the "war" in warp, so that the land is warped by war. The word may also be perceived as "war" and "plan" or "pland," compatible with the call to organize for battle; "pland" also suggests "plain" or "planed"—a leveling by war, by planes or airplanes. A sermon implies, furthermore, the need for moral guidance in such a land. The word "on" in the title conveys a message about the land, to it, for it, and also suggests simple location, as in the Sermon on the Mount, with which it bears comparison.

Jesus' Sermon and that of Brooks concern the well-being of ordinary people; both are antimaterialistic. But while the biblical Sermon celebrates love, forgiveness, and a turning toward heavenly grace, the poem invokes love combined with power ("like lion-eyes") to turn the "River" of black life and history. The "doublepod" of "the coming hell and health together" will divert the River to constructive purposes, effecting change.

> And went about the warpland saying No.
> "My people, black and black, revile the River.
> Say that the River turns, and turn the River. [ll.3-5]

Lines 4 and 5 are one of Brooks's "lifelines"; another appears in the Second Sermon. The poet calls black people to "revile" the passively accepted "Ol' Man River" of the song. (See discussion, "Paul Robeson," chapter 8). Chiasmus in line 5 expresses the subject: restraints and their reversal. Brooks's imagery is artfully simple. It liberates the reader/listener's imaginative play. Discerning universal connections, its allegory extends consciousness.

Composer Noel DaCosta presented a compelling interpretation of the poem at St. Martin's Episcopal Church in Harlem, October 28, 1979. Utilizing the breadth of a twelve-tone scale in the form of a cantata, DaCosta envisioned two male Preachers: one, a speaker intoning in a high-pitched tenor voice; the other, a bass-baritone, singing dramatically against a choral background, accompanied by a piano, organ, and carillon. In conversation with me, DaCosta, who studied poetry with Countee Cullen in junior high school, observed that his composition registers the parallel structures and repetition cited above. Taking note of the shift in mood from admonition to a soothing call for love, a lyricism expressed through the extended solo, the composer added that the shift itself typifies the hortatory style of the Negro preacher.

"The Second Sermon on the Warpland," in four sections, is dedicated to Walter Bradford. Brooks now directly addresses youth and the kind of human salvaging Bradford achieved. The salvage theme draws "After Mecca" into unity. Brooks would catch the healing moment when the wrecked lives might still be redeemed. The Second Sermon is aurally stunning. A spiritual call to battle, at times it has the feeling of a drum roll, resonating the text. Here is the first section:

> This is the urgency: Live!
> and have your blooming in the noise of the whirlwind.

Compression and imperatives enforce the rhetorical strength. The words "whirlwind" and "live," recurring in each of the remaining three sections, figure most importantly at the close: "Nevertheless, live. // Conduct your blooming in the noise and whip of the whirlwind." The last line is another of Brooks's "lifelines." It returns to the collocations of "blooming," "noise," and "whirlwind" of section 1, but changes from passive "have" to active "conduct" and imposes "whip" between "noise" and "whirlwind."

The long line projects images and concepts into a fiercely palpable present. "Conduct" connotes the ability to control circumstances, others, oneself. "Whip" suggests the punishment blacks have received. "Whip" modifying "whirlwind" ironically reverses the punitive emblem into a revolutionary weapon. The familiar whip image (note Langston Hughes's *The Panther and the Lash*) occurs in the locution "backlash," often referring to white reaction or sociopolitical overreaction in general.

Brooks affirms that entering the whirlwind will foster strength and growth. Its natural force images racial conflict in the struggle for equality. "The world is a whirlwind and the social world is a whirlwind," she observes (Hull, 39). The word summons also the prophetic "For they have sown the wind, and they shall reap the whirlwind" (Hosea 8:7) and recalls "the whirlwind of good rage" in "Riders to the Blood-red Wrath."

Throughout the poem, sounds, especially the *r*'s, strong alliteration, the alternating long and short vowels, and the rush of monosyllabic words brace the structure. Hear the second section:

> Salve salvage in the spin.
> Endorse the splendor splashes;
> stylize the flawed utility;
> prop a malign or failing light—
> but know the whirlwind is our commonwealth. [ll.1-5]

The first half of the stanza presents positive imperatives; the second half, negative ones, ending with a positive:

> Not the easy man, who rides above them all,
> not the jumbo brigand,
> not the pet bird of poets, that sweetest sonnet,
> shall straddle the whirlwind.
> Nevertheless, live. [ll.6-10]

The incantatory phrasal parallels (ll.6-8) appear in the only completely imperative section. How does the mood permeate the whole?

Brooks deploys the imperative judiciously. The next section

shifts to indicative; the fourth line ("what must our Season be, which starts from Fear?") acts as a subjunctive/indicative hinge, swinging open to imperatives of the last three lines. In section 4, the last two lines out of eighteen are imperative; the rest, indicative. Shifts of mood also move the poem: imperative for most of sections 1 and 2, it turns to indicative dominance in sections 3 and 4 and concludes with a variant of section 1's imperative statement. The beginning urgency, the swift and copious commands of section 2 invoke the style of the chanted sermon and carry into the indicative of section 3 an imperative mood. This mood, in turn, is impelled by repetition, parallelism, alliteration ("All about are," etc.), and is fully resumed in the close. It then spills into section 4, whose energetic initial verbs (*cracks, lifts*) draw imperative force.

Thus power of the imperatives serves to unify the poem. By strategic positioning, parallel structure, and repetition, Brooks manages them toward incremental resonance. The commands, moreover, carry aesthetic as well as social criticism. In section 2, negative imagery jettisons the accommodating person, the ambitious thief, and, reluctantly, tamer literary forms like the sonnet. In this regard, equestrian "straddle" supports Brooks's heroic. Epithets spark the section.

The next section surveys the terrain of egocentric despair.

> All about are the cold places,
> all about are the pushmen and jeopardy, theft—
> all about are the stormers and scramblers . . . [ll. 1-3]

But one must "Define and / medicate" the ailments taken into the storm. Prescriptive action will heal the self and society. "Season" (life) and "Fear" (where we begin the struggle) are capitalized concepts; "pushmen" (aggressive men, including drug pushers and thieves who push into residences), "stormers," "scramblers" offer the metonymous biblical forms that transfer from the epithet-dominated second section to an allegorical, universal mode. Repetition and parallelism sound insistently.

The fourth section, a complex tour de force, combines and transforms preceding elements. With remarkable concentration of vision, the poet bridges "In the Mecca" and "After Mecca."

> The time
> cracks into furious flower. Lifts its face
> all unashamed. And sways in wicked grace. [ll. 1-3]

Anger, the present "furious flower," unites with the opening lines
and rhymes of the volume. "Lifts its face," rhyming with "wicked
grace," the time now considered redeemable, recalls the beginning of "In the Mecca" where light "corrupts" the face and art
(Miës Van der Rohe) flees ("retires from grace"). But here, having
been assured (section 2) that one may "prop a malign or failing
light" as long as the "commonwealth" of the whirlwind is acknowledged, it is possible to achieve a special, "wicked" (unconven-
tional, telluric) kind of salvation. No longer inviting the reader to
sit in a corrupting light, time "Lifts its face" without shame.
Transitions—from sedentary and passive images to those of action, from corruption to integrity, from falling of fables to the lifted
face and the efflorescent time—chart the historical distance between a past and present that converge in clusters of sound and
color imagery. African heritage (the time "is tom-tom hearted"),
oranges assorted by "half-black hands," "bells," "red," "shriek,"
"sheen," "boom" rush at the senses.

Respectful reference to garbagemen ("A garbageman is dignified / as any diplomat") recalls the sanitation workers' strike in
Memphis, Tennessee, where Martin Luther King journeyed to
lead their march in 1968 and met his death. The motto on placards
carried by strikers was "I AM A MAN." (References to both the
garbageman and Big Bessie revert to "A Catch of Shy Fish.") At
the close of section 4, Big Bessie, her feet hurting, "stands—bigly
. . . in the wild weed." Her posture and location, her description
as "a moment of highest quality," stress distance and ascendance
from the opening of "In the Mecca," where fables fall and Mrs.
Sallie wearily climbs. Images of corruption, sitting, and falling are
replaced by standing and human height. The wild weed of the
unruly, common aspirations of black people roots in strength and
growth out of which Big Bessie rises, herself fulfilling the hopes
she had for her son in the previous volume. A black Everywoman
like Mrs. Sallie, Bessie also acquires a certain heroic stature.

Phrasal repetition of "in the wild weed," random slant rhyme,
wide variation in verse length, and the thundering climax of the

last line, ending with spondaic reverberation of "whirlwind" cap the poem's technical mastery. Evoking the sermonic recapitulation and biblical redundance of the first three sections, it confirms development of the grand heroic style.

Section 4's four stanzas of diminishing length (12, 3, 2, 1) define with increasing precision the theme of salvage and renewal. A touch of religious symbolism (or analogy) hovers about the linear groupings, with the number twelve suggesting evangelical disciples; three, the Trinity in Big Bessie's ascension to "a moment of highest quality"; two, the I-Thou relationship of the first person plural address—"For we are the last of the loud. / Nevertheless, live"—which succeeds the third person of stanzas 1 and 2; and the emblematic unity of the unilinear close. The verb "Conduct" is also charged with the nominal "conduct," for the exhortation is not merely to live. The nature of that existence pertains most keenly to the poet's intent as she attends to youth, growth, hope, the blossoming at any age that continues the pressure toward freedom and love.

"After Mecca," in subject, themes, imagery, prophetic/heroic content and style, and typographical features, presents a postlude to "In the Mecca," fulfilling its tragic quest with hope and redemption. Like "A Catch of Shy Fish," it coheres in addressing a central question. Experience ranges the fact and fiction of "In the Mecca"; the heroic weights "After Mecca" toward contemporary heroes and the future. Personae project in magnitude, like portraits on the Wall of Respect. Ascending the steps at the Wall dedication, Brooks becomes, through a vital exchange of energies, her own heroic presence: the poet-prophet. The two Sermons on the Warpland adapt the sermon as an art form and confirm her grand heroic style. Its religious humanism bridges art and politics, supporting the role of all three. As she says of the Wall, her own work becomes "this Scald this Flute this heavy Light this Hinge."

8
Riot,
Family Pictures,
Aloneness

On first meeting Gwendolyn Brooks in 1966, Dudley Randall was impressed by her modesty and warmth.[1] That year, the Metropolitan Detroit English Club had invited her to read at Oakland University; Randall offered to organize hospitality for the visit. Brooks had read the publisher's reviews in *Black World* (then *Negro Digest*) and thought him "fierce," she told him later. But his "pleasant expression and mild manner" impressed her otherwise. Randall was to become the poet's editor, publisher, and best friend. Brooks dedicated her first book with Broadside Press, *Riot*,[2] to Randall, "a giant in our time," and donated to the press her share of proceeds from sales. In a 1975 tribute to Broadside on its tenth anniversary, she remarked in her poem to Randall, whom she met "somewhere close to the heat and youth of the road," that even before his journey to the continent, his identity was clear: "you did not know you were Afrika."[3]

The first two broadsides that inaugurated the press were Randall's own "Ballad of Birmingham" and "Dressed All in Pink." The publisher attended the first Writers' Conference at Fisk University in 1966 and obtained permission from Robert Hayden, Melvin B. Tolson, and Margaret Walker to use their poems in the developing *Broadside Series*. The sixth Broadside, for which

Randall requested Gwendolyn Brooks's permission to publish, was "We Real Cool." This initial group of six is called "Poems of the Negro Revolt."

Randall's idealism stirred Brooks. "My strongest motivations," he writes, "have been to get good black poets published, to produce beautiful books, help create and define the soul of black folk, and to know the joy of discovering new poets. I guess you could call it production for use instead of for profit" (*BSM*, 31). The books of poetry Brooks has published with Broadside, except for *Beckonings*, appear in hardcover as well as paperbound editions. Other than the two anthologies she edited, none exceeds twenty-four pages. The size permits ease of publication, a modest capital outlay, and reasonable prices. With flexible production, current issues can receive the immediate attention that originally spurred the rise of the broadside and pamphlet during England's Puritan Rebellion.

Broadside Press heightened the influence of the black press as a whole, an influence comparable to that of the black church. The newspapers had always expressed their reader's interests.[4] Drake and Cayton, for example, point out that only one-sixth of the *Chicago Defender* editorials from November 13, 1943 to March 25, 1944, pertained to the war, and only two were bona fide "war editorials" (406-9). Nearly half examined national political issues important to Negroes; the rest concerned local topics.

Responding to this need and the need of black writers to be heard, Broadside Press expanded too quickly for its modest resources. Randall relinquished control for several years in the late seventies, then resumed his position in the eighties. Esteemed as a poet himself, in 1981 he was named the first Poet Laureate of Detroit.

Riot

The murder of Martin Luther King in Memphis, Tennessee, on April 4, 1968, was followed by a week of rioting in black ghettoes throughout the country. Chicago experienced one of the most severe outbreaks. On April 11, the Civil Rights Bill, which banned racial discrimination in housing, was hastily passed. In the same month, Haki R. Madhubuti (then don l. lee), as editor of

Black Expression, a Chicago magazine, commissioned Brooks's poem "Riot." The book's epigraph from Henry Miller appears in white print on black. Miller, in 1944, saw riot as a tragic possibility in Chicago. His musing on the Negro's continuing friendship for whites "no matter what we do to him" initiates the text's dual concern: blood-guilt and caritas.

Riot is described in the contents as "A Poem in Three Parts." It comprises "Riot," "The Third Sermon on the Warpland," and "An Aspect of Love." The first section's epigraph from Martin Luther King anticipates the political content and implies, by authorship, a religious theme: "A riot is the language of the unheard." The first two poems or subpoems are directly political; the third, indirectly so. "Riot" depicts "John Cabot, out of Wilma, once a Wycliffe," and the rioting blacks. (Brooks prefers the pronunciation of Wycliffe as "wik' lif," the short *i*'s reinforcing Wilma.) The poem is written in an objective/subjective mode (distinct from the empathy of *style indirect libre*), one that might be called "third person subjective." In Brooks it often accompanies the didactic and satiric (cf. "The Lovers of the Poor") and lends Cabot an almost Dickensian dimension. Cast into pentameter, his archetype serves Brooks formally—as the ballad already has—to contain powerful feelings and to make into myth.

"The Third Sermon on the Warpland" employs quotation differently than the First Sermon, where the composite voice addresses a congregation, "My People." Here, sermonic utterance of the "Black Philosopher" and a maxim from a past "White Philosopher" suggest a kind of dialogue by quotation. The tone, also, has shifted from encouragement and exhortation to anger. Third person (objective and subjective) orders narration, recessing Brooks's own prophetic voice. The Black Philosopher further removes the poem from the previous two Sermons by his bitter epilogue.

Yet ties of "The Third Sermon" with *In the Mecca* remain close. Characters from "The Blackstone Rangers" appear, newly developed. The third subpoem, "An Aspect of Love," relates thematically to *In the Mecca*. And of the three sections (30, 102, and 25 lines, respectively), the second extends over ten pages, conveying movement and agitation, and carrying forward the cinematographic technique of "In the Mecca."

Intricate, richly allusive, "Riot" lattices imagery and concepts through its central figure, John Cabot, archetypal bigot and snob. His typology and tastes (Jaguar, art objects, the best food and liquor) strategically mirror his own stereotyping. "John Cabot, out of Wilma, once a Wycliffe, / all whitebluerose below his golden hair," categorizes him as flag-wrapped American WASP (white Anglo-Saxon Protestant), and wryly if not mischievously relates him to the author of the epigraph, Martin Luther King. John Wycliffe was an English forerunner of the Protestant Reformation, later led by Martin Luther in Germany. Although he died naturally, Wycliffe is considered a martyr because, in 1415, his body was dug up according to the wishes of Pope Martin V, and burned. John Cabot, a name synonymous from Colonial times with prominent settlers of Massachusetts, was a fifteenth-century Genoese navigator who, interestingly, had visited Mecca. He was commissioned by Henry VII of England to find a passage to India. Thus the three Johns are linked, the contemporary one parodic of those who were brave, adventurous, and righteous. "Wycliffe" is an especially just reference, his firm anti-Church-establishment position a foil to the protagonist's ruling-class mentality. The "General Prologue" to Wycliffe's translation of the Bible (1384) reads: "This Bible is for the Government of the People, by the People, and for the People" (cf. reference to the Gettysburg Address in the Don Lee stanza of "In the Mecca").

Contrasts also implement the "failed religion" theme, already noted in "In the Mecca," opposing the bigot's corrupt Christianity to integrity of the past. Thus the first line, with fine compression, assigns the subject his unheroic attributes. The phrase "out of Wilma," moreover, suggests terminology of the stable. Brooks's only comment to me on the name "Wilma" inferred an elevated social connotation (like the Chicago suburb Wilmette), but the alternate reference is not unfamiliar to her.

The spirits of prophetic Amos and Way-out Morgan preside implacably over Cabot's portrait. Their foretold "blood bath" and "Day of Debt-pay" arrives in an apocalypse of fire, smoke, and destruction—the "fire next time" which the Lord promised Noah, in the words of the Negro spiritual.[5] Corruption and perversion of Christianity, the "failed religion" theme—actually that of a failed humanity—appear in Cabot's vain cries to God, "Don't let It

touch me! the blackness! Lord!" When it does, skepticism attaches to his "old averted doubt." At point of death, nevertheless,
he calls out, "Lord! / Forgive these nigguhs that know not what
they do," parodying Jesus' words upon the Cross, "Father, forgive
them; for they know not what they do" (Luke 23:24). An incidental
irony (also noted by Shaw): Cabot's initials are those of Jesus
Christ.

Antithesis figures largely in the imagery. Cabot's accusation
"Gross. Gross. *Que tu es grossier*" ("How gross you are") which
Brooks intends as his judgment of the scene and the rioters, may
well be observed of Cabot himself. "*Grossier*" derives from the
French *gros*, meaning corpulent or coarse. Coupled with the
"nourished white" of his skin and/or attire, "gross" emphasizes the
rich food and rich life Cabot has enjoyed ("the kidney pie at
Maxim's, / the Grenadine de Boeuf at Maison Henri"). The impoverished blacks symbolically confront these luxurious images
with "pig foot, chitterling, and cheap chili," mounting their ruggedly simple food against his spiritual coarseness. In one sense,
opposition levels both classes; in another, it reverses them. There
is crudity even in Cabot's appeal "to any handy angel in the sky."
Of course the plea to God is raised in extremis, and the poet's
sarcasm leans heavily.

Triadic structures permeate the imagery—Cabot/Wilma/Wy-
cliffe; whitebluerose; pig foot/chitterling/cheap chili—and recur.
Heavy alliteration weights the hauteur, the posturing of Cabot
images and their touch of French affectation. Cabot is anything
but heroic; the stylistic device obliquely prefigures the perverse
heroic of the mob. Yet the dominantly iambic pentameter announces blank verse, potentially a heroic meter. Despite random
and slant rhyme, however, it suggests the conventional quality of
Cabot and ironically presses him to a typological grid. Brooks uses
capitalization for satiric emphasis; "Grandtully (which is The Best
Thing That Ever Happened to Scotch)" suggests an advertising
slogan. Cabot's portrait emerges: received ideas, tastes, beliefs,
snobbery and prejudice, the vulgar pastiche of a class.

As victim and murderers converge, cause and effect blur into
broken glass, smoke, and fire. Beyond God's apocalyptic ire lies
the subject: blood-guilt, its origin, consequences, and cure.
Cabot retains his blasphemous assumption of primacy as Son of

God. His last words, parodic of Jesus, signal a lack of insight or humility and touch his final outcry with grisly humor.[6]

The rioters, frenzied and blindly raging, resemble agents of the Furies. "Riot" introduces the matter of blood-guilt in a clear, spare manner, analogous to that of Aeschylus in his triology *The Oresteia*, which studies the curse on the House of Atreus. In Aeschylus, the idea, religious or moral, coheres; in Brooks, typology serves. Both writers implicitly ask, "How, by what shall I live?" and answer.

"The Third Sermon on the Warpland" carries an epigraphic definition of "Phoenix" (from Webster's) as a bird in "Egyptian mythology" or religion. African ancestry sparks the poetic conception, mainly of "the Black Philosopher," who discusses the heritage of slavery and present bondage. The Black Philosopher is a near-composite of Brooks, Lerone Bennett, Jr., and Chancellor Williams, whose *The Destruction of Black Civilization* the poet admires.[7] Discussing the book, Williams notes: "I use the term African and Black interchangeably. . . . Because I'm talking about one race—the African race."[8] Pan-Africanism becomes increasingly patent in the later Brooks. "I call myself an African," she states.[9]

Shifting from "Riot" to a setting that recalls "Spaulding and Francois," the first stanza (a lyrical tercet like that beginning "In the Mecca," but unrhymed) broaches the ironic mood and free verse of the poem. The opening's gentle mockery dramatically succeeds the violence of "Riot":

> The earth is a beautiful place.
> Watermirrors and things to be reflected.
> Goldenrod across the little lagoon.

The Black Philosopher tells his unseen audience that "our chains are in the keep of the Keeper," less a reference to the Lord as keeper, as in "the Lord bless thee and keep thee" (Num. 6:24), than an evocation of "the day when the keepers of the house shall tremble" (Eccles. 12:3) or of the keeper who maintains in service or bondage. He remarks that "Our chains" are kept "in a labeled cabinet / on the second shelf by the cookies, / sonatas, the /

arabesques . . . , " (cf. storage of honey and bread in the third sonnet of "Gay Chaps at the Bar").

Juxtaposed allusions to European and Islamic culture and the cookies set white culture and black enslavement within the context of consumer goods, which includes the pacifying cookies—or crumbs—if one takes the image a step further. "Arabesques," besides alluding to Arab culture (ipso facto "exotic," like blacks), refers to a decorative, precarious ballet posture in which the body bends forward on one leg with the corresponding arm forward and the other arm and leg backward. In a framework reflecting sermonic scriptural quotation and discussion, the first line recalls Psalm 19, "The heavens declare the glory of God; and the firmament showeth his handiwork." The redundant construction of Psalm and tercet also relates the two. David's dedication of most Psalms to "The Chief Musician" echoes in the sonata reference and the Black Philosopher's invitation to the audience to hear "the remarkable music—'A Death Song For You Before You Die.' " The listeners, if not distracted by "cookies," would make music, "the *black*blues." He calls for action.

The poem cuts to West Madison Street where "Jessie's Kitchen," featuring "Jessie's Perfect Food," is empty. As in later work ("In the Mecca"), burning imagery holds a creative force, a new aesthetic. "Crazy flowers / cry up across the sky, spreading / and hissing *This is / it.*" Synaesthetic, the "cry" of the flowering flames perfectly realizes the riot as "the language of the unheard."

On the next page (sts. 4-5), six lines spill over into eight, presenting additional concrete images of men running and stealing. The poet enters to comment on their choice of records: eschewing Bing Crosby for Melvin Van Peebles's "Lillie" ("Lillie Done the Zampoughi Every Time I Pull Her Coattail," in the album *Br'er Soul*), racially selective plunder that distinguishes them from vandals. The following page (sts. 6 and 7) resumes the irony with "A clean riot is not," explaining in concentrated images ("long-stomped, long-straddled, BEANLESS") its political, social, and economic causes. The rioters steal a radio and pause to listen to black musicians. An easy listing of names ("James Brown / and Mingus, Young-Holt, Coleman, John") emphasizes rapport between poet and rioters, implying that culture and audience are separated only by economics.

"However, what / is going on / is going on" (st. 7), reminiscent of the opening tercet, reverses the initial sermonic procedure by folowing commentary with text. It also features the typical syncopation of black music by the line break after "what" (cf. "We Real Cool," chapter 5). Conventional alignment would have placed "what" at the beginning of line 2, thereby regularizing the rhythm. The subtle grading marks Brooks's primary attention, as she puts it, to "sound and sense."

The next page (sts. 8-10) begins with the word "Fire" set alone on the line. The poet remarks that the rioters are "lighting candles in the darkness," introducing the White Philosopher's words, "It is better to light one candle than curse the darkness."[10] Brooks's candles "curse" as the rioters themselves fiercely illuminate. The candle image transforms Big Bessie's insufficient "candles in the eyes" and the "Don Lee" stanza of "In the Mecca."

The riot fires recall the library burning in *Paterson*, Williams's pronouncement, "Fire burns; that is the first law."[11] He refers to Heraclitus' dialectical view of change as essential reality. For the pre-Socratic, fire is a constant, single process: "The way up and way down are one." Williams similarly embraces the creative elements of destruction: wind, fire, flood. He targets Eliot and Pound for adumbrating present culture with the past and prophetically intones, "So be it," while the library burns. An oppressive emblem, it is consumed in a spontaneous combustion of the imagination.

The horror of Williams's fire, paradoxically, lies in conception more than fact. It is mainly the poet's skill and emotive power (especially in Book III, 1, beginning, "I love the locust tree") that make us care. Brooks's fire, historic, is physically embedded in emotive images. Though we know little about the rioters, they have a literal presence for us.

Stanzas 9 and 10 present "The Law": "GUARD HERE, GUNS LOADED." Balance, emphasized by comma and alliteration, suggests a ready stance. Announcing the police car(s), stanza 10's unilinear disjoining hastens movement across the page in long vowels and diphthongs: "The Law comes sirening across the town." The next page (sts. 11-14) cuts to three closeups. A dead "Motherwoman," a casualty, receives a homely eulogy. Her vernacular apotheosis follows deeper into the scene: "That was a gut gal." Next, we glimpse a twelve-year-old rioter, Yancey, who triumphantly rejects "Your deathintheafternoon" with "kill 'em, bull!" Invoking Hemingway's tribute to bullfighting, *Death in the Afternoon* (1932), again spurns white values, although some whites would share Yancey's identification with the bulls.[12] Finally, like a latter-day Marcus Garvey, the Black Philosopher urges "a blackless America."

Brooks continues her tact of alternating subjective and ironic narration with objective. Alone on the opposite page, a quatrain tersely mentions the death of nine people. Many rumors chased around Chicago at the time. The *Sun-Times* advertised a special number to telephone, reproduced in the poem: " 'Rumor? check it at 744-4111.' "

"A Poem to Peanut" (st. 16, next page) eulogizes Richard "Peanut" Washington, the young man who observed in an epigraph to *In the Mecca*, "There is danger in my neighborhood." He is a Blackstone Ranger, a gang leader highly regarded among his peers as "Endorsement" and "Affirmation," Brooks notes, in addition to her acknowledgment of him in the poem, "A Signature. A Herald. And a Span." Peanut is a "Signature" or sign, identity of change. As "Herald," he is a quasi-religious emblem. As "a Span," he is youth joining past and present to the future after the riot. Emotionally and physically he spans hell (st. 6) to the heaven of the phoenix that will rise (st. 18). The capitalizations indicate elevation into the heroic. Responsible, "This Peanut will not let his men explode." Nor will the other leaders.

The Trinitarian motif figures importantly. Brooks reintroduces "Bop, Jeff, Geronimo" from "The Leaders" in "The Blackstone Rangers." She drops "Disciplines" for "Disciples" (the latter mentioned in "Gang Girls") who, in their biblical-sounding "thousandfold," gather with the Rangers and their leaders. Viewed more closely and favorably than in the previous poem, the gangs *seem* disciplined. Brooks changes the name of Gene, a leader in the "Rangers" poem, to "Lover" in the Third Sermon. The name appropriates the Christian symbolism of this section and the caritas theme which operates in tension with blood-guilt. "Rico" and "Sengali," new names, add ethnic richness to the text. By the end of the stanza, the Rangers agree that rioting "AIN'T" all upinheah!" The last word, a Black English expression of the sixties, means "hip," "with it," smart or clever. The language stresses the young men's communality.

The Rangers are said to "pass the Passion over." (Note the transition from "the passionate noon" in "The Blackstone Rangers.") The riot becomes a tragic suffering. "But WHY do These People offend themselves?" (st. 17) evokes Pontius Pilate speaking of Jesus, "I find no fault in this man" (Luke 23:4). Brooks refers to those whites who, belatedly offering help, can understand neither the rioters' apparently self-punitive rage nor their own complicity. Pilate, too, rejected his guilt and washed his hands.

On the last page (sts. 18-20), the rhyming tetrameter couplet, unique in the poem except for repeated lines, serves as inscription: "Lies are told and legends made./Phoenix rises unafraid." Rising phoenix-like from despair, the people may organize themselves, even as Blackstone Rangers and Disciples. The Blackstones are raised here from "monstrous pearl" in "The Leaders" to their identity as *black stones,* hence associated with the rock and St. Peter. The Black Philosopher closes the poem with a moving tribute to the rioters, "the hurt mute" who, for a moment, "came to life and exulted." This image reverts to the epigraph from King.

The tripartite last line, "The dust, as they say, settled," numbers two, three, and two syllables, respectively, in a wryly Trinitarian touch. The settling dust evokes the words of God to Adam, "for dust thou art, and unto dust shalt thou return" (Gen. 3:19). Enduring beyond failure, the dust has affected life. "Settling," however, also denotes compromise (remember "the parents" in *Annie Allen*). Trinitarian symbolism, with God's Judgment in "Riot" partly redeemed by Disciples and Rangers, somberly approaches the concluding poem.

"An Aspect of Love, / Alive in the Ice and Fire / LaBohem Brown" refers to Robert Frost's famous poem "Fire and Ice,"[13] which compares the virtues of ice and fire in ending the world. They become love/hate symbols, needing and destroying each other. There are male-female connotations: conventionally aggressive (hostile, rapacious) fire versus passive ice (cf. Annie's "gloves of ice" in "intermission"). Frost's personalized apocalypse relates directly to Brooks's poem. While anticipating a redemptive sequel, she, too, retrieves the anagogic symbols for the concrete and personal. She merges classical and Christian themes with an implicitly feminist and egalitarian view. Caritas is to redeem apocalyptic judgment and wrath, blood-guilt, hatred, and sacrifice. But something falls short. One thinks of Pound mourning over his lifetime's work, "I cannot make it cohere."[14] Brooks's poem coheres, but ironic wisps shy away from the union of matter and spirit, of salvation and purpose within a cohesive Black consciousness, the trilogic ideal of the whole.

Brooks's suggested persona, "LaBohem Brown," mildly refers to Puccini's heroine in *La Bohème*; Brown is the family name of Maud Martha. In the opera, Mimi quarrels with her lover and, upon their reunion, dies of consumption. The narrator's strong personality, however, implies a concealed disappointment. Brooks's autobiographical note on the poem reveals her motive for removing the first line, "It is the morning of our love," after Carolyn Rodgers called to report its appearance in a Rod McKuen poem in *Listen to the Warm* (1967). Brooks notes that hers was written before McKuen's was published, as witnessed by the dated manuscript version, reproduced in the hardcover edition of *Riot*. She concludes, "Such a horror is every writer's nightmare. Poets, doubt any 'inevitability!' " (*RPO*, 187).

An alba, the poem recalls John Donne's famous example, "The Sunne Rising," in which the lover also regrets the coming of day, and would chase away the "Busie old foole, unruly Sunne."[15] His relationship, complete, becomes the world. For Brooks, the outside world remains distinct. Donne establishes the woman as "all States," that he may be "all princes." Brooks makes the partnership equal, for she and the lover must be about the world's business. Both "are responsible props and posts," an advance over the woman's "leaning" position in *Maud Martha* and "The Blackstone Rangers."

In "An Aspect of Love" the narrator addresses her lover. Feelings, momentarily intense, illumine the couple. The "physical light" which they make in the room fulfills the Don Lee stanza of "In the Mecca." The clandestine pair cannot tarry, however, for "the world is at the window," and they must go their separate ways "down the imperturbable street." The lover, "a lion / in African velvet," seems tame, nonetheless, by virtue of the fabric.[16] The poet observes, somewhat querulously, "I cannot bear an interruption" in the "time of not-to-end." (Brooks considered changing "I" to "We," then decided not to.) Notwithstanding, dignity and sincerity of feeling come through as the lovers make the best of a difficult situation.

And yet the questions raised in the poem and the trilogy are not fully satisfied. Tantalizing possibilities remain: of resolution and renewal, of translating the metaphor of personal love into public action. Sharing goals, the lovers go out to labor separately. While comradely affection will survive like the phoenix of the previous subpoem, there has been no real apocalypse and, therefore, no new heaven and earth.

Riot is a work of complexity and vigor. The poet thrusts heroic, prophetic, and reportorial impulses from *In the Mecca* into immediacies of social chaos. A Trinitarian motif presides, roughly (and ironically) correlated as follows: Father, the Judgment of God visited upon the blasphemous earth and its emblem, John Cabot; Son, the Incarnation and Passion of the earthly riot; and Holy Ghost, the provisional caritas of "An Aspect of Love." Free verse supersedes the iambic pentameter of "Riot."

Through a wide range of personae, Brooks renders a sociohistorical situation. In so doing, she examines the national spirit, and, ultimately, its soul. The way, as she says in "In the Mecca," is "reportage and redemption." For her, to be truly reported, a riot must be compassionately understood. *Riot*'s unspoken "Why?" probes its own answer. Like Aeschylus, who ends his trilogy by subordinating justice to mercy in *The Eumenides*, Brooks takes vengeance and blood-guilt into the precincts of caritas, which transforms, however tentatively, into hope.

Family Pictures

Family Pictures collects eight poems (including a diptych and a triptych), which vary in voice, mood, and person and progress from indicative third-person objective to third-person subjective, second-person indefinite, first person, and imperative. Diction tends increasingly toward black and vernacular usage. Stylistically, even within the heroic, the book's dominant colloquial voice distinguishes a subcategory, the lesser or "plain" heroic. The contours of grand heroic, already discerned in the prophetic First and Second Sermons—alliteration and compounding, capitalization, parallelism and repetition, and the largely imperative mood—present a complex of the elevated style. Brooks, however, employs the nominative tendency in English to explore the possibilities of simple and informal language, along with other grammatical modifications (see especially "Speech to the Young" and "Young Africans").

The title *Family Pictures* recalls Walter Bradford's comment in "The Wall": "She / our Sister is." Conceiving the Black Nation as an extended family sustains the "newish" Brooks and her interpretation of Black consciousness.[17] Her lively family album represents children, political activists, theoreticians, youth workers, artists, preachers, lovers, and parents. It is dedicated to Lerone Bennett: "Mind, heart, spirit. / 'An essential sanity, black and electric.' " (See the Alfred balcony section in "In the Mecca.") The historian makes sound proposals for changes in American society and for black unity to achieve them.[18]

"The Life of Lincoln West" Brooks calls "an identity poem." Originally a prose piece, it was mentioned in early correspondence between Brooks and Lawrence (EL/GB, March 10, 1954). The editor's interest rekindled Brooks's own to develop the vignette into a longer work, but the project was abandoned. The story remained as published until it was reshaped for the Broadside volume.[19] Lincoln West offers a touching parable of the ugly duckling, although he never turns into a swan. At school he is looked upon as a monstrosity. Among his family he fails to ingratiate himself with his father. His indomitably loving and gentle nature, however, apparently registers his mother's benign neglect and nurturing acceptance.

One day at a downtown movie, a white man discovers Lincoln and loudly exclaims to his companion:

> "Black, ugly, and odd.
> You can see the savagery. The blunt
> blankness. That is the real
> thing."

Lincoln's mother begins an angry defense, then breaks off and takes her son home. But the boy consoles himself that, ugly or not, he is authentic, unique, "the real thing." Here, too, his mother's protection supplies an understated yet signal value. Lincoln's emotional strength becomes a paradigm. Difference fosters his identity which, in its painful context, defines his character. The story also draws a parallel between the stereotype thinking of the whites (spiritual kinfolk of John Cabot) and the conventions of beauty accepted by whites and blacks alike.

The prose and poetic versions of the tale are nearly identical. The transition involved a minimum of changes; Brooks arranged the prose as free verse. Even the paragraphs correspond with most of the stanzas. Since the original text is poetically spare and vivid, it transposes easily. The last line, "It comforted him," is strengthened by dropping the line following in the prose, "For almost four years it comforted him."

The child's "branching ears," "pendulous lip," and "great head" suggest Abraham Lincoln's physiognomy. The Great Emancipator's surname provokes a similar irony in "of DeWitt Williams on his way to Lincoln Cemetery," which also couples the president's name with the notion of Blackness.[20] "West" lends further irony as a putative symbol of opportunity—although the association for Native Americans would probably differ. The portrait—detailed, compassionate—staunchly inaugurates the gallery. The only poem in past tense (except for the beginning of "Paul Robeson"), it expresses a contemporary parable for the whole. Self-esteem and self-acceptance, solidarity and mutual respect are what the book is about. This is the larger significance of "The Life of Lincoln West" and its placement at the head of the volume. It quintessentially interprets the slogan "Black is Beautiful" as attitude and action and introduces a unity of vision for present and future.

"Young Heroes" is a triptych addressed "To Keorapetse Kgositsile (Willie)," a South African poet; "To Don at Salaam" (don l. lee); and to "Walter Bradford," the youth organizer from Chicago. Leadership exemplars, particularly for black youth, they inspire tributes in differing styles. The first subpoem employs an impressionistic reportorial mode with alliterative firming, repetition, and rhetorical incursions. The second and third are friendly appreciations, casual, conversational. Yet the "Don" poem, mainly in first person, is a lyric; the "Walter," mainly in second person, hews to the alliterative, epithet-making compounds of heroic genre.

These differences enrich the pieces as a group. The first gives artistic, historical, and polemical depth, with its references to aesthetics and education, political struggle, genocidal attacks on Black leadership ("Medgar Malcolm Martin and Black Panthers"), and the unsung "Susie. Cecil Williams. Azzie Jane." It begins with the exiled poet who, like the title of his poem and book, *My Name Is Afrika* (1971), to which Brooks wrote an introduction, symbolizes the homeland of Black culture. The second conveys an image of peace ("salaam" meaning "peace" in Arabic) within the self and its earthly task. "Salaam" in the title meaningfully recalls the closing of Madhubuti's introductions to two of his volumes, "As-Salaam-Alaikum," and its use of Arabic, invoking, by way of Swahili, his Pan-African views.[21] Haki Madhubuti means "precise justice" in Swahili. Earnest about his own leadership, he encourages the future heroic role of his students.

The third subpoem concerns practical application of the will to struggle, exemplified in the first, and the spiritual and theoretical ardor in the second. Walter Bradford emerges as a man of solid merits, pragmatic, dedicated, a worker in the social field of the young, specifically the Blackstone Rangers. Brooks focuses upon his qualities of leadership among the alienated who may still be fruitfully reclaimed, for themselves and for society. The three modulations in Brooks's "strategy" (in Kenneth Burke's terminology)[22] for presenting the heroic role give its "situation" dimensions of artistic perception and historical struggle, spiritual, theoretical, and intellectual form, and sturdy adaptability to daily life.

The Kgositsile poem quotes his philosophy of art and life: "*Art is life worked with.*" The simple diction uses basic verbs and adjectives, the verbs mostly monosyllabic. Successive stanzas describe the subject looking, seeing, teaching. For him, looking and feeling cohere: "To look, he knows, is to involve subject and suppliant." As *seer*, he apprehends paradoxes of the existence he would teach us to look at sympathetically. At the end, diction precipitates into the colloquial with "every fella's a Foreign Country."

"To Don at Salaam" presents the subject leaning back in his chair, vibrantly at ease. Concrete images alternate with personal response in a flow of sound: long vowels and lines suggest relaxation; short lines compress comment. Lyrical repetition in the fourth stanza, "Sometimes in life / things seem to be moving / and they are not / and they are not / there. / You are there." adroitly emphasizes place and holds in contrast the solitude of "there" (l. 5) with the wholeness of the last sentence and its subject.

Concluding the trilogy, "Walter Bradford" ruggedly proclaims the heroic style in its conversational or "plain" version. Marked alliteration, metaphor, epithet, metonym, kenning-type compound—all the stylistic attributes appear. Images are powerful, uncluttered, interrelated. Concision rests on the vigorous monosyllabic and spondaic. The poem stresses Bradford's strength, resourceful and constructive. In the first stanza, the subject opens the door to life, admits the full "Wilderness," "Whirlpool" (again, Brooks's whirlwind image) or "Whipper" of existence. "Whipper" invokes slavery and the struggle for black equality. In the next stanza, Bradford, a kind of counter-Pied Piper, opposes "the Last Trombones of seduction." Eponymous "Walter-work," reclaiming the young, is expressed in the conclusion's tough compounding:

> brick-fitter, brick-MAKER, and wave-
> outwitter;
> whip-stopper.

The succinct "whip-stopper" blocks the "Whipper" at the door. Having moved from wilderness to orderly, useful growth, the poem continues to its final appraisal of Bradford as a "Tree-planting Man." The poet invites him, in a closing word, staunchly separate: "Stay."

Headed by "Young Heroes," "Young Africans" (spelled "Afrikans" in *To Disembark*) strides into an exuberant mood of the prophetic and grand heroic. The title indicates its Pan-African impetus of common struggle against economic and political bondage. The epigraph, "of the *furious*," describes those "Who take Today and jerk it out of joint." "Jerk" has both a harsh, contemporary quality and an obsolete, yet palpable reference to the stroke of a whip, a fine irony in this context. Dynamically fusing colloquial with standard and creative language, the power and seriousness of the verse uphold the level of grand heroic.

From third person (primarily) Brooks proceeds through indicative and imperative moods, addressing both the "Young Africans" and the reader/listener, and concludes in first person plural. The free verse, irregular line length, and flexibility of voice create an exciting alternation, a rhythm of statement and expansion or commentary, which rhetorically echoes the sermonic and chanted sermonic technique observed in the First and Second Sermons on the Warpland. Linguistically and prosodically, the poem is very rich. "Blacktime," "poemhood," "hardheroic," "leechlike-as-usual," and the less individual "milkofhumankindness" liberally use compounding. Skillful play of assonance and rhyme among *time, mind, kind, chime, fine, wily,* and *wines,* combine with alliteration, internal and slant rhyme, and repetition. Wordplay among *kind, milk,* and *mind* sharply directs toward a modification of values, of kindness to be esteemed only with its intelligent and purposeful direction.

Brooks's fine ear directs the robust sound mixtures and guides the eye toward precise emphasis. Observe stanza 3, for example:

> If there are flowers flowers
> must come to the road. Rowdy! —
> knowing where wheels and people are,
> knowing where whips and screams are,
> knowing where deaths are, where the kind kills are.

Dropping the comma between the two "flowers" achieves both speed and accentuation. The lines race and the breath must pause at "Rowdy!" Alliterated *r*'s and the diphthong in "Rowdy" after the long *o* of "road" boost the raucous energy of the word. Pausing, the eye and ear focus on harsh images foregrounded by the flowers. The stanza's alliteration, repetition, and parallelism converge powerfully in the oxymoron "kind kills." The image of beauty traverses horror, pain, death, and "Changes," toward regeneration. "Flowers" of youth and beauty must come out to the road of social engagement, joining their identity to aesthetics and morality.

A revised religion presides over the "milkofhumankindness" (Lady Macbeth's musing on her husband's potential weakness,

Macbeth (1.5.16)—which must become like "wily wine"—and over "our black revival, our black vinegar," suggestive of the cloth dipped in vinegar and given to Jesus on the Cross, and of the Resurrection. Moral values reorient from endurance toward opposition.

Action generates much of the poem's energy. Abstract concepts take active and jarring verbs, as in "Who take Today and jerk it out of joint." Cognitive verbs take active and concrete images, as in "knowing where wheels and people are, / knowing where whips and screams are." Structural images abound: *joint, underpinnings, Head, jagged, wheels, Changes, spiraling, hands, blood.* Even the raw material of verbal structure, Brooks's compounding, appears in the word "mega," a combining Greek form meaning "great." The line "Must be mega, must be main" refers to kindness. Used as a word, the prefix becomes a socially charged formal device, since "main" occurs frequently in the black English vernacular expression "main man," a favorite male friend or hero. Thus ancient and modern combine in the new mythos of heroic.

"Paul Robeson" honors the great bass-baritone who died in 1976 after a brilliant career. Radical politics brought him professional hardship in the United States. In literary order, he climaxes the list of heroes. Brooks describes his ageless qualities of dignity and perseverance. His "major Voice" is an "adult Voice." Brooks's "Family," although youth-oriented, includes maturity as well. The rhyming impulse of the verse, the internal rhyme and lyrical repetitions, and the incremental force and musicality of repeated long vowels and abundant diphthongs express the music of the subject.[23] Alliteration reinforces his heroic identity.

As a singer, Robeson refused to perpetuate the stereotype of black passivity and endless forbearance. "[F]orgoing Rolling River," the seventh line, critically refers, as does the next, to "Ol' Man River," a song with which his voice was early associated. The idea of life as an inexorable process sanctions the apathy that Robeson and Brooks came to abhor. Lines 8 and 9 offer an ironic stroke of iambic pentameter. Bearing in mind that the ninth line is the pivotal center of the seventeen, we read:

> forgoing tearful tale of bale and barge
> and other symptoms of an old despond.

Brooks balances the conventional meter into a sing-song rendition, while it suggests the trochaic ambivalence noted in "The Anniad." The balanced pairing of *t*'s and *b*'s in line 8 also contributes to the monotony. Framed within free verse, the metric from the past (together with the old-fashioned "despond") seems increasingly remote. When the singer warns at the close,

> . . . in music-words
> devout and large,
> that we are each other's
> harvest:
> we are each other's
> business:
> we are each other's
> magnitude and bond.

Brooks counters Robeson's spiritual message, which includes his communal political sympathies, against an egocentric, commercial society. Not without possibilities of resolution, abstract contends with concrete: "bond," something owed, also unites; "magnitude" of Robeson's "major Voice" represents the greatness of his soul; the bondage slavery imposed upon both slave and master seeds Black solidarity; commerce ("business") and agriculture ("harvest") meet within the spiritual, biblical coupling of sowing and reaping. In "magnitude and bond," openness and strength seem to inhere in the sounds themselves, even as the labials *m* and *b* are related and, together with liquid *r*'s, convey a tactile, unifying resonance. The poet's basic theme of caritas reappears through Robeson, his restorative art, "cool and clear / cutting across the hot grit of the day."

Leaving a socially disposed art for personal affection, "Women in Love" presents a diptych of two women: one shy and reserved, the other vivacious, romantic, and apparently confident, although both share feelings of insecurity. They hold male-inspired views of their deficiencies. The first fears that she disappoints her man; the second, that whatever she may give will be insufficient. "Estimable Mable," an epigraphic couplet, implies by its formality the woman's essential ("estimable") worth. The rhyme surprises the ear. A heroic couplet, its surprising presence (and rhyme) offers an amusing footnote to the heroic poetry in the volume. Punning on "Mable," "-mable," and "able" contributes to its wit.

The second poem, "Love You Right Back," a personal lyric, rare in Brooks's later work, replies to Dudley Randall's *Love You*, dedicated to her.[24] Employing random and slant rhyme, with a refrain, the poem displays the heroic characteristics of the preceding poems. Fully capped lines end each of the two stanzas, "WILL BE NOT ENOUGH!" The inversion "BE NOT" fortifies the stanza's potent metaphor: mind and body as a human printing press. Through alliteration and phrasal parallels, the gathered energy boosts the capitalized words. These read like a banner headline, so that the public image of the press, with "symbols and seals," registers in the typography and rhythm.

Following the social and private aspects of caritas, "Song: / The Rev. MuBugwu Dickinson / Ruminates behind the Sermon" addresses the religious and updates an early Brooks poem. In "the preacher: ruminates behind the sermon," the subject reviews his own religious beliefs and thinks it must be lonely, sometimes, to be God because "Nobody loves a master." Twenty-five years later, the Protestant minister has acquired an odd ("-Bugwu" suggests insect and vernacular *bug* or bother) though stylishly African-sounding given name, keeping the Anglo-Saxon one, and has become even more skeptical. Not yet an activist, he is nonetheless aware that "Agitation is general all over America" and the world (cf. James Joyce's "snow was general all over Ireland," in "The Dead"). He counsels, "sleep through the morning three-thirties of the world," i.e., avoid facing the current revolutionary upheavals that precede an implied dawn, and he satisfies his congregation with the palliatives they crave like "a braver beer." Polonius with insight, he knows that the command "Be good . . . will not suffice because it / is neither heat nor ice," a reference to Frost (see "An Aspect of Love"). In apocalyptic times, the minister ruefully promotes the passive Sunday School lesson, which freely translates as: Sit still and don't rock the pew. The "Song," with its modified verse repetitions, ironically suggests in context the chanted sermon and African/African American call and response.

The Rev. Dickinson himself invites comparison with Gabriel in "The Dead." *Dubliners,* in which the story appears, is important for Brooks. Both characters retain their conventional roles yet see beyond them. The apocalypse envisioned by Gabriel, snow "faintly falling, like the descent of their last end, upon all the living and the dead," results from a new perception of love and truth. His shocked recognition and frustrated affection resemble Brooks's minister, who cannot reach his congregation. Dickinson foresees that social tremors will become universal, eventually reaching "that Moon" on which the American astronauts landed in 1969.

"Speech to the Young. / Speech to the Progress-Toward," dedicated to the poet's two children, Nora Brooks Blakely and HenryBlakely III, ends the volume as it begins: with youth. Emphasizing character defined by struggle, the poem features the compounds of Brooks's heroic style along with its capitals, alliteration, and spondaic vigor. The "down-keepers, / the sun-slappers, / the self-soilers, / the harmony-hushers" imaginatively use simple words, reordered into lively figures. Rhyme and slant rhyme enhance tight control. The didactic imperative combines with the colloquial tone in phrasing like "Live not for Battles Won. / Live not for The-End-of-the-Song. / Live in the along," which lacks the freshness of the beginning. This risk of facile rhyme and sentiment the poet has courted by her deliberate quest for ease of communication. As noted, she deems this goal clarity rather than simplicity and finds it in compositions like the popular song lyrics of Dory Previn.[25]

Family Pictures may be placed stylistically midway between *Riot* and *Beckonings*. It carries forward the heroic mood of *In the Mecca*, employs novel modes and continuities of strength with earlier forms, and reaffirms Brooks's thematic system. Rhetorical urgency veers away from allusion and the occasional, recondite image in previous work. While the poet clearly demonstrates the effectiveness and creativity of colloquial language, at times when used chiefly as communication it jeopardizes the heroic and, in other modes, risks weakening the verse. Brooks's vitality, focused on youth and the future, surges toward the reader, imbuing the heroic poems with ethical and social values. *Family Pictures* articulates Black consciousness as a family unit.

Aloneness

Aloneness is a children's book, less ambitious than *Bronzeville Boys and Girls*. A gently reflective poem of fifty-one lines, it projects a child's experience of solitude. The epigraph quotes Brooks's daughter Nora, who early had distinguished between loneliness and aloneness, enjoying the latter. Black-and-white illustrations accompany verses in blue script, the color absent from the second printing, to Brooks's regret. The pen-and-ink drawings by Leroy Foster present an appealing little black boy.

Feelings and sense impressions define the child's solitude. Brooks employs the indefinite "you" to merge with his narration and the tranquil copulatives of present tense. She posits loneliness as progressive, delicious at first, then decreasingly so, like a small red apple one is eating. The images are child-sized and true. Beginning with a child standing alone, "loneliness means" introduces a list of negative impressions, social and physical, the latter of color, sound, and taste. The imagined color of loneliness, "gray," has been discussed here (e.g., *Maud Martha*, *The Bean Eaters*) as a recurrent symbol of depression and death. Transition to positive "aloneness" begns with taste, the small apple, "sweet and round and cold and for just you," lexical inversion accentuating the recipient.

An instructive comparison is offered by Williams's famous poem about the plums in the refrigerator, "so sweet and so cold."[26] His self-imposed Objectivist limits, abandoned in *Paterson*, confine this early piece, where he tries to focus upon the object per se. Brooks's figurative language, on the other hand, relates a concept (aloneness) to a percept (the apple). The psychology summons Ezra Pound's definition of the image as "that which presents an intellectual and emotional complex in an instant of time."[27] Jerome Rothenberg's "deep image" later confronts limitations of the perceptual approach.[28] Clearly, the distance between text and reader is effectively bridged by emotive means, elsewhere called "sympathetic identification."[29]

Let it be noted that citation of Williams at several points in this study does not imply any "influence" by him on Brooks, who objects to any comparisons drawn between her work and his.

There are similarities, however, in attitudes toward popular diction and humanist orientation.

From the pivotal apple, Brooks turns to the image of a pond. Aloneness is "like loving a pond in summer," a simile that grasps the experience of a place and time. The water is "a little silver-dark, and kind." The child loves the silver in it and, significantly, the darkness. His world of feeling animistically binds him to what he sees. Just as he can love a "kind" pond, he can love people. In a fine lyric passage, the pond's meaning reaches him:

> Rest is under your eyes
> and above your eyes
> and your brain stops its wrinkles
> and is peaceful as a windless pond.

Aloneness sometimes vanishes into the rhythm of the "pulse and nature." The contemplative act provides a core of sanity, to be reinforced in traveling outward. Giving the child mental space as a basic living space reveals the ground of mental growth.

The poem ends with a dialectical conception of aloneness, "Whose other name is Love." Open to nature, in touch with its own yearnings and impressions, the self respects its reality. There, in the fruition of sensitive maternal listening and the assurance of being heard, even its deepest solitude escapes isolation.

Riot and *Family Pictures* carry forward the hopeful announcements of *In the Mecca* and prophesy a salvageable future. Together with *Aloneness*, all bespeak the presiding maternal concern of Brooks, who generalizes the warmth of a mother on to her people. Her ability to think and feel as a child, a rioter, a heroic figure mark a psychic extension. She has not "put away childish things" but carries past, present, and future together as a wholeness, "an essential sanity" that ballasts and moves her work steadfast into open waters.

9

Later Works

While *Riot* and *Family Pictures* crest the progressive mood of the Civil Rights Movement, "In Montgomery"[1] describes something new. Ever "a Watchful Eye, a Tuned Ear, a Super-Reporter," Brooks was commissioned by *Ebony* magazine in 1971 to report on black life in Montgomery, Alabama. Her startling prescience of the new decade supports Pound's view that poets are "the antennae of the race."

The seventies retreated from the activist sixties. Revelations of government corruption, climaxed by the resignation of President Richard Nixon; the end of the Vietnam War; a weariness with politics coupled with satisfaction by modest gains in civil rights; concentration upon daily needs—jobs; a nostalgic and escapist mentality; these factors influenced the national mood and black life. Referring to the seventies as "a decade of American disillusionment,"[2] Russell Baker satirically cites public boredom and frustration (in both one reads anger) regarding current scandals. Specific changes, some minor (such as the return to hair-straightening among black women) and some major (such as the decision by the Johnson Publishing Company to suspend *Black World* [1977] because of falling circulation), Brooks found significant and disturbing. Dismantling of the magazine's intellectual and spiritual leadership reflected a general trend, at least on the surface, toward conformity. Brooks's thematic responses, expressed through verse journalism, the heroic/prophetic, and children's literature, augment her ongoing interests, evident since *A Street in Bronzeville.*

"In Montgomery"

"In Montgomery" ranks with "In the Mecca" as one of Brooks's most serious and sustained efforts. Its 677 lines are exceeded only by "In the Mecca" 's 807. The main artistic problem for Brooks was the manner of approaching the material. Accompanied by Moneta Sleet, Jr., a prominent black photographer, she was sent to interpret the contemporary social milieu in what was once the scene of historic civil rights agitation.

While "In the Mecca" underwent radical changes over a period of years, "In Montgomery," the labor of several weeks, was mainly the product of three days' intensive effort. During the week of her stay in Montgomery, she retired to the Croydon Hotel, where she sequestered herself for seventy-two hours, thinking through and laboring over the material she had collected. To gather the data she had addressed strangers at streetcorners, bus stops, and elsewhere in the town, questioning them about past and present. Reluctant to consider the work a poem, she feels she has extended the limits of journalism. It seems equally just, however, to conclude that verse journalism has furthered the limits of poetry.

Brooks maintains the prophetic voice and the grand heroic style, largely sermonic and often in the chanted genre, combining their black and white elements through a montage of interviews, sense-impressions and observations, reporting, and an excellent photographic coverage with captions supplied by the poet. The color photos illustrate the text and, together with Brooks's sensitive comments and *Ebony*'s attractive layout, capture the poetic vision. No analysis can re-create the visual impact of divinely tragic comedy, with photographs instead of Gustave Doré illustrations. In place of Dante's guide Virgil, however, we have the camera eye of the poet/prophet confronting the wilderness.

Brooks introduces her first-person account with quick impressions of Montgomery. The free verse rhymes minimally and at random. In the opening couplet,

> The first thing I saw at Court Square corner
> was black men, lifting that bale. . . .

visual referents merge with aural ones: the syncopated rhythm; the song "Ol' Man River" where the blacks "lift that bale," accepting servitude. (Remember Paul Robeson "forgoing Rolling River.") The two lines, heavily spondaic, balance the stresses of "black men" with "that bale."

In stanza 2 the poet reflects upon the past of the Civil Rights Movement, the great expectations of "civilrightsmen," whose sheathed anger "hit it out as hatchets with velvet on. . . . With sometimes the hatchets hacking through." The stanza is paragraph indented, as is the penultimate one, sharpening the parallel between opening and closing couplets.

"White white white is the Capitol," gleaming in the photographs, is stanza 3's opening image, intensified by omission of commas. Alternating commentary with observation, contrasting long past (slavery, Confederacy), near past (civil rights), and present (reactionary, retrogressive), Brooks's method clearly details "the special poetic grammar"[3] of the chanted sermon—its repetition and parallel syntactic structures, the influence of the Bible, gospel songs, the "English of the American South," and black English vernacular. The chanted sermon, moreover, shares important features with the heroic style, including the tendency toward Anglo-Saxon, alliteration, epithet, and strongly stressed rhythms. (See the introduction to the Sermons on the Warpland.)

Next, Brooks offers a wry, quasi-epical invocation to the muse. The work will "cite in semi-song / the meaning of Confederacy's Cradle" (st. 4). Her muse, however, is updated classical: the spirit and struggle of black people. She registers disappointment in stanza 6:

> I came expecting
> the strong young —
> up of head, severe,
> not drowsy, not in-bitten, not
> outwitted by the wiles of history.

The last two lines recall the title *The Ayenbite of Inwyt (The Remorse of Conscience)*, translation of a medieval French classic, a source for Geoffrey Chaucer's Parson's Tale in *The Canterbury Tales*. Sounds—harsh and strong, compounding, the simple yet subtle word-play (on "in" and "out"), and the suggestion of litotes ("not drowsy, not in-bitten," etc.) give an Anglo-Saxon flavor to this passage.

Brooks's incantatory repetitions, like Whitman's "syntactical parallelism,"[4] ally with music as much as sermon. Stanzas 5, 6, and 7 begin with "I came expecting"; stanza 8 replies with, "I did not come expecting. . . . " Following these lists, "Montgomery is a game leg. After such walking! . . . After such Talking! . . . after such Feeling" (st. 9) suggests call and response, an antiphonal structure noted as common to African music and Protestant lining-out of hymns and appearing in the blues. Stanzas 8 to 10 are the prophet upbraiding; stanza 11 reviews the religious background of the city's greatness. By stanza 12, "Leaning" and "Lostness" (from stanza 8) become capitalized; "Empty-stare / and Final-howl-of-the-wind and Dragging-flag and Whiner" are added, among other figures. "Leaning" and "Lostness," representing apathy, rise to highly charged metonymy, typical of the Brooks heroic insignia. (Cf. Maud Martha's and Mary Ann's "leaning"; "props and posts" in "an Aspect of Love.")

Transition at stanza 12 demonstrates Brooks's genius in orchestrating the sermonic, conversational, and reportorial. Beginning with "Yet / into what country shall any go / and find *no* Likely thing?" the biblical tone carries through the metonymic typology ("Leaning," "Lostness"), among whom "there were to find / Justin / and Leon and Mildred, Dolores Boateng," and others whose interviews appear in the poem. Thus the first eleven stanzas are introductory; the twelfth, a hinge; and from the thirteenth to the twenty-second, individual portraits of varying lengths comprise each stanza. Stanza 23, "Wanted: / The Fine Hand of God. . . . " hinges another transition to a panorama of people, the street scene, individual remarks, but now in glimpses that quicken toward the final section. At stanza 33, the poet herself joins the action: "I ride on a bus," where she sees a self-imposed segregation in effect. The irony lies, of course, in the history of the Montgomery Bus Boycott of 1955-56, begun by Rosa Parks, a black woman who sat down in the white section of a bus on December 1, 1955. Martin Luther King, Jr., organized the successful boycotting of public mass transportation in the city. The next stanza (34) is set in the Dexter Avenue Baptist Church, where King began his pastorate in 1954 and "gave the True Bread" to his people. Now, says Brooks, "It is served quietly / to 'The Beautiful People' of Montgomery. / Here is a hat made of red flowers." The sequence of hat (resonantly red and flowered), wigs, and neat, fashionable people, following the "True Bread" of King and the "quiet" serving of the bread by Murray Branch, the minister, provides a disingenuous view of the congregation as it sings "I Am Thine, O Lord (Draw Me Nearer)." Recall the people singing "Sunday hymns like anything" in Little Rock, in "The Chicago *Defender.*" "The Christian religion is a SINGING religion," observes Reverend Branch.

The several thematic strains converge past and present from stanza 34 through the close at 37. The stanzaic total, two years short of King's age when he was assassinated, implies curtailment of achievement. (Cf. discussion of the number 33 in "The Chicago *Defender.*") Brooks concludes in a couplet, "Martin Luther King is not free. / Nor is Montgomery," referring to his words of August 28, 1963, at the Lincoln Memorial. "Free at last" ends King's eloquent "I Have a Dream" speech, which extols American ideal democracy and world brotherhood. The phrase inscribes his marble tomb in Atlanta, also a capital, near the site of the Ebenezer Baptist Church, where he and his father carried on their ministry.

Having boarded the bus at stanza 33, Brooks has already prepared the final joining of religious, secular, and structural elements of the poem and its message. As "Super-Reporter" she tellingly selects and interprets facts. Describing the imperturbable young Justin, first black page in the legislature, she notes wryly that "the plaque on the wall at the entrance shakes a little." She sees, "at the top of a mountain of sand," a black youth "astride the Future!" and, with further symbolism, a brown dog lying dead in the middle of the street.

The Civil Rights Movement and advances and the forgiveness implicit in black overtures toward integration with whites ("This blackness forgave what it would not forget," stanza 11) invoke various biblical precepts. Saliently, Jesus' new commandment

"That ye love one another" (John 13:34) accompanies the whirlwind image, "They have sown the wind, and they shall reap the
whirlwind" (Hosea 8:7), importantly restored to its context. The
quotations remind of a mournful and angry God, remind that
Israel may still be redeemed by faith and that "Weeping may
endure for a night, but joy cometh in the morning" (Psalms 30:5).

Brooks tours "History City," interviewing the young and the
old: prominent citizens like E. D. Nixon, who organized the
Montgomery Improvement Association in 1955, and invited Martin Luther King to help lead the bus boycott; ordinary working
people; "bean-eaters" (st. 29). Nixon's impressions are dour. Noting the need for jobs, he feels the young are no longer interested
in politics. Devout Sallie Townsend believes social improvements
will continue. Leon Hall works with young people and hopes they
will seek education and organize themselves. Idessa Williams
feels that the "Great days" are over and Montgomery is dead. A
black member of the legislature, Thomas Reed, stresses the need
for leadership. Many reminisce nostalgically about the Boycott
days. Others, like Connie Harper, Justin's mother, work con-
structively in small ways. Most seem satisfied with minor gains;
few retain a combative spirit. Architectural serenity belies the
past of civil rights black-white confrontations. Richly mounted
color, sound, and speech, evoke the texture of Montgomery life.

The poetic voice of the Super-Reporter unifies diverse moods
and modes. And like the "Chicago *Defender*" newsman, who
expects to find demons in Little Rock, Brooks arrives with preconceptions that prove largely illusory. But while the *Defender* reporter represents his "Editor"/judge/Deity, Brooks embodies the
prophetic. Following the E. D. Nixon interview, she notes
ruefully: "Wanted: / The Fine Hand of God. / Marching Songs
for the People, in a / Town That Could Be (But Ain't) Your Own"
(st. 23).

Music and rhythm blend the sermonic/prophetic, reportorial,
and conversational strains. Typography also helps organize. Capitalization amplifies voice and slogans, like the sign carried by a
black man, "HELP KEEP MONTGOMERY CLEAN." The sign
obliquely recalls those which read, "I AM A MAN," carried by
Memphis sanitation workers in their 1968 strike. Captions for the
photographs are italicized; incidental boldface within the text

communicates emphasis and tone. Despite much literal tran-
scription, the interviews carry poetic rhythms. Even occasional
excesses—like the talky speech—seem exactly right. The main
speakers' insights and emotions animate the tableau into a self-
commenting text.

"In Montgomery" is a major work. Its verse journalism con-
structs reportage of a grand heroic order. Rhetorical and musical
repetitions from the chanted sermon bridge poetry and prose.
Contemplative, angry, inquiring, sorrowful, remonstrating, its
aggrieved prophecy vivifies a motley continuum of past and present. Like a restless wraith of the Civil Rights Movement, tracing
its faded purposes, Brooks wanders through sunny streets domi-
nated by the "White white white" Capitol. But Montgomery's
workers and doers, the subjects of her lengthiest interviews,
cannot energize the apathy, disguised and revealed in the daz-
zling light.

Report from Part One

Gwendolyn Brooks's poetic sensibility imprints her prose. Engagement with the present, the young, and the future liven her
unusual autobiography, remote from the retrospective norm. Dudley Randall helped organize the manuscript, which Brooks referred to in conversation with me as originally "a mess." But the
mixture of poetically compact reminiscence, observation, trav-
elogue, aperçus, reflection, commentary on her own poems,
excerpts from her book reviews, memorabilia, correspondence,
and an "autobiography" by her mother, Keziah Brooks, using her
daughter's persona, assembles a potpourri of alert vitality, sui
generis. It ends with a touching eulogy of the family dog, Fluffy,
who, in 1971, was the first of "Our Family" to die. "He made us all
kinder" (*RPO*, 215). "Reverence for life," in Albert Schweitzer's
phrase, taps the poet's religious wellspring.

Vigor, wonder, openness imbue Brooks's experience. Thus it
should not surprise that only about one-third of her material
specifically addresses the past. The remainder—a twenty-page
account of her first visit to Africa in 1971; interviews with Paul M.
Angle (1967), George Stavros (1969), and Ida Lewis (1971); notes
on published poems and miscellaneous items—stresses her re-

cent and current life and thought and becomes an urgent call to action.

World War II, so prominent in her poetry, seems puzzlingly absent, although the gap may partly reflect the *Black Metropolis* analysis of *Chicago Defender* editorials (see previous chapter). Nevertheless, Brooks regrets the omission, especially since a dear friend was killed in action (see dedication to *Annie Allen*). She plans to rectify this lacuna and others in a sequel.

The Tiger Who Wore White Gloves
or What you are you are

Brooks's first book with Haki Madhubuti's Third World Press is a work for children, dedicated to Nora, "THE FIRST TIGER," and to Henry Jr., "THE DELINEATOR." While *Bronzeville Boys and Girls* individually surveys the children of a community, *Tiger*, like *Aloneness*, is a single poem. The three differ in tone and style. *Aloneness*, meditative, is basically in free verse; *Tiger*, homiletic, returns to the rhyme of *Bronzeville Boys and Girls* and clips an insistent dimeter and trimeter pattern of rhyming couplets. Visually, *Tiger's* fully capped letters are often multicolored, tilted, and irregularly sized. Its bold graphics by Timothy Jones include illustrations that highlight the action. The nine-by-twelve-inch format frames the tiger who crouches on the cover. Couplets break and scatter through the drawings, sharing freshness with images and rhymes.

Tiger is a beast fable and represents, like the mock heroic of "The Anniad," Brooks's application of an older literary genre. It may be considered within the rich heritage of animal tales in African American folk literature, their subjects ranging from jungle animals to "Br'er Rabbit." Like beast fables, African tales are usually didactic. They offer a variety of objectives, including "strategies for survival."[5] Brooks's title implies human folly, a subject typical of the genre descended from Aesop, a semilegendary Greek slave, possibly African. Fables flourished during the Middle Ages and were particularly favored for sermonic use. The seventeenth-century interest in wit and satire was hospitable to the fable, notably those of the French poet Jean de la Fontaine. The form has always been popular; its multilevel content appeals to children and adults.

Brooks's tiger wears white gloves to be fashionable; companions shame his egregious behavior. The strength of the tiger accompanies his stripes, emblem of the lash, while his toenails extrude through the gloves. The theme is self-accceptance and pride. Yet a contradiction intervenes. Although the tiger would conform to an impractical, alien style, he is pressured to conform to "natural" group standards. One might argue that the group embodies principles of natural development, an Aristotelian sense of inherent purpose or *telos* or final cause. Just as "All men by nature desire to know,"[6] the purpose of a tiger may be determined by its qualities as a felid. Brooks writes: "IT'S NATURE'S / NICE DECREE / THAT TIGER FOLK / SHOULD BE / NOT DAINTY, / BUT DARING, / AND WISELY WEARING / WHAT'S FIERCE AS THE FACE. / NOT WHITENESS AND LACE!" Living creatures must develop their attributes and esteem them: the tiger qua tiger; the human qua human. As metaphor, the gloves represent phenomena like the return to hair-straightening which, for Brooks, resumes subservience to white values.

White gloves are ascribed to female behavior, "THE WAY IT ALWAYS WAS, AND RIGHTLY SO," a role restriction unpalatable to feminists. The illustrations support the linking of the gloves with white culture. Apart from the ludicrously attired tiger, only doll-like little white girls "WITH MANNERS AND CURLS" are so outfitted. In the group of active girls, one is black, riding on the back of a white child's tricycle, neither weaing gloves. The common association is with decorum and restraint, protection against grimy reality, and disguise (or withholding) of power.

Tiger's lesson in self-valuation will have special import for black children. As part of a minority with a history of repression in this country, they need to resist being overwhelmed by the dominant culture. White children will also find pleasure and profit in reading *Tiger*, even though a feminist might have reservations. Nevertheless, the book effectively serves its modest purposes.

Beckonings

This subdued-looking volume (brown and beige cover, parchment-colored paper) presents a heterogeneous collection of twelve poems, discussed here in their sequence. It begins with an

⸍ for the poet's late brother, Raymond Melvin Brooks, who ⸗⸗⸗⸗ in January 1974. He had served in World War II and was only fifty-five at the time of his death. His line drawing of his sister appears on the back cover of *Beckonings,* along with a quotation from Hoyt W. Fuller praising the poems. The poet is not happy with the inclusion of "Horses Graze" and "'When Handed a Lemon, Make Lemonade,'" realizing that neither suits the rest thematically. Both are excluded from *To Disembark.* She approves of "Horses Graze," however, as an independent poem.

"Raymond Melvin Brooks" sets the tone. Elegiac yet positive, its free verse links the poet's conversational and incantatory modes. Brooks describes a man whose warm relationships have chiefly articulated his creativity. His talent for "jeweling use and the usual" combines art with life in the union Brooks admires and applies. Celebrating his virtues, the poet indirectly mourns the truncated potential she confronts in the next poem and in the last.

"The Boy Died in My Alley," dedicated to an anonymous "Running Boy," allegorizes a tragic shooting in Brooks's neighborhood. First published in *Black Scholar,* the poem originates in separate incidents involving two black youths. One, Kenneth Alexander, a high honors student in Nora Blakely's Hirsch High School graduating class, was killed running from a policeman (*RPO,* 205). The other, a boy observed running in Ghana, 1974, was the subject of discussion between Brooks and Henry Blakely. Blakely felt that the child could be written about in his momentary pleasure, rolling his bicycle wheel along the road. Brooks disagreed, convinced that black poets should be "exhaustive," taking the whole life to its end, to distinguish the fate of blacks from that of whites. Both black youths, in their running, become symbols of "impulse, not achievement," she told me. The body of the Ghanaian boy will submit to its "collected disease and deprivation"; his life will end prematurely, unfulfilled, like Kenneth and the "Running Boy."

In the poem, a policeman investigating the victim's identity questions the poet/narrator. Unlike *To Disembark,* where each stanza of the modified ballad (except for the concluding couplet) takes a separate page, the simple, conventional sequence here seems more apt.

> The Boy died in my alley
> without my Having Known.
> Policeman said, next morning,
> "Apparently died Alone."

Taking no article, "Policeman" becomes typological; "Boy," also generically capitalized, becomes specific as well. (Capitalization summons Wordsworth's tragic "Boy of Winander" in *The Prelude*, Book V, 364-97, who died before the age of twelve.) "Boy," furthermore, a deprecating form of address sometimes used by whites, may allude ironically to a black man. The "man" in "policeman" echoes this linguistic counter, assuming the Black English definition as a white. The victim's cries of "Father!" "Mother! / Sister! / Brother" reinforce the impression of a youth.

Instead of reductively pitting oppressive society against the boy, Brooks places the opposition within her consciousness. By ignoring the "Shot," she "joined the Wild and killed him / with knowledgeable unknowing"; seeing him "Crossed," she "did not take him down." Urban-style detachment toward one who "ornaments my alley" turns to assumption of responsibility. Solitary martyrdom reddens the alley floor, announcing blood-guilt. The theme, personally intensified, reverts to *Riot*. Lyrical repetitions, compounding ("futurefall"), alliteration, and capitalization combine to give the poem heroic stature.

The attack on selfishness continues with "Five Men / Against the Theme / 'My Name is Red Hot. / Yo Name Ain Doodley Squat,' " dedicated to friends: Hoyt W. Fuller, Lerone Bennett, Jr., Dudley Randall, Haki R. Madhubuti, and Lu Palmer (a Chicago journalist). The quotation is a rhyme heard in games— often rope-skipping—of black children. Brooks's free verse scores childish egocentricity and eulogizes men whose work benefits black people. The first line directly attacks competitive egoism, which typifies capitalist society and the dominant white culture: "This is the time of the crit, the creeple, and the makeiteer." Here is the very process of vernacularizing. Alliteration, epithet, and incantatory repetitions heroically imprint the poem. "Our warfare," says Brooks, "is through the trite traitors" who perpetuate destructive beliefs in empty political promises; they are like children who repeat rhymes, ignorant of their social connotations. Compounding and imagery sardonically focus; witness "ice-committees" and "suburban petals." The poem ends with a repeated "We are thankful for steel" (contrasted with the "tin-foil" of the culture), omitted in the *To Disembark* revision (see below). Brooks mildly syncopates, ending four consecutive lines with "through" (like the epistrophic *Wes* of "We Real Cool"), emphasizing what must be overcome.

"To John Oliver Killens in 1975" laments the retreat from " 'black solidarity' " (diminished by quotation marks) and appeals for leadership to the brilliant novelist, paradigm of commitment to black unity: "John, / look at our mercy, the massiveness that it is not." (In *To Disembark*, the verse addresses "John Killens," the surname adding a near-oxymoron, and the opening stanza comes later.) "Mercy" alludes to the Hebrew meaning of his given name, "God is gracious." Killens, hailed in alliterative free verse of the heroic mode, is "a mender," a man in whom kindness is an "eye-tenderizer, a / heart-honeyer." The first compound may be the one questionable instance in Brooks's creative usage since, on the literal level, the image is strained. "Heart-honeyer," on the other hand, recalls Melville's reference to Plato as a "honeyhead." Prufrock's "I grow old . . . I grow old" lurks in the first stanza's "we / grow colder; we / grow colder. / See our / tatter-time."

"Steam Song" introduces other aspects of love. Its ironic inscription, "Hostilica hears Al Green," refers to the emotionally suasive style of the popular black singer. His voice mollifies the intense Hostilica. The "Song" boiling up the blood lets off the "steam" of the ballad. Black English appears in the invariant verbal form (it *sing*, it *make*, it *boil*). With *is* centered in its line, Hostilica declares, "My man is my only / necessary thing," a belief that Brooks emphatically does not share (Hull, 22). Invariant *be*, moreover, would have weakened the statement.[7]

"Elegy in a Rainbow" recalls childhood. Inscribed as "Moe Belle's double love song," the name invokes "Moe Belle Jackson" of the "Hattie Scott" sequence. Here, correspondence between the lost anticipation of Christmas and the intangible presence of the Black Nation suggests an emotional bridging between personal and social identities. The speaker asserts that closely examining Christmas past "might nullify the shine." (The sentiment parallels

Lamb and Keats at Benjamin Haydon's "Immortal Dinner," December 28, 1817, toasting with disapproval Sir Isaac Newton, whose *Optics* had supposedly destroyed the "poetry" of the rainbow.) Describing her own childhood Christmases, Brooks conveys that, while their mystery and illusion added beauty, their familial warmth gave joy (*RPO*, 40-43). Moe Belle concludes simply:

> Thus with a Love
> that has to have a Home
> like the Black Nation,
> like the Black Nation
> defining its own Roof
> that no one else can see.

A worksheet for the poem, exhibited by the National Institute of Arts and Letters at Brooks's induction, May 19, 1976, reveals several changes. The most important alters "friendship" to "Love" (l. 1, above), acknowledging the Black Nation's familial structure, to be realized through faith.

"A Black Wedding Song," an epithalamion (or "prothalamion," as Edmund Spenser would have it), is dedicated to three young couples on their wedding day. This two-part "weapon-song" (printed as one in *To Disembark*) wishes them continued strength for the social and personal battles ahead. "Keep it strong. / Keep it logic and Magic and lightning and Muscle" (ll. 4-5). The heroic shifts from mainly grand to the second part's plain, which becomes more personal as it offers warning and wisdom ("I wish you the daily forgiveness of each other") and wryly lists dangers from the envying "World" that "tangles tongues, / mashes minds." The burden on kindness to "romp or sorrow along" seems heavy. Brooks's concept of "the along," however, as in "Speech to the Young" (below), is crucial to her stalwart philosophy. The controlling combat image, its cast of mock heroic recalling "The Anniad," effectively commemorates a serious theme: relationships must struggle to endure.

"Horses Graze" surprises by its content. A pastoral, unique in Brooks, its potent charm lies in childlike impressions. She, whose "Sunday chicken" becomes a sacrificial emblem; whose Maud

Martha spares the mouse and attains grace; who eulogized her dog, Fluffy, in her autobiography; who, in my presence, was concerned that a tiny moth be liberated from a house rather than killed, pays here a high tribute to natural life. The pristine opening lines express the animals in sense-images:

> Cows graze.
> Horses graze.
> They
> eat
> eat
> eat.

Patient listing of one word below the next depicts the persistent chewing, the unmoving quiet of the animals as they feed. ("Their graceful heads / are bowed / bowed / bowed."). The beasts are "nobly oblivious" to the adversary ways of the world. Their needs for sustenance met,

> And at the crest of their brute satisfaction,
> with wonderful gentleness, in affirmation,
> they lift their clean calm eyes and they lie down
> and love the world. [ll. 20-23]

This is the heart of the forty-line poem, its tranquil core where lines spread out as the animals rest, its theme—the familiar caritas—metamorphic. The work rises in an arc from simple to complex and returns to simple perceptions of the nursery-rhyme-like second stanza. The animals converse with each other, are satisfied with their ground, not wishing to be "otherwhere." Their wisdom inhabits an immaculate sense of the world. The first stanza ends:

> Perhaps they know that creature feet may press
> only a few earth inches at a time,
> that earth is anywhere earth,
> that an eye may see,
> wherever it may be,
> the Immediate arc, alone, of life, of love.

"Anywhere earth" reminds of Williams's "anywhere is every-where."[8] Brooks's poem is like a still center of the volume, an ideal reality beyond sorrow and conflict, elegy and heroic. Without sentimentalizing the animals, her alchemy of the innocent eye transmits their wisdom.

Notably, for the first time in a book, the poet spells "Afrika" with a *k* (st. 2). (See also "Sammy Chester" and "Boys. Black," below.) Brooks explains that there is no sibiliant *c* before vowels in African languages; the alternate spelling seems "more authentic." Repetition of "know" in the second stanza relates the vertical physicality of "eat / eat / eat" and "bowed / bowed / bowed" to the horizontal of the animals' "they know and know and know" (fol-lowed by the conclusion, "there's ground below / and sky / up high"). Verticality distinguishes sense impressions, itemized like sums for addition, from continuity of thought, where the horizon-tal also intensifies the meaning.

The vertical/horizontal dimension brings to mind "coupling," Samuel R. Levin's psycholinguistic concept of aural and semantic elements, particularly as they occur in rhyme.[9] Extending the theory *visually*, we note thematic coupling of vertical and hori-zontal: the sky to which the animals lift their clean eyes and the ground upon which they lie down and love the world. The two directions, each revealing heaven and earth, mind and matter, intersect. Verticality dominates the beginning, horizontality the middle; the longest lines correspond with the midpoint of the structural arc suggested above and retract to the brevity of the beginning. The motifs convey a pacific quality since, for the eye, vertical and horizontal tend to stay in the plane. The poem's unities, concrete and abstract, realize one of Brooks's most for-mally absolute works.

" 'When Handed a Lemon, / Make Lemonade,' " with the humorous credit "(title by Anonymous)," is a motto Brooks calls one of several "little life-lines taped to my closet wall" (*RPO*, 64). This slight, amusing song advises children, "There is always a use / for lemon juice." As she notes in her " 'Last' Speech to the Court of Two," Henry Jr. and Nora, "Remember: unhappiness e-ventually becomes something else—as does everything" (*RPO*, 63). The poem's practical tone differs from the volume's energetic appeals to the young.

"Sammy Chester Leaves 'Godspell' and Visits *Upward Bound* on a Lake Forest Lawn, Bringing West Afrika," in common with several other Brooks titles, bears the specificity of Wordsworth's "Lines Left upon a Seat in a Yew-Tree, Which Stands Near the Lake of Esthwaite, on a Desolate Part of the Shore, Commanding a Beautiful Prospect."[10] Brooks's journalistic caption, in full capitals, like the rest in this volume and *Riot*, suggests a headline. "Sammy Chester" conveys the currency of Africa in the poet's thought. She equates her subject's birthplace, Chicago's West Side, with West Africa. Mischievously placing the returned actor, Brooks depicts him rejecting "Lake Forest limplush," the "limp," luxurious ("plush," "lush") setting of the city's expensive and racially segregated suburb. "Godspell," a quasi-religious musical with an integrated cast and a message of universal love, and Chester's proletarian blackness are anomalies in Lake Forest. "*Upward Bound*" refers to the Upward Bound Programs, which afford special educational opportunities to black youth throughout the United States. The name also ironically connotes upward social mobility. The West Side become West Afrika breaks heroically "free of the / plastic platitudes— / free of the / strange stress, ordained ordure and high hell."

Following poems of childhood, youth, marriage, and parental advice, "Friend" presents mature companionship. The first line of the fifth stanza, "It is the evening of our love," relates the piece to "An Aspect of Love," which, before revision, began "It is the morning of our love." The latter poem's irony recedes; instead of rising to walk "in different directions," the lovers walk together. Friendship ("Friend" capitalized) supplants passion ("Evening is comforting flame. / Evening is comforting flame"), as the poet prescribes (Hull, 39). Verse repetitions of simple declarative sentences, together with the dominant copula, convey stasis and serenity. Structurally, the fourteen lines (sonnet length) balance into five stanzas: 4, 1, 2, 2, 5. The first two stanzas equal the last and, if combined (they are semantically close), form two stanzaic pairs of reversed length: 5, 2, 2, 5, furthering the tranquil pairing motif.

"Boys. Black," identified as "a preachment," closes the volume. (See also *To Disembark*, below.) This extraordinary work of sixty-three lines, which first appeared in *Ebony*, August 1972,

constitutes the longest piece in *Beckonings*. Control and development of the grand heroic style, imperative, sermonic, yet maternal, ally it with the First and Second Sermons on the Warpland.
In free verse, with internal and slant rhyme and repetitions, it
accommodates pentameter at several points where the ample,
familiar rhythm braces the didactic content. Variety includes the
multi- or polyrhythmic features noted in *In the Mecca*; resonances
range from the complexity of African drum music to Anglo-Saxon
sound and stress.

> Boys. Black. Black Boys.
> Be brave to battle for your breath and bread.

The strong, spondaic chiasmus of the opening line joins the
concepts of youth and blackness. As in "The Boy Died in My
Alley" (and "of DeWitt Williams"), "Boy" is shadowed by white
deprecation so that the word indirectly yet proudly invokes black
men. Brooks rouses the youths to consciousness of their power
and its origin, "your Poem, AFRIKA." "Up, boys. Boys black.
Black boys," she urges. Compression, spondaic stressing,
chiasmic repetition, and alliteration focus the energy of command. "Boys" functions as symbol, as does "Running Boy" of the
first poem.

An increasingly sophisticated compounding includes wider
use of the oxymoronic ("leaplanguid," "dwarfmagnificent,"
"busysimple"), pervasive alliteration, some metonymy ("a Thorough," "a There"), and active, imperative verbs like "invade,"
"take," "sharpen," "force." Imagery is strong, earthy. The poet
assures the boys of fertile ground beneath "pseudo-ice," ground to
be cultivated, hatchets to be sharpened, "sludge" and wild scen-
ery to be traversed and overcome. The African jungle becomes a
controlling image, subsuming attributes of fertility and summer
weather. These emblems of identity oppose the winter of present
discontents.

The philosophical crux of the poem contrasts God's law and
power with that of the boys. They must "legislate" a steadfast,
"inward law" in developing racial consciousness; they must adapt
"force"—a central verb inclining toward the nominative and suggesting a body of men prepared for action. Stanza 2 exhorts the
boys to "Force into the green." This "symbol of land for nation-

establishment and a symbol, too, for live faith in our young,"[11] among the Black Nationalist colors of green, black, and red connotes youth and the latent power of growth lying below "pseudo-ice," the false winter of despair. "Force through the sludge" occurs once in stanza 4 and twice in stanza 5, where God's erratic ways accompany faltering contemporary leadership. Religious skepticism overtakes Brooks as she hastens the young men to their task:

> Because
> the eyeless Leaders flutter, tilt, and fail.
> The followers falter, peculiar, eyeless too.
> Force through the sludge. Force, whether
> God is a Thorough and a There,
> or a mad child,
> playing
> with a floorful of toys,
> mashing
> whatwhen he wills. Force, whether
> God is spent pulse, capricious, or a yet-to-come.

The eyeless leaders lack moral vision. They "flutter"—like the shades that Virgil and Dante compare to the falling autumn leaves.[12] They "tilt," suggesting a knightly charge with a lance on horseback, or the tilt of a pinball machine, connoting chance, or a seesaw. But possibilities come to naught; the leaders "fail." There is an intimation, too, of Milton's *Samson Agonistes*, "Eyeless in *Gaza* at the Mill with slaves" (l. 41), emblem of the temporary loss of power. Brooks worries, however, about the blind leading the blind. "Peculiar," which evokes the "Peculiar Institution" of slavery, may also refer to "Leaders," making them, like their followers, unfree.

Brooks relates *force, through, thorough, there, floorful* by fine aural and semantic modulations. Epithets for God are unfavorable. By proximity and association, the word *sludge* connects with *God* by means of *through* and *thorough. Thorough* means painfully exact. Its archaic meaning is through; both are nominally current in *thoroughfare, throughway,* deriving from the Old English *thuruh* and from Old Norse *thrō,* a trough. In addition to the common adverbial definitions of *through*, as noun it means pipe, trough, coffin, or material that passes through a sieve during the flour-milling process, suggesting negative connotations, as with *sludge*. *Through/thorough* also recalls, "I am the way, the truth, and the life: no man cometh unto the Father but by me" (John 14:6). In later association, "Thorough" names the tyrannical policy of Sir Thomas Wentworth (later the Earl of Strafford), applied by Archibishop Laud, who instituted the inquisitorial Star Chamber during the reign of Charles I. The excesses were followed by the Puritan Revolution, a succession pertinent here. J. R. Green's fascinating account of Strafford's arrest informs, "The keeper of the Black rod demanded his sword as he took him in charge."[13]

God may also be *There* (not necessarily Omnipresent, one of the three major attributes) so that even if approachable, he is not *here*. As a "mad child" he functions below the level of the boys, who are asked to "See, say, salvage" (recall "salvage" in the Second Sermon). They must themselves become Tellers who will lead and prophesy. Potentially, they are salvation. For all practical purposes, whether mad, immature, "spent pulse" (as opposed to the boys' vital pulse in stanza 1), or possibility—as presently conceived—God is dead.

The poet warns the youths to "beware the imitation coronations" (st. 6), which replace one set of illusions with another. They must beware, also, "the easy griefs" whose momentary impact fades, like the tragedy of "ATTICA" (loud in full caps). Brooks refers to the New York State prison where, on September 13, 1971, Governor Nelson A. Rockefeller ordered 1,500 state troopers to quell a rebellion of unarmed prisoners. During the air and ground assault, forty deaths resulted, those of thirty-one prisoners and nine guards and civilian employees taken hostage.[14]

The biblical "thy" appears in the next stanza (7) where the boys are asked not to "shock thy street, / and purse thy mouth, / and go home to thy 'Gunsmoke,' " the latter a popular Western television program. The chiding usage fulfills the critical religious tone of stanza 5. Thus Brooks removes force from an association with growth (st. 1), to an attack upon muddy or muddled thinking and passivity (st. 4), to short-lived protest against the Attica massacre (st. 7), and then to a television fantasy that dissipates the youths' creative and combative energies. The poet maternally entrusts her loving faith to the boys, that finally they might transform it into "an engine" and "a Black Star," beckoning.[15] Brooks herself becomes the dynamic force in the leaderless situation. Assumption of the heroic and prophetic role has developed organically within the poem.

Brooks has expressed dissatisfaction with *Beckonings* as a transitional work. Agreeing with criticism of its stylistic variety and seeming shift of heroic subjects from female in early work to male from the late sixties on (Hull, 19-40), she even rejects its selection of poems. Yet the volume amplifies the heroic style, which it flexibly composes with other modes. Recalling *Family Pictures* in themes and familial tone, it similarly moves away from the allusive and further recesses the ironic mode. Brooks tends toward clarity in her sense of the perspicuous, toward music, linguistic invention, use of the vernacular and black speech—all informed by a didactic impulse to communicate emotively. Reaching "taverners"[16]—her symbol for commanding immediate attention, an ability she appreciates in Haki Madhubuti, Sonia Sanchez, and Robert Burns—has been the long-term objective of her poetry. This aim parallels the achievement of her mentor Langston Hughes as a people's poet. Brooks's unmediated voice addresses her people and the need for leadership. Appealing directly to youth and to maturity, she answers her own challenge.

Primer For Blacks

Although Brooks wrote occasional and commissioned pieces between 1975 and 1980, such as the elegy for Governor Otto Kerner of Illinois, which she read at his funeral in 1976, she did not publish a volume of poetry during that time. Health problems, concern over black disunity, personal loss, and the distressing suspension of Broadside Press marked those years. Brooks helped her mother with the publication of *The Voice and Other Short Stories* (1975), a garland of lively reminiscences, stories, reflections, and family photographs (including Brooks) and wrote its

preface. Mrs. Brooks's failing health and her death in 1978 burdened the poet's consciousness.

Primer For Blacks, a chapbook of "Three Preachments," affirms the positive nature of Brooks and her art. Published wholly
under her own aegis, Black Position Press (its name taken from
her magazine), the book renews the social nexus of her work. A
notable addition to the important small press movement, it constitutes a feminist statement. Brooks's own category of "preachment" links the book with "Boys. Black." as basic to her canon.
The works in this volume, the first to appear without a personal
dedication, have been immensely popular in public readings.

"Primer For Blacks," the first poem, sounds the grand heroic
in a stirring summons to love and esteem the spectrum of Blackness: "All of you— / you COLORED ones, / you NEGRO ones,
. . . you half-Blacks, / you wish-I-weren't Blacks, / Niggeroes and
Niggerenes. // You." "To Those Of My Sisters Who Kept Their
Naturals, *Never to look a hot comb in the teeth*" speaks to black
women in the diction of plain heroic, praising those who "have not
bought Blondine," whose "hair is Celebration in the world!"
"Requiem Before Revival," a prose poem essay, seeks to answer
the need for "the essential Black statement of defense and definition."

The book gives Brooks much satisfaction. "I like what the
poems say," she told me in Chicago on July 7, 1980. "They say
what I mean. It is an insistence that Blacks have some gumption
about themselves, and that they like themselves and stop imitat-
ing whites."

To Disembark

This anthology brings together Brooks's work from the sixties to
the eighties. *Riot* and the main portions of *Family Pictures* and
Beckonings are joined by a fourth section of new poems, "To the
Diaspora." Several important revisions will be noted.

The volume is dedicated "To Dudley Randall. With Affection
and Respect," and introduced by "In Memoriam: Edgar William
Blakely," an elegy for Brooks's "righteous and radiant" brother-in-
law. The title, *To Disembark*, alludes to the Black diaspora. The

theme carries through in "To the Diaspora," its original version written for Dudley Randall on the Tenth Anniversary of Broadside Press. Cut and honed, the new poem retains its vigor while broadening to include all African Americans: "You did not know you were Afrika." It urges "into the places rough to reach," to complete, in the words of the percussive close, "Your work, that was done, to be done to be done to be done."

The other poems also feature courage and resistance. "Music For Martyrs" eulogizes Steve Biko, "Biko the Emerger / laid low," who was, the epigraph states, "killed in South Africa for loving his people." "A Welcome Song For Laini Nzinga" greets the birth of Haki Madhubuti's daughter, "coming through the rim of the world" in 1975. "To Black Women" praises black women who fight yet "create and train your flowers still." "To Prisoners" stirringly calls for "Dark gardening / in the vertigo cold. / In the hot paralysis," for "cultivation of strength to heal and enhance . . . in the chalk and choke," the final phrase its last line. Brooks regularly visits prisons throughout the country; her work is enthusiastically received.

Of the two major revisions from *Beckonings*, "To John Killens" combines the muscular beginning of "Five Men Against the Theme" with "To John Oliver Killens in 1975" and augments them into a powerful new work. Drastic revision occurs in "Another Preachment." It presents edited updated selections from "Boys. Black," adding "Gilligan's Island" (from television) and "the NFL" (National Football League) as distractions and substituting for "Attica" "Afrika," the latter mentioned at the beginning of both poems and now the focus. The later version is probably best viewed as a different poem. Its opening and conclusion, however, severely cut, miss the introductory resonance and closing affirmation of "Boys. Black."

Very Young Poets

In 1980 Brooks published *Young Poet's Primer*, a useful, concise manual addressed mainly to high school and college students. The first book under her new imprint, Brooks Press, it was followed in 1983 by *Very Young Poets*, "Dedicated to all the children in the world." Twenty "Little Lessons," one to a page, give practical, simply worded advice about writing, reading, and subject matter. "Poems do not have to rhyme!" they begin, and end with "Remember that poetry is your Friend!"

"Eight Poems for Children" reinforce the lessons. The engaging free verse encourages looking at the world and books themselves with love and wonder. "Books Feed and Cure and Chortle and Collide," published as "A Bookmark" in 1969, praises the power of books, their "drumbeats on the air." The last poem, "To Young Readers," observes that "Good books . . . are keys and hammers, / ripe redeemers, / dials and bells and / healing hallelujah." Its final stanza announces:

> Good books are good nutrition.
> A reader is a Guest
> nourished, by riches of the Feast,
> to lift, to launch, and to applaud the world.

The Brooks heroic rhythms abide in robust affirmation. The poet routes her appeal outward through a child's basic experience. Mentor and mother, she renders a clear, encouraging guide that would benefit aspiring adults as well as very young poets.

10
A Major Poet

In contemporary poetry, the world of the poem is often conceived as a beleaguered fortress against the real world; to enter one is to depart from the other. This limits the material of reality for the work and requires a choice between the two as means or end. Whether weighted toward solipsism or manipulation, the tendency results in an exclusive poetry, usually offered with matching poetics and criticism. The art of Gwendolyn Brooks makes no such dichotomy. It includes the world, its poetic emblems, and us. We are not merely to be ranked and shaped with the raw data of existence. We matter, in the vital properties of our thought, feeling, growth, and change, so that the poem becomes an interaction in a mutual process, socially resonant.

There is significance in the rock as symbol for Eliot, Pound, Williams, and Stevens; significance in fire and whirlwind as symbols for Brooks. Whatever the historical and social origins, which may be legitimately examined, the difference goes to the substance of their respective works. For Eliot, "The Rock" means traditional Christian faith; for Pound, "Rock-Drill Cantos" reveal the sources of poetic faith, which imbricate a Confucian-type order of language, literature, and the state. In Williams, permanence is also critical: love is "a stone, endlessly in flight"; the poem raises "the most perfect rock and temple, the highest / falls" (*Paterson*, Book II, 3). Despite the risk (the falls) that must be faced in creating beauty, the ideal—though distant from Eliot's "still point of the turning world" (*Burnt Norton*)—is stability. The rocks themselves speak, but the poet denies prophecy in his quest for "the thing itself." Fire and flood purge toward a new synthesis, where past and present, locus and myth may combine, like the unicorn tapestries of Book V.[1] For Stevens, as Joseph N. Riddel observes, the rock "defines the life of the mind as a world of reality existing in analogy with, yet independent of, the indifferent materiality of things."[2]

Brooks's religious faith is ambivalent regarding the supernatural, yet it is deeply humanistic. Her apocalyptic imagery has a counterpart of stability, but its force is dynamic; its permanence, change. "Divorce"—from nature, as decried by Williams and followers like Charles Olson; from God, as mourned in Eliot; from excellence in art, as scorned by Pound; from mind, as chided by Stevens—is transformed by Brooks into a concern with divorce from human dignity. Her work cries out against the subjugation of blacks, which may have inflicted more physical than spiritual damage, while it has hurt whites spiritually. Brooks embodies caritas, expressed in the poetic voice as it articulates a racial and communal vision. Hers is a unified sensibility, pragmatic and idealistic, shaped, in part, by the needs which it ventures to meet. This kind of artistic courage, risking "the highest falls," is shown by a poet of the first rank, a major poet.

Brooks meets the criteria for major status on all four levels: craft and technique; scope or breadth; influence of the work in style, content, or productivity, upon others; and influence of the poet upon others. Technically, we have examined her mastery of form and cultivation of new and renewed forms. She has extended language itself, as Whitman did, by imaginative compounding, word-coinage, and use of black English vernacular. She belongs to that select category Pound called "the inventors," the highest classification of poets who create and expand formal limits and, thereby, taste itself.[3] Development toward a genre of contemporary heroic poetry, offering distinctive style and language, may be considered Brooks's outstanding achievement. Various types of heroic, exemplified by several other black poets, are examined elsewhere.[4] Yet Brooks's heroic, direct though subtle, comprehensive in sensibility and range, whether "grand" or "plain," socially responsive and evangelically fused, makes her work a paradigm of the genre.[5] The unique authority with which she speaks to her people is based in mutual affection and esteem and a historically viable sense of kinship. Her call to Black pride, even when chiding or dismayed, has a familial intimacy. This kind of rapport hovered over the Fireside Poets who supported the Union during the Civil War. For the earlier tradition of literature in English, the configuration is Miltonic and Romantic, the poet as artist and activist. For the native tradition of the American and African American folk preacher, it is sermonic and communal.

A further complex of antecedence has been suggested: the Homeric bard, the Anglo-Saxon scop, the African griot, the balladeer. We have noted Black roots in African and African American culture: religion, religious and secular music (the latter emphasizing blues and jazz), language, and the legacy of oral tales and verbal artistry. Yet even here, we have chiefly studied formal intersection with content: visual, aural, semantic, and psycholinguistic elements that absorb and transcend boundaries of time and place. At what point or line do we separate blues from ballad? Where do we locate the ancestral balladeer: in Britain? New Orleans? Harlem? When does gut become "the slipping string" of a Stradivarius? And what of the sonnet—when it becomes a "sonnet-ballad"? Can we usefully ghettoize our cultural traditions?

> . . . Look at her! Look at her!
> my space thought. She is one of us—
> she is none of us. She is
> herself, as we are,
> particles of now.[6]

Brooks is now. "Bees in the stomach, sweat across the brow. Now." She *is* our multiethnic, multiracial American artistic heritage.

And so the implicit attempt here has been to find continuities and parallels, conscious or unconscious, and non- or minimally culture-bound aspects. These have sometimes confronted a criticism that ignores or dismisses what it does not understand and that reads differences as deficiencies. Brooks's poetry partakes in a dynamic continuum. Cultural cross-fertilization and—to borrow from anthropology (Darwin via Ashley Montagu)—its resulting "hybrid vigor" have fostered greatness in British and American literature and language, notable in periods of cultural ferment such as the Renaissance and our own.

While examining Brooks's heroic style in terms of "contemporary fact," the background of African and African American culture, and the British and American poetic tradition(s), we should also bear in mind its relation to the American democratic impulse. Brooks's work, like that of the entire genre, shares idealistic strains of the culture, notable, for example, in the early Emerson and Whitman, and in Thoreau. Observe the continuity with Whitman, who wrote in 1888: "One main genesis-motive of the 'Leaves' was my conviction (just as strong to-day as ever) that the crowning growth of the United States is to be spiritual and heroic."[7] The words call our subject, her art infused with the historic, communal quest for emancipation and leadership.

Brooks participates in the Black Rebellion, identified by Bennett as "one of the longest and most varied upheavals by black people in the twentieth century."[8] Her life and work illustrate his claim that "Blackness is the real repository of values Euro-Americans proclaimed and never lived," or—in the word rightly popular among blacks—repository of the American *soul*. Beyond Blackness, therefore, and the growing sense of a pan-African heritage, we arrive at spirituality, emphasized by Du Bois and more recently by Chancellor Williams. Speaking of Africa, the latter notes:

> our land, rather than any other land, was called the *spiritual* land, the land of the Gods by the non-African world. . . . So that we have been a very religious people, a very humble people. What reason for it overall is kind of difficult to understand because the same religion—which is an admirable quality, in our world—turned out to be that by which we were victimized.[9]

Brooks's ambivalence toward Christianity stems partly from its very compatibility with the African tradition of humility and acceptance. One recalls Whitman's apt prediction: "There will be soon no more priests. Their work is done . . . the gangs of kosmos and prophets en masse shall take their place."[10]

It is Brooks's fundamental humanism that prevents her from

being trapped either in the Victorian conflict between religion and science or in the twentieth-century dilemma of reconciling spirit, idealism, and optimism with science, determinism, and pessimism.[11] For Brooks, ideals are the given of existence, whether or not supernaturally endowed, and the task is to create a humane society in the benign image of an extended family. She is sophisticated enough to understand the vicissitudes of progress, and determined enough not to submit to a weary pessimism. Her gentle, amused mien accompanies a fervent seriousness. The prophetic role, once assumed, is not to be put aside. In periods of confusion or disintegration, it orders vision. Since the prophet traditionally expects little or no honor in his or her own country, neither appreciation nor recognition are prerequisites for the task.

Perhaps Gwendolyn Brooks's most important contribution to the philosophy of literature is the challenge of her work to the cul-de-sac of the antiheroic ironic mode, as defined by Northrop Frye,[12] retaining its intellectual virtues while moving toward reentry into the mythic/heroic. In this process, she also gathers historical strands of romantic and mimetic or realistic modes along with the ironic, into the heroic abode of epic genre. Frye's definition of epic is useful here. He writes, "The function of the epic, in its origin, seems to be primarily to teach the nation, or whatever we call the social unit which the poet is addressing, its own traditions."[13] Madhubuti (*RPO*, 22) perceptively refers to *In the Mecca* as Brooks's "epic of black humanity." Writing in *The Reason of Church-Government*, Milton discerns two types of the genre: the "diffuse"—that of Homer, Virgil, and Tasso—and the "brief model" of the Book of Job. If, therefore, we follow Madhubuti's insight and Barbara Kiefer Lewalski's example, in which she assigns Milton's own category to *Paradise Regain'd*, we may similarly classify the 1968 volume as a "brief epic."[14]

Brooks has not codified her transition to heroic as an "Adamic" celebration of the individual, to use the terminology of Roy Harvey Pearce.[15] In his useful study, Pearce distinguishes an Adamic mode, embodied in Whitman and culminating in Stevens, and a mythic mode, also historically continuous, realized in Eliot. It would seem, however, that the political impulse of Whitman is distant from Stevens's detachment. Brooks is Whitmanic in a way she cannot be Stevensian. Faith in self, projected nationally, politicizes awareness. This diverges radically from poetic faith as a commitment to art, ultimately one's own. Nor can she be Eliotic, with a mythos based on stabilizing a society that she is bent upon altering. In her quest of heroic and its prosody, Brooks transforms the aristocratic concept of the hero or heroine from the conventional status of super-being—as Frye accepts the perspective for his heroic/mythic historical mode—toward redemption of that which is more compatible with the Judeo-Christian tradition of humble origins of beauty and power.

The creative by-product of Brooks's local and national efforts has been to encourage the making of poems. She has personally established a prodigious number of prizes and awards for poetry, funded student trips to Africa, anthologized, subsidized, and promoted student work. Her readings and workshops, undertaken on regular, cross-country travels, convey her to prisons and reformatories, as well as to schools, universities, and other environments. Whether journeying or at home in Chicago, she communicates the drama of current affairs with a concern that begins in the spirit. Her faithful representations of black experience define the nature of its white context. She enriches both black and white cultures by revealing essential life, its universal identities, and the challenge it poses to a society beset with corruption and decay.

Beyond critical analysis, we decide that we like a work, or we don't; we like a poet, or not. We care about the poetry of Gwendolyn Brooks in great measure because it cares about us and the existence we share. It does not lose us in a labyrinthine psyche, or make us claustrophobic to get out of life, or tax our patience with chronic self-pity. Its warmth is more immediate, for the most part, than that of Eliot, Pound, Williams, or Stevens. A social act, it hones an art of utility and beauty, at home in the world. Brooks is a "Figure of Outward,"[16] her later work Projective in Charles Olson's sense of stance and voice and breath itself informing a poetry of vital connections. Its human terrain recalls John Dewey's observation that Williams found so compelling: "The local is the only universal, upon that all art builds."[17] At the same time, Brooks's travels, her span of interests and enterprise, give her work a cosmopolitan breadth. She contributes a beauty of wholeness, of a fully articulated human being whose compassionate intelligence, wit and humor and anger transcend their tragic awareness.

It is especially just that Brooks's familial perspective on the Black Nation renders her animating quality. As we read her poems, we feel their indivisible affection, their cohering power. Acknowledging them, "an essential sanity, black and electric," we recognize a national resource, needed now.

Notes

Introduction

1. Charles Olson, "Projective Verse" (1950), rpt. in *Selected Writings*, ed. Robert Creeley (New York: New Directions, 1966), 16. Creeley's sentence formulates Olson's theory.

2. Harry Shaw's *Gwendolyn Brooks* (New York: Twayne, 1980) discusses the work thematically in terms of "death, the fall from glory, the labyrinth, and survival" (preface).

3. George Stavros, "An Interview with Gwendolyn Brooks" (1970), rpt. in *Report from Part One* (Detroit: Broadside Press, 1972), 166.

4. Clenora F. Hudson, "Racial Themes in the Poetry of Gwendolyn Brooks," *CLA Journal* 17 (Sept. 1973): 16.

5. George E. Kent, "The Poetry of Gwendolyn Brooks" (1971), rpt. and enl. in *Blackness and the Adventure of Western Culture* (Chicago: Third World Press, 1972), 104-37.

6. John A. Williams, "The Harlem Renaissance: Its Artists, Its Impact, Its Meaning," *Black World* 20 (Nov. 1970): 18.

7. For aspects of heroic other than those discussed here, including the slave, the "trickster," and the outlaw, see Lawrence W. Levine's *Black Culture and Black Consciousness: Afro-American Folk Thought from Slavery to Freedom* (Oxford: Oxford Univ. Press, 1977), chap. 6, "A Pantheon of Heroes." See also the "toasts," epical poetic narratives (378-80), noting especially the folklore studies by Roger D. Abrahams, such as *Deep Down in the Jungle: Negro Narrative Folklore from the Streets of Philadelphia* (Chicago: Aldine, 1964).

8. See discussion of the period in Lerone Bennett, Jr., *The Challenge of Blackness* (Chicago: Johnson, 1972), 14-18. See also Addison Gayle, Jr., ed., *The Black Aesthetic* (Garden City, N.Y.: Doubleday/Anchor, 1971).

9. Matthew Arnold, from "On Translating Homer: Last Words," 1862.

10. Stephen Henderson, *Understanding the New Black Poetry: Black Speech and Black Music as Poetic References* (New York: William Morrow, 1973).

Note especially "Structure," 28-61. Clarence Major's *Dictionary of Afro-American Slang* (New York: International Publishers, 1970), offers a convenient guide to the specialized vocabulary.

11. W. E. B. Du Bois, *The Souls of Black Folk* (1903; rpt. New York: Washington Square Press, 1970), chap. 14.

1. Biographical

1. Claudia Tate, ed., *Black Women Writers at Work* (New York: Continuum, 1983), 46.

2. Keziah Wims Brooks, *"The Voice"—And Other Short Stories* (Chicago: Harlo Press, 1975).

3. Kent, *Blackness*, 112-13. See also his "Portrait, in Part, of the Artist as a Young Girl and Apprentice Writer," *Callaloo* 2 (Oct. 1979): 74-83. Kent worked on a biography of the poet until his untimely death in 1982.

4. Gloria T. Hull and Posey Gallagher, "Update on Part One: An Interview with Gwendolyn Brooks," *CLA Journal*, 20 (Sept. 1977): 32.

5. Ida Lewis, "Conversation: Gwen Brooks and Ida Lewis: 'My People Are Black People,'" *Essence* (April 1971); rpt. in *RPO*, 167-82.

6. Phyl Garland, "Gwendolyn Brooks—Poet Laureate," *Ebony* 23 (July 1968): 48-56.

7. Blakely's first book of poems, *Windy Place* (Detroit: Broadside Press, 1975), was warmly reviewed by George E. Kent in *Black World* 24 (Sept. 1975): 85-87.

8. The term "Negro Renaissance" originated with Alain L. Locke in his anthology *The New Negro* (New York: Boni, 1925), where he located its core as Harlem.

9. Brooks no longer recommends Hillyer's book as a primer for poets (Kent, *Blackness*, 35). She has expressed to students and to me her approval of Elizabeth Drew's *Poetry: A Modern Guide to Its Understanding and Enjoyment* (New York: Dell, 1959).

10. See especially Langston Hughes, *Good Morning, Revolution*, ed. Faith Berry (Westport, Conn.: Hill, 1973).

11. Jean Wagner, *Black Poets of the United States: From Paul Laurence Dunbar to Langston Hughes* (Urbana, Ill.: Univ. of Illinois Press, 1973), 477.

12. Frank Harriott, "The Life of a Pulitzer Poet," *Negro Digest* (later *Black World*) (Aug. 1950): 14-16.

13. The title is taken from a poem by Linwood Smith, "This is For You," dedicated to Brooks, in *To Gwen With Love*, ed. Patricia Brown et al. (Chicago: Johnson, 1971), 90.

14. Paul M. Angle, *We Asked Gwendolyn Brooks* (Chicago: Illinois Bell Telephone, Summer 1967); rpt. in *RPO*, 146.

2. A Street in Bronzeville

1. Gwendolyn Brooks, *A Street in Bronzeville* (1945), rpt. in *The World of Gwendolyn Brooks* (New York: Harper and Row, 1971).

2. Summaries of the pertinent Gwendolyn Brooks correspondence from the Harper and Row files (1944-58 in Author Files at Princeton University Library; 1959 to present in New York) will appear at the beginning of each chapter. References will be made in the text, with the sender's initials first, as follows: Gwendolyn Brooks, GB; Elizabeth Lawrence, EL; and other personal initials as will be clearly indicated by the context.

3. Lawrence was addressed as "Miss Lawrence" in the correspondence from 1944 to 1946 when, in February, formal salutations were dropped by the writers. The letters display a graceful decorum and warmth on both sides.

4. Cf. the attitude expressed in the March 1969 interview with George Stavros (*RPO*, 147-66), where the politics of Blackness support a new order of aesthetics.

5. St. Clair Drake and Horace R. Cayton, *Black Metropolis: A Study of Negro Life in a Northern City*, vol. 2, rev. and enl. ed. (1945; rpt. New York: Harper and Row, 1962). See especially ch. 14, "Bronzeville."

6. See Donald Phelps, "Depressed Art 2: Tone," *For Now*, no. 8, 84-96, n.d., for a useful distinction between "style," "the after-thought of critics," and "tone," "the recognition by language of its skin."

7. Shaw sees the theme in terms of "The Labyrinth," which is the title of ch. 5 in his study (94-130). Also see Introduction, n. 2, above.

8. Louis Simpson, reviewing Brooks's *Selected Poems* (*New York Herald Tribune Book Week*, Oct. 27, 1963, 27), takes the opposite view. Expressing doubts that a Negro can "write well without making us aware he is a Negro," Simpson declares, "if being a Negro is the only subject, the writing is not important." Richard Wright's observation may be cited in rebuttal: "The Negro is America's metaphor." Shaw, on the other hand, focuses on Brooks's portrayal of the "Black Microcosm," title of his ch. 8.

9. Richard Wright, "Early Days in Chicago," *Cross-Section 1945: A Collection of New American Writing*, ed. Edwin Seaver (New York: L.B. Fischer, 1945), 306-42.

10. Herbert Hill, ed., *Soon, One Morning* (New York: Knopf, 1963), 326.

11. Houston A. Baker, Jr., "The Achievement of Gwendolyn Brooks," *CLA Journal* 16 (Sept. 1972): 23.

12. Kent, *Blackness*, 117-18.

13. W. E. B. Du Bois, *The Gift of Black Folk: The Negroes in the Making of America* (1924; rpt. New York: Washington Square Press, 1970). See ch. 7, "The American Folk Song."

14. Shaw points out that Brooks's "poetry is aligned with the black tradition of artful ambiguity and indirection and therefore communicates with a sub-conscious sophistication that is not possible with expression made solely on the conscious level," 183.

15. Tate, *BWW*, 46.

16. Arthur P. Davis, "The Black-and-Tan Motif in the Poetry of Gwendolyn Brooks," *CLA Journal* 6 (Dec. 1962): 90-97.

17. Ben A. Franklin, "Three Held in Dispute Over Textbooks," *New York Times*, Sept. 19, 1974, p. 14, cols. 1-3.

18. "It is a lonesome Glee," no. 774, in *The Complete Poems of Emily Dickinson*, ed. Thomas H. Johnson (Boston: Little, Brown, 1960), 378.

19. For another perspective on this poem and others, see George E. Kent, "Aesthetic Values in the Poetry of Gwendolyn Brooks," in *Black American Literature and Humanism*, ed. R. Baxter Miller (Lexington: Univ. Press of Kentucky, 1981), 75-94.

20. F. Scott Fitzgerald, *The Great Gatsby* (1925), rpt. in *Three Novels* (New York: Scribner's, 1953), 70.

21. Henderson, *Understanding the New Black Poetry*, 48. John T. Shawcross, in "Names as 'Symbols' in Black Poetry," *Literary Onomastic Studies* 6 (1978): 49-61, deepens the critical dimension here. He observes black poetic uses that, "moving from being allusion to symbol to 'symbol,' involve a loss of essential meaning and an accrual of separate and special meanings" in "geography, politics, and music (specifically jazz)," and notes that Henderson's introduction comments "do not engage this dimension of the poetry" (151).

22. Kent also sees Hughes's influence here and in "when Mrs. Martin's Booker T.," "a song in the front yard," "patent leather," "Hattie Scott" (*Blackness*, 108). Henderson writes that Sterling A. Brown "invents" a new form, the melded "blues-ballad" (50-51).

23. See LeRoi Jones (Amiri Baraka), *Blues People: The Negro Experience in White America and the Music that Developed from It* (New York: Morrow, 1963), for a useful survey and interpretation of the blues and jazz.

24. This is pointed out in James A. Emanuel's enlightening article "Renaissance Sonneteers," *Black World* 24 (Sept. 1975): 32-45, 92-97.

25. See W. K. Wimsatt and Monroe C. Beardsley, "The Concept of Meter: An Exercise in Abstraction," *PMLA* 74 (1959), rpt. in Seymour Chatman and Samuel R. Levin, eds., *Essays on the Language of Literature* (Boston: Houghton Mifflin, 1967), 91-114, in which the authors discern a tension between abstract syllable stress and the concrete, strong stress of the meter. One of the best arguments against the metrical-foot approach is presented by Otto Jespersen's "Notes on Metre," written in 1900 (rpt. in Chatman and Levin, eds., 71-96). Jespersen locates verse rhythms in everyday speech. He dismisses as "fallacies" the concepts of syllabic meter and of the foot and the notion of two grades of stress, long and short, finding at least four and perhaps more.

26. Discussing this sonnet as disillusionmennt with religion and noting the star's remoteness, Shaw concludes, "The subtle implication is that religion's excessive impracticality makes it not only worthless for the black man in the labyrinth but indeed, with its narcotic wiles, part of the labyrinth itself" (120). Brooks, ignoring her disavowed ending of "The Chicago *Defender*" (ch. 5) and the powerful "Riders" (ch. 6), confirms this negative view. "I can't think of anything I've written that speaks sweetly of religion," she maintains (*BWW*, 46). Gladys Margaret Williams, in her sensitive analysis "Gwendolyn Brooks's Way with a sonnet," *CLA Journal* 26 (Dec. 1982): 215-40, reads the first eight lines of "firstly inclined" as "an invocation to Liberty" (225).

27. Referring to I. A. Richards's useful distinctions between tenor and vehicle, Babette Deutsch, in defining *symbol*, observes, "It may be regarded as a

metaphor with a rich but indefinite tenor." *Poetry Handbook: A Dictionary of Terms*, 4th ed. (New York: Funk & Wagnalls, 1974), 178.

28. Cowper, beset by problems of sanity as well as belief, characterized himself as a "stricken deer" in *The Task*; his mock heroic genre foreshadows *The Anniad*.

29. Seaver, ed., *Cross-Section 1945*, 82.

3. *Annie Allen*

1. Gwendolyn Brooks, *Annie Allen* (1949); rpt. in *WGB*. Citations from the omnibus volume.

2. J. Saunders Redding, "Cellini-like Lyrics," *Saturday Review of Literature*, Sept. 17, 1949, 23, 27.

3. Phyllis McGinley, "Poetry for Prose Readers," *New York Times Book Review*, Jan. 22, 1950, 7.

4. Stanley Kunitz, "Bronze by Gold," *Poetry* (April 1950): 52-56.

5. Rolfe Humphries, "Verse Chronicle," *Nation*, Sept. 24, 1949, 306. Curiously, Humphries had written Brooks "a wildly enthusiastic review (*A Street in Bronzeville*) which he *severely* tempered before publishing it in a newspaper!" (GB).

6. For helpful discussions of compression, see Samuel R. Levin, "The Analysis of Compression in Poetry," in *Foundations of Language* 7 (1971): 38-55; and "Some Uses of the Grammar in Poetic Analysis," in *Problems of Textual Analysis*, ed. Pierre R. Léon et al. (Montreal: Didier, 1971), 19-31. Jeanne Kammer's thoughtful essay "The Art of Silence and the Forms of Women's Poetry," in *Shakespeare's Sisters: Feminist Essays on Women Poets*, ed. and introd. by Sandra M. Gilbert and Susan Gubar (Bloomington: Indiana Univ. Press, 1979), takes a feminist view of poetic compression as silence.

7. Nikki Giovanni, "To Gwen Brooks from Nikki Giovanni," *Essence* 1 (April 1971): 26.

8. Gwendolyn Brooks, "The Birth In A Narrow Room," in Langston Hughes and Arna Bontemps, eds., *The Poetry of the Negro, 1746-1949* (Garden City, N.Y.: Doubleday, 1949), 191.

9. The identical observation appears in Mary Helen Washington's " 'Taming All That Anger Down': Rage and Silence in Gwendolyn Brooks's *Maud Martha*," *Massachusetts Review* 24 (1983): 453. Contrary to the thesis here, she believes that "Brooks, in her poetry, seldom endows women with the power, integrity, or magnificence of her male figures" (461). For a differing view, see Beverly Guy-Sheftall, "The Women of Bronzeville," in Roseann P. Bell, Bettye J. Parker, and Beverly Guy-Sheftall, eds., *Sturdy Black Bridges: Visions of Black Women in Literature* (New York: Doubleday/Anchor, 1979), 157-70.

10. Northrop Frye, *Fearful Symmetry: A Study of William Blake* (1947; rpt. Princeton: Princeton Univ. Press, 1969), 168, 278.

11. Hortense J. Spillers, whose keen ear catches a possible punning on "Aeneid" and correctly refers to Annie's "mock heroic journey," views Brooks's work as "a poetry of cunning, laconic surprise." She declares, nevertheless, "In

her insistence that common life is not as common as we sometimes suspect, G.B. is probably the democratic poet of our time." "Gwendolyn the Terrible: Propositions on Eleven Poems," in Gilbert and Gubar, eds., *Shakespeare's Sisters*, 233-44.

12. Louis I. Bredvold, ed., notes in his introduction to Lord Byron, *Don Juan and Other Satirical Poems* (New York: Odyssey Press, 1935), "The comic epic of Italy reflects the intellectual anarchy, the Epicureanism, the comfortable worldliness of the Renaissance" (xxii).

13. Stanley Eugene Fish develops this thesis, suggested by Joseph H. Summers's concept of "the guilty reader," in *Surprised by Sin: The Reader in "Paradise Lost"* (London: Macmillan, 1967) and in other writings.

14. Anon., *Beowulf.* I have cited the verse translation by C. W. Kennedy and the simplified transliteration which appear in *The Literature of England: An Anthology and a History*, vol. 1, rev. ed., G. Woods, H. Watt, G. Anderson, eds. (Chicago/New York: Scott, Foresman, 1941), 20, 32.

15. Dickinson, *Complete Poems*, 249.

16. In Hudson, "Racial Themes," 16-20.

17. Gladys Margaret Williams, in "Gwendolyn Brooks's Way with a Sonnet," points out: "Readers who know the vigorous life of Chicago and Harlem streets and have seen vital women resisting anyone's efforts to force their movements in directions they do not care to take . . . are cued to the kind of woman Cousin Vit must have been" (238).

18. Sojourner Truth, "What Time of Night It Is" (1853), rpt. in *Feminism: The Essential Historical Writings*, ed. Miriam Schneir (New York: Random House/ Vintage, 1972), 96-98.

19. Edna St. Vincent Millay, Sonnet 4, in *The Harp-Weaver and Other Poems* (New York and London: Harper and Brothers, 1923), 53. Cf. "Priscilla Assails the Sepulchre of Love," ch. 6.

4. *Maud Martha, Bronzeville Boys and Girls*

1. Gwendolyn Brooks, *Maud Martha* (1953), rpt. in *WGB*, 125-306.

2. Henry James, *The Art of the Novel: Critical Prefaces*, introd. R. P. Blackmur (New York: Scribner's, 1934).

3. Gertrude Stein, *Three Lives* (1909; rpt. New York: Random House/ Vintage, 1958).

4. Annette Oliver Shands, "Gwendolyn Brooks as Novelist," *Black World* 22 (June 1973): 22-30.

5. Langston Hughes, "Dreams," in *The Dream Keeper and Other Poems* (New York: Knopf, 1932), 7.

6. See Stephen Crane, *Maggie: A Girl of the Streets* (1893). The impressionistic descriptions of theatrical performances that Crane ironically calls in the novel "transcendental realism," uniting Maggie, the audience, and the performers, are recalled in this chapter.

7. Gwendolyn Brooks, *Bronzeville Boys and Girls* (New York: Harper and Row, 1956).

8. "Cynthia in the Snow," from *Bronzeville Boys and Girls* by Gwendolyn Brooks, p. 8. Copyright © 1956 by Gwendolyn Brooks Blakely.

9. See my "Ivan Foñagy and Paul Delbouille: Sonority Structures in Poetic Language," *Language and Style* 6 (Summer 1973): 206-15 for a discussion of two opposing views: vocal sounds as meaningfully iconic—for which there seems to be important evidence—or as accidental and learned.

5. *The Bean Eaters*

1. Gwendolyn Brooks, *The Bean Eaters* (1960), rpt. in *WGB*. Citations from the omnibus volume.

2. Harvey Curtis Webster, "Pity the Giants," *Nation* 195 (Sept. 1962): 96. For the effect of this review on *Selected Poems*, see the discussion of correspondence in the next chapter.

3. Gwendolyn Brooks, "*Black Books Bulletin* Interviews Gwen Brooks," with don l. lee, *Black Books Bulletin* 2 (1974): 28-35.

4. Reference to Emmett Till in Susan Brownmiller's *Against Our Will* is misleading and, in view of the facts outlined here, grotesque. As Alice Walker notes in her Letter to the Editor *(New York Times Book Review*, Nov. 30, 1975, 65-66), "Emmett Till was not a rapist. He was not even a man. He was a child who did not understand that whistling at a white woman could cost him his life."

5. I have depended upon *Facts on File*, 15 (1955): 324, 412, 418 and my own recollection of newspaper accounts of the case.

6. See also John T. Shawcross, "Some Literary Uses of Numerology," *Hartford Studies in Literature* 1, no. 1 (1969): 50-62, for useful inquiry.

7. C. Eric Lincoln, *The Negro Pilgrimage in America: The Coming of Age of the Black Americans* (New York: Bantam, 1967), ch. 6, "Northern Migration," 84-106.

8. "Reed" is the name of several American statesmen; John Reed, the Communist journalist and author of *Ten Days That Shook the World*, might also be thought of as a referent. But since these men are white, and Rudolph's name and identity are clearly defined within the poem, there is no need to look outside it.

9. Gwendolyn Brooks, in Kamili Anderson, "*Belles Lettres* Interviews," *Belles Lettres,* Jan./Feb. 1986, 9-10.

10. Note Hughes's ambivalence toward Christianity, his "Goodbye, Christ," and later retraction, wishing "that Christ could come back to save us all" (*GMR*, 36-37, 135).

11. Cf. "Sammy Chester" and ch. 9, n. 10. Brooks's journalistic and didactic impulses combine here. Both aspects recall Wordsworth, who writes in a letter of 1808 to Sir George Beaumont, his friend and patron, "Every great poet is a Teacher: I was either to be considered as a Teacher or as nothing." As quoted in M. H. Abrams, *The Mirror and the Lamp* (New York: Oxford Univ. Press, 1953), 329. Note capitalization.

12. Lerone Bennett, Jr., in his introduction to *To Gwen With Love* (Chicago: Johnson, 1971), 3, reads the subject as a woman.

13. Ezra Pound, "The Study in Aesthetics," from *Lustra* (1915), rpt. in *Personae* (1926); (rpt. and enl. New York: New Directions, 1971), 96-97.

14. "We Real Cool," from *The Bean Eaters*. Copyright © 1959 by Gwendolyn Brooks. Rpt. in *WGB*, 315.

15. Brooks's current evaluation of her poetry emphasizes this aspect: "My works express rage and focus on *rage*" (*BWW*, 43).

6. *Selected Poems*

1. Gwendolyn Brooks, *Selected Poems* (New York: Harper and Row, 1963).

2. Webster, "Pity the Giants," 96-97. See the reservation mentioned in the previous chapter's correspondence (page 101).

3. Cf. Levine: "Throughout the century of freedom, guile and wit remained necessary and ubiquitous tools with which to confront the dominant culture" (380).

4. See *National Geographic*, Oct. 1954, 487-517.

5. Stevens's essay (1942); rpt. in *The Necessary Angel: Essays on Reality and the Imagination* (New York: Random House/Vintage, 1951), 3-36.

6. "[O]ld tennis player," from *Selected Poems* by Gwendolyn Brooks, 125. Copyright © 1963 by Gwendolyn Brooks Blakely.

7. Frye, *Fearful Symmetry*, 223.

8. I use the word "gay" in its current, additional denotation, which is distinct from its original usage in this poem, in "Gay Chaps at the Bar" and elsewhere in Brooks.

7. *In the Mecca*

1. Gwendolyn Brooks, *In the Mecca* (New York: Harper and Row, 1968); rpt. in *WGB*. Citations from *WGB*.

2. Addison Gayle, Jr., "The World of Gwendolyn Brooks," *New York Times Book Review*, Jan. 2, 1972, 4.

3. James N. Johnson, "Blacklisting Poets," *Ramparts*, 7, no. 9 (1968): 54.

4. C. Eric Lincoln, as quoted in *The Autobiography of Malcolm X* (1964; rpt. New York: Grove Press, 1966), 444.

5. John Bartlow Martin, "The Strangest Place in Chicago," *Harper's Magazine* 201 (Dec. 1950):86-97; rpt. in *This is Chicago: An Anthology*, ed. Albert Halper (New York: Henry Holt, 1952), 42-60.

6. Ibid., ed. note, 42. A laboratory was planned for the site, which now extends the Illinois Institute of Technology.

7. See William Labov, "Contraction, Deletion, and Inherent Variability of the English Copula," *Language*, 45 (Dec. 1969); rpt. in *Language in the Inner City: Studies in the Black English Vernacular* (Philadelphia: Univ. of Pennsylvania Press, 1972), ch. 3. (See also n. 7, ch. 9, below.) A more general guide is J. L. Dillard, *Black English* (New York: Random House/Vintage, 1973). Its controversial thesis traces Black English to African sources via pidgin English and Creole.

8. The issue is raised in M. L. Rosenthal's review, "In the Mecca," *New York Times Book Review*, March 2, 1969, 14-16. He writes: "It is as though, despite the familiar squalor and violence and terror . . . it would be unbearable to point up a native son's guilt as well." Rosenthal is perturbed by Brooks's "stylistic distortions" such as alliteration, internal rhyme, and "whimsical and arch observations that distract from its horror almost as if to conceal the wound at its center."

9. The sermon appears in Martin Luther King, Jr., *Strength to Love* (New York: Harper and Row, 1963), 58-66.

10. Robert Sommers argues against "hard" or vandal-proof architecture in *Tight Spaces: Hard Architecture and How to Humanize It* (Englewood Cliffs, N.J.: Prentice-Hall, 1974), 1-3, 7-19, 111-14.

11. See the anthology edited by Dudley Randall and Margaret G. Burroughs, *For Malcolm: Poems on the Life and Death of Malcolm X* (Detroit: Broadside Press, 1969). Randall's Introduction ends: "Malcolm was a man, and for being a man he was murdered" (xxii).

12. Malcolm X, assisted by Alex Haley, *The Autobiography of Malcolm X* (New York: Grove Press, 1964). The book admirably spans black life and aspiration, expressed in this unique man.

13. For further discussion of the poems, see William H. Hansell, "Aestheticism vs. Political Militancy in Gwendolyn Brooks's 'The Chicago Picasso' and 'The Wall,' " *CLA Journal* 17 (Sept. 1973): 11-15; and R. Baxter Miller, "Does Man Love Art?" in *Black American Literature and Humanism*, 95-112.

14. James Weldon Johnson's, *God's Trombones: Some Negro Sermons in Verse* (London: Allen and Unwin, 1929), 12.

15. Bruce A. Rosenberg, *The Art of the American Folk Preacher* (New York: Oxford Univ. Press, 1970), 117.

16. William H. Hansell, discussing the "Third Sermon" in "The Role of Violence in the Poems of Gwendolyn Brooks," *Studies in Black Literature* 5 (Summer 1974): 21-27, recalls W. E. B. Du Bois's statement, "We have woven ourselves with the very warp of the nation" (*The Souls of Black Folk*), and points out that the warp is "the foundation or supporting thread in weaving." As such, it suggests that "blacks have been essential to the United States even though forced to live a warped existence and denied credit for their contributions."

8. *Riot, Family Pictures, Aloneness*

1. Dudley Randall, "The Poets of Broadside: A Personal Chronicle," *Black Academy Review* 1 (Spring 1970); rpt. in Floyd Barbour's *The Black Seventies*, and in *Broadside Memories: Poets I Have Known* (Detroit: Broadside Press, 1975), 8-9, which includes a report on the Press by Melba J. Boyd. Cited in the text as *BSM*.

2. Gwendolyn Brooks, *Riot* (1969), followed by *Family Pictures* (1970), and *Aloneness* (1971); all published Detroit: Broadside Press.

3. Gwendolyn Brooks, "For Dudley Randall," *Black World* (Jan. 1976): 91.

4. Drake and Cayton, *Black Metropolis*. See especially ch. 14, "Bronzeville," and ch. 15, "The Power of Press and Pulpit."

5. See James Baldwin's prophetic *The Fire Next Time* (New York: Dial, 1963).

6. For an interesting description of black humor, which relates it to Freudian views of aggression and "tendentious" criticism, see Levine, *Black Culture and Black Consciousness*, ch. 5, "Black Laughter."

7. Chancellor Williams, *The Destruction of Black Civilization*, rev. and enl. (1971; Chicago: Third World Press, 1974).

8. George Kent, "George Kent Interviews Chancellor Williams," *The Black Position* no. 3 (1973):35.

9. Tate, *BWW*, 47.

10. Ascribed to Rabindranath Tagore and adopted by the Christophers, a Catholic lay organization, the motto appears in Adlai Stevenson's famous eulogy of Anna Eleanor Roosevelt.

11. William Carlos Williams, *Paterson*, Book III, 2 (New York: New Directions, 1963), 137.

12. Tom Lea's *The Brave Bulls* (Boston: Little Brown, 1949), for example, presents bullfighting from the perspective of the bulls.

13. Robert Frost, *The Poetry of Robert Frost*, ed. Edward Connery Lathem (1921; rpt. New York: Holt, Rinehart, 1969), 220.

14. Ezra Pound, Canto CXVI, *The Cantos of Ezra Pound* (New York: New Directions, 1972), 795-96.

15. John T. Shawcross, ed., *The Complete Poetry of John Donne with an Introduction, Notes, and Variants*, 2nd ed. (New York: Doubleday/Anchor, 1971), 93.

16. Cf. Hughes's image, "You're no tame lion," in "Roar China" (*GMR*, 118-19).

17. See the important study by Herbert G. Gutman, *The Black Family in Slavery and Freedom, 1750-1925* (New York: Random House/Vintage, 1976), esp. chs. 7 and 8. Gutman offers a revision (see esp. 212, 556 n. 4) of certain conclusions in Melville J. Herskovits's pioneering *The Myth of the Negro Past*, 2nd ed. (Boston: Beacon, 1958). See the latter's ch. 6, esp. pp. 182ff., for discussion of the African "extended family" and its survival among African Americans.

18. See esp. introd. and chs. 1 and 2, *The Challenge of Blackness*.

19. "The Life of Lincoln West," in Herbert Hill, ed., *Soon, One Morning: New Writing by American Negroes, 1940-1962* (New York: Knopf, 1963), 317-19.

20. See also Safisha N. Madhubuti, "Focus on Form in Gwendolyn Brooks," *Black Books Bulletin* 2 (Spring 1974); 24-27, for discussion of these descriptive phrases.

21. See don l. lee (Haki R. Madhubuti), *Directionscore: Selected and New Poems* (Detroit: Broadside Press, 1971), 87, 148. For more recent statements of his views, see "From the Beginning: The Decision Is to Fight," *Black World*, March 1976; rpt. in *Enemies: The Clash of Races* (Chicago: Third World Press, 1978), ch. 1; also my "Black Nationalism and the Poet Activist," *Western Journal of Black Studies* 9 (Summer 1985): 106-14.

22. See Kenneth Burke, *The Philosophy of Literary Form: Studies in Symbolic Action*, 2nd ed. (Baton Rouge, La.: Louisiana State Univ. Press, 1967), for his description of the poem as a "strategy" to approach an existential situation.

23. S. N. Madhubuti, "Focus on Form," 26, aptly perceives the "deep pitch and undulating rhythm of Robeson" as expressed by the poet's "conscious alternation of open and voweled syllables (the long 'o') and closed voweled syllables ('ing')" that "connects, through alliteration, the vowel motifs."

24. Dudley Randall, *Love You* (London: Paul Breman, Autumn 1970).

25. See her lyrics in *On My Way to Where* (New York: McCall, 1970-71).

26. "This Is Just to Say," in William Carlos Williams, *The Collected Earlier Poems* (New York: New Directions, 1951), 354.

27. Ezra Pound, "A Retrospect" (1913), rpt. in *Literary Essays of Ezra Pound* (New York: New Directions, 1968), 4.

28. Rothenberg's "deep image," connected with "perception as an instrument of vision" that looks to "a compassionate comprehension of the world" (cf. Wordsworth's "height of feeling intellect"), is discussed in "Jerome Rothenberg and Robert Creeley: An Exchange. Deep Image and Mode," *Kulchur* 2 (Summer 1962): 28-42.

29. See my essay, "On the Poetics of Charles Olson," *For Now*, no. 15 (n.d.): 40-56.

9. Later Works

1. "In Montgomery," *Ebony*, Aug. 1971, 42-48. Other works discussed in this chapter: *Report from Part One (RPO,* as previously cited); *The Tiger Who Wore White Gloves* (Chicago: Third World Press, 1974); *Beckonings* (Detroit: Broadside Press, 1975); *Primer For Blacks* (Chicago: Black Position Press, 1980); *To Disembark* (Chicago: Third World Press, 1981); *Very Young Poets* (Chicago: Brooks Press, 1983).

2. Russell Baker, "Sunday Observer," *New York Times Magazine*, April 4, 1976, 9.

3. Rosenberg, *The Art of the American Folk Preacher*, 101-8.

4. Harvey E. Gross, *Sound and Form in Modern Poetry: A Study of Prosody from Thomas Hardy to Robert Lowell* (Ann Arbor: Univ. of Michigan Press, 1964), p. 5.

5. Levine, 99. The author gives examples of practical advice in the slave tales, such as behavior toward a master. He describes the antecedent African tales as similarly instructive, imbued with moral prescriptions.

6. Aristotle, opening of *The Metaphysics*, in *The Basic Works*, ed. Richard McKeon (New York: Random House, 1941), 689.

7. See Labov, *Language in the Inner City*, for discussion of the copula and invariant *be*, 41-53, and ch. 3, 65-129. (See also n. 7, ch. 7, above.)

8. William Carlos Williams, *Paterson*, Book V, 3 (New York: New Directions, 1963), 273.

9. Samuel R. Levin, "Coupling," ch. 4 in *Linguistic Structures in Poetry* (The Hague: Mouton, 1962), 30-41. This useful concept is also applied to the

visual in my William Carlos Williams paper, "Sight and Sound in *Paterson*, Book Two, Parts I and III: Some Aspects of Technique" (in manuscript).

10. William Wordsworth, *Selected Poems and Prefaces,* ed. Jack Stillinger (Boston: Houghton Mifflin/Riverside, 1965), 12-13. Geoffrey H. Hartman, in "Wordsworth, Inscriptions, and Romantic Nature Poetry," in Frederick W. Hilles and Harold Bloom, eds., *From Sensibility to Romanticism* (London: Oxford Univ. Press, 1965), 389-413, identifies the poetic genre of the "nature-inscription" in discussing this poem. He notes the link between inscription, epigram, and the journalistic broadside ballad, whose title was often elaborate and concrete.

11. Brooks, *RPO*, 46. The poet describes here the black concept "Kwanza," developed by Ron Karenga, based on an African holiday, as an alternative to a commercial Christmas. During the week beginning December 26, homes are decorated in "black representing the blacknation, the red representing our shed blood," and green.

12. See Allen Mandelbaum, verse trans., *The Aeneid of Virgil* (Berkeley: Univ. of California Press, 1971), VI.402-16. See also his verse trans., Dante, *Inferno* (1980), III.112-17.

13. J. R. Green, *A Short History of the English People,* 2 vols. (1915; rpt. London: Dent/Everyman; New York: Dutton, 1945), 2:503. Green's classic nineteenth-century account (1874), especially of the Puritan Rebellion, is dramatically vivid as well as scholarly.

14. See coverage by Tom Wicker, beginning Sept. 14, 1971, in the *New York Times.*

15. William H. Hansell, in "Essences, Unifyings, and Black Militancy: Major Themes in Gwendolyn Brooks's *Family Pictures* and *Beckonings*," *Black American Literature Forum* 11 (Summer 1977): 63-66, suggests that "Black Star," in addition to its spiritual connotations, may refer to Marcus Garvey. The leader of the "Back to Africa" Universal Negro Improvement Association planned to travel there with his followers on a steamship of the proposed "Black Star Line."

16. See Stavros (*RPO*, 152) and Hull (20-23) interviews.

10. A Major Poet

1. For an excellent discussion of this relation, see Louis L. Martz, "The Unicorn in *Paterson*: William Carlos Williams," in *William Carlos Williams: A Collection of Critical Essays,* ed. J. Hillis Miller (Englewood Cliffs, N.J.: Prentice-Hall, 1966), 70-87.

2. In *The Clairvoyant Eye: The Poetry and Poetics of Wallace Stevens* (Baton Rouge: Louisiana State Univ. Press, 1965), 32.

3. Pound, "How to Read," in *Literary Essays*, 23.

4. Excerpts and adaptations from *Black Poets: The New Heroic Genre: Critical Inquiry and Interviews,* a study aided by a National Endowment for the Humanities Fellowship, appear in *Black American Literature Forum* (on Baraka, Fall 1982; Randall, Winter 1983); *Greenfield Review* (Jayne Cortez, Summer/Fall 1983); *Time Capsule* (Brooks, Summer/Fall 1983); *Western Journal of*

Black Studies (Madhubuti, Summer 1985); and are forthcoming (1986) in *MELUS* (Sonia Sanchez) and *Thirteenth Moon* (Brooks).

5. The view, first taken in my doctoral dissertation (1976, CUNY), appears also in "Gwendolyn Brooks: The Heroic Voice of Prophecy," *Studies in Black Literature* 8 (Spring 1977): 1-3 (first presented at NEMLA, Pittsburgh, April 1977); "Cultural Challenge, Heroic Response: Gwendolyn Brooks and the New Black Poetry," paper given at NPCA, Baltimore, April 1977.

6. D. H. Melhem, from "Hudson Continuum," *Confrontation* 30-31 (Nov. 1985): 286.

7. Walt Whitman, "A Backward Glance O'er Travel'd Roads," preface to *November Boughs*, in *Complete Poetry and Selected Prose*, ed. James E. Miller, Jr. (Boston: Houghton Mifflin/Riverside, 1959), 453.

8. Bennett, introduction, *The Challenge of Blackness*, 2.

9. In "George Kent Interviews Chancellor Williams," 32.

10. Whitman, Preface to 1855 edition of *Leaves of Grass*, 425.

11. Charles Child Walcutt, *American Literary Naturalism: A Divided Stream* (Minneapolis: Univ. of Minnesota Press, 1956), in studying transcendental and scientific sources of naturalism, perceptively discusses the dilemma as the central problem of twentieth-century thought.

12. Northrop Frye, *Anatomy of Criticism: Four Essays* (Princeton: Princeton Univ. Press, 1957). See the First Essay, "Historical Criticism: Theory of Modes," 33-67, for Frye's concept of mythic, romantic, high mimetic, low mimetic, and ironic modes. In the mythic, the hero is divine, superior in kind and degree to the audience; in the ironic, he is inferior.

13. Frye, *Fearful Symmetry*, 316.

14. Barbara Kiefer Lewalski, *Milton's Brief Epic: The Genre, Meaning and Art of "Paradise Regained"* (Providence, R.I.: Brown Univ. Press, 1966).

15. Roy Harvey Pearce, *The Continuity of American Poetry* (Princeton: Princeton Univ. Press, 1961).

16. Charles Olson dedicates *The Maximus Poems* (New York: Jargon/Corinth, 1960) to Robert Creeley, "the Figure of Outward."

17. As quoted in William Carlos Williams, *The Autobiography* (New York: Random House, 1951), 391.

Bibliography
of Works by
Gwendolyn Brooks

With Harper and Row, New York

A Street in Bronzeville, 1945. Reprinted in *The World of Gwendolyn Brooks* (1971).

Annie Allen, 1949. Reprinted in *The World of Gwendolyn Brooks* (1971).

Maud Martha, 1953. Reprinted in *The World of Gwendolyn Brooks* (1971).

Bronzeville Boys and Girls, 1956. Illustrations by Ronni Solbert.

The Bean Eaters, 1960. Reprinted in *The World of Gwendolyn Brooks* (1971).

Selected Poems, 1963.

In the Mecca, 1968. Reprinted in *The World of Gwendolyn Brooks* (1971).

The World of Gwendolyn Brooks, 1971.

With Broadside Press, Detroit

We Real Cool. Broadside Series, no. 6, 1966. Reprinted from *The Bean Eaters*.

The Wall. Broadside Series, no. 19, 1967.

Riot, 1969.

Family Pictures, 1970.

Aloneness, 1971. Illustrations by Leroy Foster.

Black Steel: Joe Frazier and Muhammad Ali. Special Broadside, 1971.

Editor, *A Broadside Treasury*, 1971. Includes "Martin Luther King, Jr.," Memorial Broadside.

Editor, *Jump Bad: A New Chicago Anthology*, 1971.

Report from Part One, 1972. Prefaces by Don L. Lee and George Kent.

Beckonings, 1975.

With Keorapetse Kgositsile, Haki R. Madhubuti, Dudley Randall, *a capsule course in Black Poetry Writing*, 1975.

Other Publications

"We're the Only Colored People Here." *Portfolio*, no. 1 (Summer 1945), leaf 13.

"Death of the Dinosaur"; "One Wants a Teller in a Time Like This"; "Memorial to Ed Bland." *Cross-Section 1945: A Collection of New American Writing*, edited by Edwin Seaver. New York: L. B. Fischer, 1945, 82-83.

"The Birth in a Narrow Room." *The Poetry of the Negro, 1746-1949*, edited by Langston Hughes and Arna Bontemps. Garden City, N.Y.: Doubleday, 1949, 191.

"The Life of Lincoln West." *Soon, One Morning: New Writing by American Negroes, 1940-1962*, edited by Herbert Hill. New York: Alfred A. Knopf, 1963, 317-19. [The volume also contains biographical material (316, 326) and reprints from published books.]

"The Assassination of John F. Kennedy." *Chicago Sun-Times*, December 19, 1963.

"I See Chicago." Commissioned by Illinois Bell Telephone, 1964.

"Perspectives." *Negro Digest* 15 (July 1966): 49-50.

"In Montgomery." Photographs by Moneta Sleet, Jr., and captions by the author. *Ebony* 26 (Aug. 1971): 42-48.

"Thank you (A love note to all the components of *To Gwen With Love*)." *Black World* 21 (Nov. 1971): 42.

Editor, *The Black Position*. Annual, beginning 1971.

"Boys. Black. a preachment." *Ebony* 27 (Aug. 1972):45. Reprinted in *Beckonings*, 1975.

The Tiger Who Wore White Gloves, or What you are you are. Illustrations by Timothy Jones. Chicago: Third World Press, 1974.

"Of Flowers and Fire and Flowers." *Black Books Bulletin*, 3 (Fall 1975):16-18. [Review of a projected second edition of *A Broadside Treasury* (edited with Dudley Randall).]

"For Dudley Randall." *Black World* 25 (Jan. 1976): 91.

Primer For Blacks. Chicago: Black Position Press, 1980.

Young Poet's Primer. Chicago: Brooks Press, 1980.

To Disembark. Chicago: Third World Press, 1981.

"Black Love." *Ebony* 36 (Aug. 1981). Reprinted as separate publication, Chicago: Black Position Press, 1982.

Very Young Poets. Chicago: Brooks Press, 1983.

"24 Poems from Four Decades." Anthology compiled by Gwendolyn Brooks and D. H. Melhem. [Tribute issue includes "The Sundays of Satin-Legs Smith," all of *Riot,* and articles on Brooks by Dudley Randall and D. H. Melhem.] *Time Capsule* 7 (Summer/Fall 1983):16-25.

Blacks. Chicago: The David Company, 1987. [In press] [Comprises *A Street in Bronzeville, Annie Allen, Maud Martha, The Bean Eaters,* "New Poems," *In the Mecca,* selections from *To Disembark,* and *The Near-Johannesburg Boy and Other Poems.*]

Index